A
DEPENDENT
PEOPLE

Description of the Town of Newport, Rhode Island
By JOHN MAYLEM a native of it*

A Town laid out ten furlongs—good
With houses like the people—wood
Save here and there an Edifice
of Brick and Stone and Mortar. yes.
A goodly Church of Cedar So!
Two Presbyterian meetings poh!
A Quaker house with Stables ah!
Two anabaptists ditto la!
A Dancing School and Town House hie!
A synagogue of Satan—fie!
A Castle too, a building—where?
G-d d-m you Sir! Why in the air.
A Gallows too without the City
To hang all rogues but theirs, O pity!

* "Notes in Newport in 1768," *Rhode Island Historical Society Collections,* 12 (1919), 51.

A
DEPENDENT
PEOPLE

NEWPORT, RHODE ISLAND
IN THE REVOLUTIONARY ERA

ELAINE FORMAN CRANE

New York
FORDHAM UNIVERSITY PRESS

© Copyright 1985, 1992 by FORDHAM UNIVERSITY PRESS
All rights reserved.
LC 92–6808
ISBN 0–8232–1112–6

Library of Congress Cataloging-in-Publication Data

Crane, Elaine Forman.
A dependent people : Newport, Rhode Island in the revolutionary
era / Elaine Forman Crane.
  p. cm.
Includes bibliographical references and index.
ISBN 0–8232–1111–8. — ISBN 0–8232–1112–6 (pbk.)
  1. Newport (R.I.)—History.   2. Rhode Island—History—Revolution,
1775–1783.   I. Title.
F89.N5C8 1992
974.5'702—dc20   92–6808
                                                                        CIP

Printed in the United States of America

FOR C.
FROM A.

ABBREVIATIONS AND SHORT TITLES

Commerce	*Commerce of Rhode Island, 1726–1800*. Collections of the Massachusetts Historical Society. 7th Series., Nos. 9 and 10. Boston, 1914, 1915.
Diary	*The Literary Diary of Ezra Stiles*. Ed. Franklin B. Dexter. 3 vols. New York, 1901.
Documents	*Documents Illustrative of the Slave Trade*. Ed. Elizabeth Donnan. 4 vols. Washington, D.C., 1930–1935.
Itineraries	*Extracts from the Itineraries and Other Miscellanies of Ezra Stiles, D.D., LL.D., 1755–1794*. Ed. Franklin B. Dexter. New Haven, Conn., 1916.
NHS	Newport Historical Society, Newport, Rhode Island
NM	*Newport Mercury*
NYHS	New-York Historical Society, New York, New York
PRO	Public Record Office of Great Britain, London
RICR	*Records of the Colony of Rhode Island and Providence Plantations*. Ed. John Russell Bartlett. 10 vols. Providence, 1862.
RIHS	Rhode Island Historical Society, Providence, Rhode Island

Editorial Note

In order to preserve the integrity of the eighteenth-century manuscripts which have been quoted, original spelling has been retained throughout. For the same reason, conformity of citations has given way to exact replication of address. For example, letters to or from Godfrey and John Malbone will be cited as being sent or received by either Godfrey and John Malbone or G and J Malbone, depending on the way the names appear in the original document.

CONTENTS

TABLES

ILLUSTRATIONS

ACKNOWLEDGMENTS

The list of people to whom I am indebted for this book is extensive. Since I did not make a note of each person's contribution over the course of research and writing, I fear there will be omissions, and for that I apologize. The following people and institutions, however, have given advice, support, time, and encouragement, for which I am very grateful.

My friend and husband Stephen must receive the largest share of thanks since his part of this adventure consisted of giving up vacations, helping with research, and acting as a sounding board through all the initial writing, revisions, and frustrations that are inevitably part of a book. At the same time, the book would not have been possible without the help of Mrs. Gladys Bolhouse, Curator of Manuscripts at the Newport Historical Society. She knows more about the history of Newport than anyone I have met, and I feel fortunate that I could avail myself of her knowledge of the manuscript collection. The other indispensable person at the Newport Historical Society was the librarian, Mrs. Madeline Wordell, who always seemed to find the books I needed when I could not find them myself. The rest of the staff at the Newport Historical Society were always helpful, ready to answer questions, and interested in what I was doing. The same can be said for Richard Champlin at the Redwood Library, and Rabbi Theodore Lewis of Touro Synagogue.

The alphabetical typescripts of census and tax data compiled by an unofficial staff member of the Newport Historical Society, Mr. Joseph W. Blaine, were valuable research tools.

Since this study of Newport started out as a doctoral dissertation at New York University, it is altogether appropriate to thank my mentor, Professor Patricia Bonomi, as well as the other committee members, David Reimers and Thomas Bender, who helped me to refocus the narrative and argument. The credits at New York University would be incomplete without noting that it was in Bayrd Still's splendid course in urban history that I first became interested in this remarkable colonial town.

Professors John Murrin and Lynne Withey were particularly helpful and encouraging. By reading the manuscript and suggesting that I probe more deeply into certain areas, they sent me in directions I would not have thought of myself. Professors Philip Curtin and Stanley Engerman lent their assistance to the very difficult—and controversial—section on the slave trade, and I thank them both.

I also wish to thank the staffs of the Rhode Island Historical Society, Newport County Court House, Rhode Island State Archives, Library of Congress, New York Public Library, and New-York Historical Society. Similarly, my appreciation is extended to the National Society of the Colonial Dames of America for their grant which enabled me to spend time in Newport for purposes of research.

My appreciation extends also to the Editor of Fordham University Press, Dr. Mary Beatrice Schulte, whose professional abilities are unmatched, and who worked above and beyond the call of duty to help produce the best possible book.

Finally, a statement of gratitude to the late Clinton Rossiter whose enthusiasm for history and delight in reconstructing the past was infectious.

PREFACE TO THE PAPERBACK EDITION

IT IS PROBABLY A GOOD IDEA for every writer to review his or her work after a lapse of several years because time and distance permit a more dispassionate assessment of a thesis than when the author and the original manuscript were constant companions. Having just completed such a critique, I am able to report (with some sense of relief, I might add), that in the seven years since *A Dependent People* was published, no newly discovered manuscript or recently issued book has created a need to modify its basic conclusions. At the same time, were I to explore the same subject today, I might give greater emphasis to topics which were only touched upon, and I might ask—and try to answer—questions that were not even raised seven years ago.

With the benefit of hindsight and further reading, I am not at all certain that I said enough about the prevailing attitude that influenced Newport's revolutionary expectations and actions. I am as convinced today as I was seven years ago that economic grievances precipitated Newport's entry into the war, yet today I would broaden that assertion to include a discussion of the intellectual baggage which made economic issues a raison d'être for rebellion. As I argue in the book itself, self-interest was surely a motivating value, but how did this component fit into the total equation: Why would one person perceive that his self-interest was best served by "ideal" British duties and yet another see those same duties as a threat to his very survival? And what did survival mean in the context of eighteenth-century Newport? Was it simply having enough to eat, or was survival equivalent to upward mobility and prosperity? In short, what in their collective mentalité—what in the cumulative experience of this seaport town—made the hasty pursuit of profit more important than standing membership in the British empire?

It occurs to me now that the absence of a strong Puritan legacy might relate in some way to these questions. Strict Puritan doctrine demanded economic moderation and the suppression of self-interest for the good of the whole. But as tempting opportunities presented themselves, the history of seventeenth-century Massachusetts became, at least in part, a story of the conflict between expanding mercantilism and undiluted Puritanism. If it took almost a century for mercantile interests to prevail in Massachusetts, however, Rhode Island merchants achieved predominance in far less time. The original settlers of Newport found Boston's brand of Puritanism incompatible with their own as early as 1639, and once they left their guilt on the Massachusetts side of the border, they had little reason to contain their accumulation of wealth. Revolutionary Newporters were merely heirs to a longstanding economic tradition in which a just price and low interest rates had little meaning even in theory.

A Puritan legacy in Massachusetts (and the near absence of one in Newport) may also explain the proliferation of pamphlet literature in Boston during the 1760s and 1770s, and the dearth of such position papers in Newport during the same period of time. Newporters never felt the necessity of justifying their actions in constitutional or ideological terms because they were never bound by an intellectual heritage that constrained their acquisitive instincts.

Pursuing this line of thought still further, I would speculate today—as I did not seven years ago—that the revolutionary confrontation between Congregationalists and Anglicans might be explained in the above context. The Anglicans were the furthest removed from Puritan economic guidelines while at the same time they were, as a group, the most affluent members of the Newport community. This combination of factors may have antagonized the Congregationalists whose resentment toward the economic achievements of their Anglican brethren was translated into rebellion. Does this interpretation make Newport's experience in the revolutionary era a class struggle? Not exactly, but perhaps it brings that argument out of total oblivion.

One other subject that deserves a more thorough analysis than I gave it in 1985 concerns personal relationships. If church affiliation was, as I believe it to have been, the key to revolutionary allegiances, how did this affect intra-family relationships? Were ordinary marital tensions heightened when husbands and wives supported opposing camps? What sort of strains were siblings subject to when they argued for—and even fought for—different sides? And how did parents treat a son or daughter whose revolutionary commitment differed from their own?

A final observation: if I am still comfortable with the basic argument of the book, I am less satisfied—indeed, I admit to wincing—at the sexist language that slipped by seven years ago. Please note, therefore, that I had men *and women* in mind in the last paragraph on page 2, and on pages 49, 50, and 55, "tradesmen" should read "tradespeople."

ELAINE FORMAN CRANE
January 1992

A
DEPENDENT
PEOPLE

Sea Captains Carousing in Surinam by JOHN GREENWOOD CA. 1758

Several prominent Rhode Islanders are portrayed in this tavern scene, including Captain Nicholas Cooke, smoking a pipe at the far side of the table and deep in conversation with Captain Esek Hopkins. A second Hopkins—Stephen—spills rum over the sleeping Jonas Wanton, while Ambrose Page vomits into Wanton's pocket, oblivious of the discomfort he will soon feel at his rear. On the right, Nicholas Power appears to be knighting someone who might be Godfrey Malbone, Jr. Behind them, Greenwood has painted himself into the picture, candle in hand, making a hasty retreat.

INTRODUCTION

NEWPORT, RHODE ISLAND, may be the oldest city on the North American continent. On the other hand, it may not be. For half a century a controversy has raged over whether Newport was—or was not—the site of a Viking settlement. The believers rest their convictions on an old stone tower which stands somewhat inconspicuously near the center of town, and which bears a striking resemblance to thirteenth-century Norse structures.[1] The skeptics, sad to say, have archaeological evidence on their side, and it is generally agreed today that the tower was built as a mill in the last quarter of the seventeenth century by Governor Benedict Arnold on whose land it stood.

The controversy over the tower is not surprising, however, since Newport has been surrounded by controversy for a good part of its history. Indeed, its very founding stemmed from a dispute between certain dissidents and the inflexible founding fathers of Massachusetts Bay.[2] In 1638 several alleged Antinomian sympathizers, led by John Clarke and William Coddington, avoided certain banishment from the Bay Colony by following Roger Williams into the wilderness of Rhode Island. Williams negotiated the purchase of Aquidneck Island from the Indians for Coddington's group and watched as they established a toe hold at Portsmouth on the northern end of the island. In the following year, Ann Hutchinson's followers wrested political control from this small band, and because it was easier to move on than fight, Coddington's group paddled to the southern end of Aquidneck where they established a more substantial foothold quite close to Newport harbor. It is unlikely that this particular location was a happy accident, since the settlers were aware of the harbor's excellent reputation and growing use in the coastal trade. Satisfied that this was a promising spot for a permanent settlement, these nine men "agreed and ordered, that the Plantation now begun at this South West end of the Island shall be called Newport. . . ."[3]

By midsummer 1639 plans were well under way to lay out the town's streets, houses, and highways, and by the end of the year, commissioners had already approached Portsmouth with plans for a union of the two Aquidneck communities. A year later the plan was implemented, with William Coddington of Newport chosen governor for a "yeare, or till a new be chosen" —a term having a certain air of indefiniteness about it.[4] At the same time, a deputy governor, four assistants, and various treasurers, secretaries, and constables were elected with similar conditions of office. Within four years this union was expanded to include Providence and Warwick, and Rhode Island had secured a Parliamentary charter under which John Coggeshall of Newport was elected the first chief executive of the colony. Despite some political sleight of hand by William Coddington, Charles II granted Rhode Island a royal charter in 1663, which bound the towns together once for all, and which remained in effect until 1843.[5]

With these esoteric details of governance satisfactorily resolved, the inhabitants of Newport could get on with the day-to-day business of city building. This was less difficult in Rhode Island than it had been in Massachusetts because the infant colony was blessed with several natural advantages that Massachusetts sorely lacked. The early settlers of Newport were familiar enough with the Narragansett region to know that its soil was remarkably fertile compared to the rocky, unproductive ground that plagued the visible saints of Massachusetts Bay. Boston had a good harbor, but people generally agreed that Newport's was better. Not only was it more protected, but since the harbor was situated in the path of the gulf stream, it rarely froze. According to at least one account, Newport was " 'a coat warmer in winter and a coat cooler in summer than Boston.' "[6] Moreover, the several islands surrounding Newport were free of the wolf packs that constantly threatened to devour cattle and sheep on the mainland.

In the end, of course, the success or failure of the experiment depended on the people involved, and happily for Newport, the early settlers were experienced pioneers. They had expertise in mercantile, political, and agricultural affairs on both sides of the Atlantic,[7] and they knew the necessary ingredients for a successful venture. Of greater significance, perhaps, is that they were fairly wealthy men, able to buy and develop large tracts of land which in time would produce surpluses to pay for essential manufactured goods from abroad. Agriculture, the sheep and cattle industry, and commerce grew hand-in-hand as this astute first generation of Newport merchants began the never-ending search for commercial markets. The founding and development of Newport was never a haphazard affair. An excellent harbor, kind weather, fertile land, few predatory animals, and shrewd men combined to open the way to Newport's prosperity. By the end of the seventeenth century, a visitor noted that Newporters lived "plentifully and easily."[8]

As Newport continued to thrive over the next decades, the town's reputation as a lively, freethinking community attracted a variety of people. James Franklin, Benjamin's brother, set up his press in Newport in 1726, after Boston officials became inhospitable. A few years later the philosopher George Berkeley arrived with his own cultivated coterie and was delighted to find a community receptive to and stimulated by new ideas. In the 1730s his influence led to the formation of the Society for the Promotion of Knowledge and Virtue (more commonly known as the Philosophical Club) and, a decade later, of Redwood Library. Architect Peter Harrison made his way to Newport in time to design Redwood Library and elope with the pregnant daughter of one of Newport's leading merchants.[9] Harrison's brilliant architectural skills made up for his breach of etiquette, and he went on to design the Brick Market Place and Touro Synagogue, all three of which still stand as a tribute to this farsighted designer.

Since Roger Williams' spiritual descendants refused to eject anyone from the colony for nonconformity, by mid-century Quakers were rubbing elbows with Jews, Huguenots, Anglicans, Catholics, Presbyterians, and Baptists. There was neither time nor motivation for religious persecution in Newport, and "notwithstanding so many differences," there were "fewer quarrels about religion than elsewhere, the people living peaceably with their neighbors of whatever profession." Despite the amicable relations, however, all the dissenters agreed that "the Church of England is second best."[10]

There can be little doubt that Newport prospered as a result of Britain's neglect. By ignoring British navigation laws and pursuing a policy of free trade long before Adam Smith made it fashionable, the community was able to expand its commerce and its borders as the eighteenth century advanced. Even the European colonial squabbling (King George's War, 1744–1748, and the French and Indian War, 1756–1763) gave Newport traders an opportunity to make a little extra money on the side. In both wars merchants fitted out privateers and sent them after French ships. Unfortunately for the British, when the Newport vessels encountered French ships carrying molasses, sugar, and rum, the parties engaged in commerce rather than conflict.[11] Treason? Call it good business.

Historians cannot point to any particular year in which Newport entered its so-called golden era, but by 1760 the seaport was basking in unparalleled prosperity. Commercial activity dominated the community, which had long since ceased to depend on its own hinterland for exportable products. Few would have guessed that scarcely sixteen years later it would lie wasted, a desolate monument to the change in British imperial policy. The explanation for Newport's decline lies in the town's singular dependence on the sea surrounding it, a dependence based not merely on trade, but on Britain's benign neglect as well. Because the Atlantic dominated Newport's economy so completely, the city felt the impact of the new British mercantile restrictions in the 1760s and 1770s more keenly than any other American community. Once the British decided to reorganize the empire, once the Sugar Act was passed and the customs apparatus strengthened in order to enforce both it and succeeding legislation, Newport's trials began in earnest.

Furthermore, if the town was dependent on a healthy commerce, the townspeople themselves were dependent on each other. No one group, not even the merchants, could succeed without the support of the others. In short, the single-minded concentration on trade involved the entire community in an interdependent chain of relationships which worked to the benefit of all. How uniquely vulnerable the whole network was to outside pressures was demonstrated by the British as they destroyed Newport's entire socio-economic structure by imposing commercial restraints. Frustrated by the knowledge that obedience to the mercantile laws meant self-destruction, the townspeople turned on each other in fear and confusion. Cooperation gave way to rancor, and discord replaced harmony. Challenged by one crisis after another, the majority of Newporters allied themselves with rebel forces in a desperate attempt to forestall British "tyranny" and extend their age of glory.

Like the events themselves, this study is confined to a short span of years. Because Newport's decline was so precipitous (and unexpected), emphasis has been placed on the basic forces which affected Newport's rise, and on the influences which led to its decay. For an understanding of what happened at that time and place, three major and interrelated topics have been explored: the basis of Newport's economy, the effect of that economy on individuals and groups within the community, and the consequences of Great Britain's role in this late–eighteenth-century drama.

In so defining the parameters of the study, other topics—interesting, but unrelated to the matter at hand—have been ignored. In short, the threads of history have been woven selectively because many aspects of Newport's development are not relevant to this particular tale. No attempt has been made to untangle all the knotty issues of town government, political haggling, educational facilities, or religious practices. Topics that are only peripheral to the main thrust of the story have been excluded for the sake of continuity and cohesiveness.

This is a story about the relationship of the sea, the townspeople, and the British. As such, the political revolving door commonly known as the Ward–Hopkins controversy has little connection. As an internal struggle in which the power of the governorship was at stake, it is important to the political history of Rhode Island, but not to the Revolutionary era. However, the early confrontation between recalcitrant royalists and budding whigs (which set the scene for the political divisions of the Revolutionary years) is an essential component of the narrative. Similarly, although a general discourse on religious principles (or the lack thereof) in eighteenth-century Rhode Island would be extraneous, the growing acrimony between the Anglican Church and competing religious groups is important here. The development of educational institutions or municipal services sheds no light on Newport's struggle for survival during America's best and worst of times.

What follows is a social and economic study of Newport in the 1760s and 1770s which will clarify the seaport's rebellious stand against England at that time. Part I sketches all the commercial patterns of the community and demonstrates the overwhelming dependence Newporters had on the unrestricted use of the sea. At the same time, the section focuses on molasses, rum, and slaves, which, during these years, took on a special role in the economic life of the town. No other seaport was as dependent on these three items of trade. Part II deals with Newport as an eighteenth-century urban community where the sea created particular patterns of development. Using evidence extracted from census data, tax lists, estate inventories, and other quantifiable material, the pages examine demographic characteristics, social institutions, and relationships among various groups. Part III superimposes the new British policies on the town and analyzes the communal response to these threats.

While Part I is concerned primarily with the commercial life of the community, the following section turns to the people themselves and discusses the unique interdependence of all groups—rich and poor, men and women, whites and blacks. If these pages suggest an harmonious community, Part III reveals the stresses and tensions that increased dramatically after 1763 and threatened the town's cohesion. Here it becomes clear that given Newport's structure and economic base—given its dependence on the sea—British imperial policy in the decade before the Revolution had a devastating effect. Rebellious and uncompromising, the town was torn apart over the question of livelihood *vs.* loyalty. The American Revolution was a civil war in Newport, Rhode Island. It was stimulated by economic considerations which in turn created dissension and disorder. The issues were resolved only after a long and costly war which brought a weakened Newport the independence it demanded but could no longer enjoy.

NOTES

1. The defense of the Viking theory is best summed up by Philip A. Means, *The Newport Tower* (New York, 1942) and Hjalmar P. Holand, *America, 1355–1364: A New Chapter in Pre-Columbian History* (New York, 1946), Part I. Irresistible refutation is provided by W. S. Godfrey, Jr., "The Newport Puzzle," *Archaeology*, 2 (1949), 146–49, and "Newport Tower, II," ibid., 3 (1950), 82–86, as well as by Samuel Eliot Morison, *The European Discovery of America: The Northern Voyages, A.D. 500–1600* (New York, 1971), pp. 72–75.

2. The most detailed study of early Newport (to 1647) is found in *A Documentary History of Rhode Island,* ed. Howard Chapin, 2 vols. (Providence, 1916, 1919). For a more recent interpretation of the early years, see Carl Bridenbaugh, *Fat Mutton and Liberty of Conscience* (Providence, 1974).

3. RICR, I 88. The nine original settlers were William Coddington, Nicholas Easton, John Coggeshall, William Brenton, John Clarke, Jeremy Clerke [Clarke], Thomas Hazard, Henry Hull, and William Dyer.

4. RICR, I 100.

5. Coddington angered the unsuspecting Newporters by surreptitiously obtaining an English patent making him governor of Aquidneck Island and in effect separating Aquidneck from the rest of the colony. A flurry of protests caused the commission to be revoked in 1653.

6. Quoted in Bridenbaugh, *Fat Mutton,* p. 13.

7. Ibid., p. 15.

8. "Travel Diary of Dr. Benjamin Bullivant [1697]," *New-York Historical Society Quarterly,* 40, No. 1 (January 1956), 58–60.

9. Sydney V. James, *Colonial Rhode Island: A History* (New York, 1975), p. 240.

10. George Berkeley to Sir John Percival, Mar. 28, 1729, Redwood Library, Newport.

11. Howard W. Preston, *Rhode Island and the Sea* (Providence, 1932), p. 61. Bostonians, enraged at Newport's unpatriotic behavior, began to seize Newport vessels, forcing the Newporters to retaliate in kind. " 'The Lord protect Capt. Hughes, they

greatly thretten him at Newport. . . . [It] is said they are fitting out a Privateer to go after him, a mad thing.' " John Hancock to Capt. Bastide, June 2, 1747, as quoted in W. T. Baxter, *The House of Hancock: Business in Boston, 1724–1775* (Cambridge, Mass., 1945), p. 94*n*.

I

"A Good Voyage and Safe Return"

By the second half of the eighteenth century, the colonies could boast of several commercially successful communities. Philadelphia had already challenged Boston's pre-eminence as America's largest and most important urban center, and New York was not far behind. Newport—with fewer people and a smaller volume of trade—assumed that it made up in quality what it lacked in quantity. These northern seaports had much in common with each other: their mercantile activities and their prosperity were inseparably intertwined, and they claimed a degree of material comfort for the majority of their residents unimaginable a century earlier. Their class structures were also comparable: wealth was increasingly channeled into the hands of fewer people, while each community was faced with a growing number of inhabitants unable to provide for themselves. And even if Newport was an island of nonconformity in a sea of congregational orthodoxy, it could look farther south and take comfort in the heterogeneity of New York and Philadelphia.

But if these towns exhibited certain basic features common to all, they were also dissimilar in many respects. As their imported merchandise varied, their processing industries followed suit. Charters and hence forms of government differed from place to place—ethnic diversity, yes, but a special blend of cultures and religions in each location. Courts throughout the colonies relied on the common law, but that law was often uncommonly applied. Colonial currency was pegged to the British pound sterling, but each community ran into its own peculiar problems with specie *vs.* a paper currency.

Newport's ascendancy as well as its decline was intricately linked both to its position as a seaport and to the precise nature of the goods loaded and unloaded on the piers. Philadelphia imported grain and milled flour; Newport imported molasses and distilled rum. New York imported dry goods and sold luxury items to the carriage trade; Newport acted as the essential middleman, collecting cargoes from all who would sell, and redirecting them to whoever would buy. Of all these commerce-oriented towns, only Newport was heavily involved in what is referred to as the "triangular trade." Although there were many possible three-legged routes, only one is commonly associated with that phrase. In this infamous triangle, Newport merchants sent rum to Africa where it was exchanged for slaves who were sold in the Caribbean for molasses to be returned to Newport for distillation into rum.

Thus, although the basis of Newport's economy was trade, the characteristics of that trade and its subsidiary industries differed from that carried on by Newport's competitors to the north and south. Moreover, "a good Voyage and safe return"[1] was essential not only to the merchants but to the townspeople as well. To Newporters a good voyage meant a safe return—and *physical* safety may not have been uppermost in their minds.

"Any Scheme of Trade"

I F IN SOME WAYS Newport was like any other eighteenth-century urban seaport, the geography of Rhode Island gave it one singular characteristic: comparatively speaking, Newport had no hinterland. Roughly ⅛ the area of Massachusetts, and 1/47 the size of New York, Rhode Island alone could not supply Newport, its commercial center, with enough local products to develop a thriving Atlantic trade.[2] To compound this difficulty, Rhode Island merchants were constantly short of cash because, as Dr. William Hunter explained, "This colony produces nothing that will procure a Dollar in any of the Nightbouring provinces."[3] Despite these problems, the colony's commerce was flourishing by the mid-eighteenth century because Newport's merchants managed, nonetheless, to assemble cargoes from other colonies to supplement Rhode Island cattle, horses, and cheese.[4] The town's unique predicament did not go unnoticed, however, and in one of many reports, customs officials pointed out that "the exports from hence are most collected from the neighbouring Colonies; the natural productions of its own, being quite insufficient to support its navigation."[5] Merchants were willing, as they themselves often said, to consider "any scheme of trade."[6]

In a Report to the Board of Trade in 1741, Governor Richard Ward indicated that Rhode Island's commerce was not only varied but widespread: "We have now one hundred and twenty sail of vesseles belonging to the inhabitants of this colony, all constantly employed in the trade; some on the coast of Africa, others in neighboring colonies, many in the West Indies, and a few in Europe."[7]

Merchants rarely specialized geographically. There were few, if any, whose dealings were limited only to England, southern Europe, the West Indies, the American coast, or Africa. Newporters could not afford to be that selective. With war and less predictable disasters a constant threat, it was not good business to restrict trade to one corner of the globe. Governor Stephen Hopkins was quite accurate when he stated that "these people . . .

look out for markets in every part of the world within their reach."[8] And with few exceptions, the geometrics of that trade changed little over two centuries. Triangular patterns calling for Newport, Nantucket, and Tenerife at each point alternated with squares composed of Newport, Jamaica, South Carolina, and London. Additional stopovers in Virginia and Surinam turned that square into a hexagon.

There was nothing haphazard about either the ports of call or the merchandise traded. If stops included Maine and Newfoundland, it was because planters in the West Indies paid good cash for northern dried fish to feed their slaves. And if the sloops and brigantines docked at Philadelphia or Baltimore before proceeding to the Caribbean, it was because those same West Indians needed flour. Shingles from New Jersey, livestock and corn from Connecticut, pitch, tar, hoops, staves, and headings from the Carolinas also found ready markets in the islands. Lumber from Honduras and spermaceti oil from Nantucket were in demand in London and were sold there in return for manufactured and luxury items.

Part of the game was timing: knowing when and where to send the various cargoes. Indeed, the success or failure of a voyage hinged on information, specific and current information, concerning markets. For this reason merchants were in constant correspondence with their factors and captains, and a captain arriving at any port was expected to send an account of his voyage and the state of the markets to his owner as soon as possible. These reports indicated whether slaves were commanding a higher price on Jamaica or Barbados. They relayed information concerning the scarcity of molasses on Guadaloupe or its abundance on Martinique. A profitable voyage depended on a merchant's learning that Kingston Harbor was glutted with dried fish, while Charleston had only a meager supply. If logwood or mahogany were lying on London docks unsold, there was no point in sending more.

It was not enough to know that a given commodity was in short supply, however. The merchant was also dependent on the availability of certain merchandise, and some products were only seasonal. Wheat was unobtainable until the end of October; pork could not be procured until the first of December. Even sugar cane was harvested only at certain times of the year. Oil sold best in England before Christmas, but what if the whales refused to cooperate?

A corollary of communication was speed. Time and time again, a captain would be advised to "make all dispatch possible."[9] Competition between merchants was keen, and it was a simple law of supply and demand that the first vessels to arrive in port with needed cargo would command the highest prices. Also, in a specie-starved economy, the early arrival could demand cash on the spot, while the laggard might be forced to settle for produce—on credit at best. "Capt. . . . Bowers and Ellery having got in but a little time before us had supply'd the first Run of the market and carried off the Ready cash . . . ," wrote Captain John Knowles from his ship in Montego Bay.[10]

Although in the seventeenth and early-eighteenth centuries English goods made their way to Newport from Boston, by the mid-eighteenth century these manufactured and luxury items flowed into Newport either directly from London or via New York. This shifting trade route suggests a desire by Newporters, unenthusiastic about their Massachusetts neighbors to begin with, to shed their dependence on Boston. As early as 1739 merchant John Banister experimented with a direct trade between Newport and London so that Newporters could "make themselves Independent of the Bay Government to whom they have a mortal aversion."[11]

After the French and Indian War, Newport's commerce underwent further expansion. Island markets such as Hispaniola, Guadaloupe, and Martinique increased in importance; whaling vessels left Newport in greater numbers, and new opportunities in Virginia and South Carolina diverted Newport slavers from the West Indies. Rhode Island products such as spermaceti candles, cheeses, and Narragansett pacers took up more space both above and below deck. Even the "poor and unmerchantable" Rhode Island tobacco found a home in the Caribbean.[12] Iron and iron products became important commercial articles. Newport merchants imported and exported pig iron in increasing amounts between 1768 and 1772, and by 1771 they were the largest exporters of cast-iron goods in the colonies. Since exports of pig iron frequently exceeded imports of that commodity, perhaps some of the ore was produced locally. How frequently the Iron Act was flouted is impossible to say.[13]

New clearance records continued to be set year after year until the mid-1770s when, according to historian Bruce Bigelow, Newport reached the pinnacle of its commercial prestige.[14] Moreover, if the ratio of shipping tonnage to population is an indication of the importance of trade, commerce had become proportionately more significant to Rhode Island than to the other colonies by 1770.[15] A wide-ranging commerce was so "essentially necessary" to the Newport merchant that even the customs officers admitted that "the least Obstruction becomes prejudicial, perhaps fatal to him."[16] The community was overwhelmingly dependent on the sea for its growth and prosperity—as well as for certain vital resources, such as wood, without which no eighteenth-century community could survive.[17] Governor Joseph Wanton had good reason to say that the inhabitants of Newport were "principally supplied with the necessities of life by water."[18]

The display of imported goods extended far beyond the necessities of life, however. Chocolates, jams, and brandies lined the shelves of Nathaniel Coggeshall's store, while leather-bound books and silver buckles awaited ready cash at Peleg Thurston's shop. Bolts of blue and red duffels, crimson and black tammies, and green and scarlet friezes dazzled the eye and waited for the skillful hands that would turn them into elegant clothing.[19]

If European products were distinguished by their infinite variety, West Indian imports were notable for the opposite reason: they remained unvaried. Sugar, molasses, and rum flowed from the islands to Newport, to the exclusion of nearly everything else.[20] Loaded with these commodities, Newport vessels sped back from the Caribbean to sell the cargoes. Not only did the molasses trade stimulate the rum industry in Newport—as evidenced by the increasing number of distilleries—but the trade between Newport and neighboring colonies expanded as well.[21] As early as 1741 Governor Richard Ward noted that "the neighboring governments have been in a great measure supplied with rum, sugar, molasses and other West Indian goods by us. . . . Nay, Boston itself, the metropolis of Massachusetts, is not a little obliged to us for rum and sugar and molasses. . . ."[22] But it was Governor Hopkins who summed up the importance of molasses and rum most succinctly: "This distillery is the main hinge upon which the trade of the colony turns."[23]

Although it is clear that Newport merchants imported more molasses and rum than anything else, the extent of that importation during the eighteenth century is not known. The Molasses Act of 1733 and the Sugar Act of 1764 imposed duties on these goods, thereby stimulating merchants to devise means by which they could import them without paying the odious taxes.[24] All that can be said for certain is that there was an enormous volume of molasses, rum, and sugar flowing into Newport—some legally, some illegally, and it is impossible to tell which route was better traveled.

Despite the lack of accurate records there are nonetheless some sources that shed light on the question of how Newporters disposed of their large quantities of molasses and rum. Statistically speaking, Stephen Hopkins left the best record. In a written protest to the rumored Sugar Act, Hopkins laid out the details of Newport's commerce.[25] According to his figures, during the year 1763 Newport employed 352 vessels in the coasting trade and sent 183 ships to foreign ports (which included Europe, Africa, and the West Indies). Breaking the latter figures down, Hopkins maintained that 150 of those vessels headed for the West Indies and 18 went to Africa. Hopkins informed the commissioners that these 18 vessels carried 1,800 hogsheads of rum which had been distilled in Rhode Island. He implied that this was the sum total of rum distilled there, which was misleading to say the least since Newporters themselves were known to enjoy mugs of that beverage now and then.

At the same time, Hopkins admitted that Rhode Island imported 14,000 hogsheads of molasses annually, only 2,500 of which came from the British islands. Since a measure of molasses yielded almost the same measure of rum, if Newport ships carried only 1,800 hogsheads of rum to Africa, that left over 12,000 hogsheads of molasses in Rhode Island. What became of this molasses? Much of it was consumed in Newport. In addition, the governor indicated that although some of it was shipped to Massachusetts, New York, and Pennsylvania to pay for goods which made up the cargoes Newport sent to the West Indies and Europe, the rest was sold in the southern colonies.

Basically what all this means is that Newport imported vast quantities of molasses, and distilled some of it into rum for home consumption and export to Africa. The surplus molasses was sent off to the other colonies, which used it in cooking and to satisfy their craving for sweets. As Newport sent molasses down the coast in ever-increasing quantities, Rhode Island's sister colonies became her most important trading partners in terms of volume.[26]

2

"The First Wheel of Commerce"

LTHOUGH A GREAT DEAL OF MOLASSES went to other colonies, a
significant amount of rum was shipped to Africa and exchanged there
for slaves who were brought to the Caribbean and southern mainland colonies. It was the profit from this triangular trade in particular which
attracted attention in the pre-Revolutionary era. As a spur to secondary industries, and as a prime source of hard money, the trade in molasses, rum, and
slaves became a dominant feature in the decade before the Revolution when
Newport emerged as a "commercial metropolis."[27] Despite lingering skepticism about the authenticity of the triangular trade, evidence from Newport
points not only to its existence but to its significance in terms of profit as
well.[28] This last point is extremely important because the merchants of Newport, in company with other New England traders, were finding it increasingly difficult in these years to pay for goods imported from England. Much
to their delight, they found that profits from the slave trade could alleviate
this problem. As one Newport correspondent explained in 1762:

> I know no other method you can take to do this, than that which is taken by
> most people who have remittance to make to London[,] that is by a Guinea
> Voyage— That trade has been carried on from this Place with great success,
> and is still the only sure way of makeing remittances. Their Cargoes are
> Chiefly rum which can be procured here for the Currency of the Colony,
> and at a lower price too than in any other port of America. . . . Some mer-
> chants here have made vast sums of money by the Guinea Trade lately; they
> have ordered their slaves directly from the Coast to Monto Christo [His-
> paniola] where they received a higher price for their Negros than in any of
> our Islands. . . . But what added greatly to the profit of the Voyage was their
> loading their Vessels from the mount with sugar.[29]

Although it must be acknowledged that the greater part of Newport's trade
was intercolonial, the triangular trade represented a crucial element in the
economy. For this reason and because of the historiographical controversy

over the triangular trade, it is appropriate to examine that aspect of Newport's commerce in greater detail.

Historians find it difficult to pinpoint the first slaving venture out of Rhode Island, but the initial voyage seems to have been in 1649 when William Withington bought part-interest in a ship appropriately named *Beginning* and sent it off to Barbados, "Guinney," and Rhode Island via the West Indies.[30] It left from Portsmouth, rather than Newport, but Newport slavers were probably not far behind.

Until 1696 the monopoly held by the English Royal African Company theoretically excluded independent American slave traders, and this may be one reason why the Rhode Island slave trade was small during the seventeenth century. The Royal African Company lost its monopoly at the turn of the century, and England obtained the Spanish assiento in 1713. These two events worked hand-in-hand to stimulate the trade between Newport and Africa since the English colonies were now permitted to act as carriers for the Spanish.[31] Evidence suggests that Rhode Islanders themselves looked to 1723 as the year in which they became irrevocably committed to the slave trade. Until that year, according to Governor Stephen Hopkins, "the negroes upon the [African] coast were supplied with large quantities of French brandies; but in the year 1723, some merchants in the colony first introduced the use of rum there, which from small beginnings soon increased to the consumption of several thousand hogsheads yearly. . . ."[32]

There is no way of knowing precisely how fast the slave traffic out of Newport grew in the following years, but the latest studies indicate that it increased in importance as the eighteenth century wore on.[33] Governor Hopkins explained to the Board of Trade in 1764 that for the previous thirty years the colony had sent about 18 vessels to the African coast annually. Customhouse records, reprinted in the *Newport Mercury*, indicated that between 1763 and 1774 anywhere from 15 to 22 vessels cleared Newport each year for Africa.[34] Furthermore, these figures do not reflect the total number of vessels involved in the slave trade at that time. Customs records in the newspaper itemize 13 African ventures in 1763, but Governor Hopkins claimed that Newport sent 18 ships to Africa in that year, and he was closer to the truth.[35] According to another source, in 1763 Newporters were "very large adventurers" in the slave trade, their fleet consisting of "20 sail of vessels, computed to carry, in the whole, about 9,000 hogsheads of rum."[36]

The exact number of ships involved in the slave trade from Newport will probably never be known because existing records from Newport showing African clearances account for only a portion of that trade. Since the publication of Philip Curtin's study of the transatlantic slave trade, other historians using additional documents have demonstrated a greater participation in the carrying trade by North Americans generally and Newporters particularly. Estimates based on carefully documented evidence indicate that American slavers averaged 30 voyages yearly in the 1760s and still more in the 1770s.[37]

But while there is agreement among historians on Newport's primacy in that trade, the number of voyages sponsored by Newporters remains conjectural—despite the most recent attempts at quantification. This is due to the nature of the supporting evidence, which is non-quantifiable except to the extent that it suggests an increase in the number of voyages attributable to Newport vessels. For example, some Newport slavers cleared for Africa from other ports, leaving evidence of their destination only in the form of correspondence. In May 1772, the Champlins gave Captain Samuel Snell the latest news about the Newport slave trade and added that "[Captain] Lin Martin is gone to Philadelphia to fit cannot sale from thence 'till July."[38] Correspondence between merchant Stephen Ayrault and his captain Nathaniel Whitting puts Whitting on the African coast in early 1774, but there was no African clearance for Whitting from Newport.[39] In a letter dated February 1772, Newport customs officers noted that James Clarke, "an inhabitant of this place," had arrived in Newport from Brunswick, North Carolina, where his vessel had been cleared for Africa.[40] Clarke, who was both captain and owner of the *Expedition*, had, according to the account, "carried on from hence for some Years a Constant Trade to Senegal. . . ." Clarke was indeed a Newport resident, and his "constant trade" with Africa is all the more notable since it fails to surface in Newport clearance records.[41]

It is hardly surprising, however, that a Newport slaver would clear from North Carolina for Africa. Newport sorely lacked wood and naval stores, and North Carolina was rich in both. Where better to repair a ship and pick up rum casks? Newport clearance records show several entries each month for North Carolina. If James Clarke found it convenient to clear from there to Africa, other Newporters may have done the same.[42] Furthermore, at least one Newporter, Aaron Lopez, sold slaves in North Carolina—slaves purchased in Jamaica.[43] This fact points to yet another reason why only the lower limits of Newport's participation in the slave trade can be determined: because there was a small secondary—or indirect—slave trade between the Caribbean and the North American mainland as well as an inter-Caribbean trade, it is difficult to estimate with any precision how many Newport vessels were involved in these variations of the traffic.[44] Indeed, how often were slaves brought into Newport directly from Africa and then exported to the southern colonies or the Caribbean?[45]

Other deviations from the basic triangular pattern could also prevent a Newport vessel from being counted as a slaver. For instance, a vessel cleared from Newport to the West Indies might, in fact, have been embarking on the first leg of a voyage that would subsequently take it to Africa. If a captain loaded his ship in Newport with New England fish, candles, hoops, and staves, what was to prevent him from selling his cargo in the Caribbean, filling his hold with rum, and sailing for Africa? If his second stop was the African coast, he could even circumvent the Sugar Act, which prohibited American *importation* of foreign rum, not its purchase. The spirit of the Sugar Act may have been violated, but the spirits below deck were surely worth the breach.[46] Documents discovered thus far confirm only one eighteenth-century voyage following this route, but this is likely due to a paucity of records rather than to a dearth of voyages.[47]

Indeed, it is not too farfetched to suggest the possibility of a shuttle between the West Indies and Africa.[48] Orders from an owner to a captain were often open-ended; they might direct him to deposit his African-bought slaves in the West Indies, with the stipulation that further orders would await him on his arrival at a particular island in the Caribbean. It is conceivable that these subsequent orders directed the captain back to Africa for another slaving voyage, particularly since captains from Newport occasionally mentioned seeing other captains from their home town on the African coast for whom there appear to have been no reported clearances from Newport.

The voluminous correspondence between owners and captains of slavers leaves little doubt, however, that the triangular pattern was the route most frequently followed by Newport merchants. So involved were they in the traffic that it would have surprised them greatly to hear that the triangular trade has been exposed as a myth.[49] They would have argued otherwise in light of their method of paying English suppliers: "In Respect to the Debt that may be due from us to you, we propose to discharge it by converting our next importation of molasses into a Cargo of Rum, which we shall send to the coast of Guinea for the purchase of slaves, which we shall order to the W. Indies to be there sold for Bills of Exchange and remitted to you."[50]

Newport also had the dubious distinction of being more heavily engaged in the slave-carrying trade than other colonial ports. Customhouse records indicate that a greater number of vessels left Newport for the African coast than from any other American port. By 1770, they conducted well over 70% of the trade. Boston, Newport's closest rival, showed a poor second throughout the 1760s and 1770s.[51] Indeed, Newporters were engaged in something more than eighteenth-century urban rivalry when they boasted that their city was " 'America's answer to Bristol.' "[52] Reaching the same conclusion—from firsthand observation—was the Rev. Samuel Hopkins, whose voice thundered from the pulpit of the First Congregational Church in Newport. "Rhode Island," he despaired in 1776, "has been more deeply interested in the slave trade . . . than any other colony in New England. . . ."[53]

Historians have spent little time inquiring into Newport's role in the slave trade, possibly because of the lack of quantifiable evidence, and possibly because whatever the actual number of slaving voyages, this trade represented only a small part of Newport's total commerce. Bruce Bigelow's entry and clearance figures for 1763, 1764, 1773, and 1774, tabulated from the *Newport Mercury*, show that Newport's coastwise and West Indian trade far surpassed the African trade in terms of numbers.[54]

These figures are deceiving, however. First of all, as explained above, there were more slaving voyages than the newspaper clearances suggest. Although Bigelow counted 14 African clearances in 1773, Jay Coughtry documented 20 voyages in that year.[55] Secondly, most of the slave trade involved a triangular pattern, which means it was three-legged rather than two-, and this omission also distorts Bigelow's figures. Thirdly, a number of coastal clearances were for ships that were returning to their home ports, which means that they were not owned or captained by Newporters at all. Finally, since many of the coastal clearances were either for fishing boats or for those making short runs to nearby Connecticut for wood and other provisions, they simply cannot be compared on a one-to-one basis with a slaving venture in terms of importance, cost, or profit.[56] If the figures are to be used at all, they should be used, not to deny the importance of the African trade, but to emphasize the disproportionate significance of these comparatively few ventures. The key question is the importance of the slave, rum, and molasses trade to the development of Newport as a commercial center, not how many slave ships cleared Newport each year. Surely it is more relevant to explore the effect this traffic had economically and socially on the community. In 1787, Mr. Hopkins was ready with an answer:

> The inhabitants of Rhode Island, especially those of Newport, have had by far the greater share in this traffic, of all these United States. This trade in human species has been the first wheel of commerce in Newport, on which every other movement in business has chiefly depended. That town has been built up, and flourished in times past, at the expense of the blood, the liberty, and happiness of the poor Africans, and the inhabitants have lived on this and by it have gotten most of their wealth and riches.[57]

As an avowed abolitionist, Hopkins may have overstated his case somewhat, but it can hardly be denied that the slave trade played a prominent role in Newport's pre-war prosperity.

The slave trade was inextricably bound up with rum because rum was the liquid currency used by Americans to purchase slaves on the African coast. Occasionally some tobacco changed hands, but by and large rum was bartered, to the exclusion of other commodities. So well were people aware of this that the term "rum vessel" was used synonymously with "slave ship."[58] Newport merchants obtained rum either by distilling it from imported molasses or by importing it directly from the Caribbean. Since the French sugar planters undersold the English, and the English did not produce the amount of molasses needed for Newport's growing commerce and home use anyway, Newport merchants naturally turned to the foreign islands for both molasses and rum.[59] Unfortunately for the merchants, both commodities were subject either to duties or to seizure if they came from the foreign sugar islands. But molasses and rum were so necessary to the Newport economy that merchants routinely ignored both duties and prohibitions either by smuggling or by bribing their way through customs.[60] Their expertise and skill in this business may be monuments to Yankee ingenuity, but they are also great frustrations to historians. In short, any eighteenth-century document purporting to show the amount of trade between Newport and the sugar islands is likely to have been greatly understated.

Even the governor of Rhode Island, Stephen Hopkins, was not above tampering with the statistics to cover up the enormous quantities of illegal rum and molasses flowing in and out of Newport. In his Remonstrance to the Board of Trade protesting the Sugar Act (1764) Hopkins supposedly laid out the details of Newport's commerce. His figures varied significantly from the clearance records as reported in the *Newport Mercury*, and if pressed, Hopkins would have found it difficult to explain them. For instance, Hopkins claimed that in 1763 18 vessels cleared Rhode Island for the African coast carrying 1,800 hogsheads of rum which had been distilled in that colony. At that time 1,800 hogsheads were the equivalent of approximately 180,000 gallons.[61] Since prime males at that time were selling for 130 gallons each, this would mean that those 18 ships could buy and bring approximately 1,385 slaves to the American continent. Divided among the 18 ships, the number of slaves would average 77 per ship. Even on the assumption that there were several more on board because women and children could be purchased for fewer gallons, evidence indicates that slaving captains usually left the coast of Africa with more slaves aboard.[62] There is no way of calculating precisely how many slaves were taken from the African coast and removed to the West Indies or southern colonies via Newport vessels, but records suggest that ships averaged more than 77 slaves. To cite only a few examples: the *Newport Mercury* on July 9, 1764, reported that Captain Robert Elliot of Newport had sailed from Africa to the West Indies with 160 slaves on board, and the *Massachusetts Gazette and News Letter* of April 4, 1765, announced the departure of Captain James Warner, master of another Newport slaver, from the coast of Guinea with 104 slaves. In 1772, Captain Samuel Tuell purchased 95 slaves, and the next year William English crossed the Atlantic with 104 slaves on board.[63]

Furthermore, the latest and most exhaustive studies suggest that American ships carried an average of anywhere from 106 to 130 slaves during the 1760s and 1770s.[64] Therefore, if Newport slavers were bringing more slaves to the West Indies than Hopkins indicated, there can be little doubt that more rum was leaving Newport to be exchanged for those slaves. Since Governor Hopkins was at a disadvantage when it came time to explain the amount of imported molasses and rum, he had every reason to minimize the amount of rum exported from Newport.

Across the ocean, Bristol merchants engaged in the slave trade began to feel that New England rum gave Newporters a competitive advantage in the race for profits. As African demand for rum increased, it became less expensive to purchase slaves in rum equivalents than in the fabrics or East India goods with which the Bristol merchants traded.[65]

In any event, rum exportation to Africa was not of "relative unimportance"[66] to the economy of Newport, especially in light of the importance given to the trade as a source of hard money by Newporters themselves. In terms of human merchandise, Jay Coughtry has verified the transportation of over 30,000 slaves between 1760 and 1775 in Newport-owned vessels, while Roger Anstey calculated that the North American colonists together brought over as many as 74,000 during those same years.[67] Thus, if Coughtry's figures are used as an absolute minimum, and Anstey's estimates are anywhere near accurate (and they are based on very convincing evidence), Newport merchants—who transported the largest share by far of this cargo —must be held accountable for the exportation and sale of at least 40,000 slaves in the fifteen years prior to the war. This was indeed a "major factor" in the town's economy, despite assertions to the contrary.[68]

Hopkins was right when he observed that molasses, rum, and slaves were the cornerstones on which Newport's temporary prosperity was built. Supporting this assessment is the fact that Newport was the only major colonial urban center with a favorable balance of trade with the West Indies in 1769.[69] Since Newport ships carried more slaves from Africa to the West Indies than did those from other American ports, it is possible that this particular aspect of Newport's commerce swung the balance of payments in its favor. Governor Hopkins certainly intimated as much when he noted that "by this trade alone" £40,000 in remittances were made from Rhode Island to England yearly.[70]

Hopkins confined his analysis to 1763–1764. After some alleged sluggishness in the latter years of the decade, the African traffic blossomed in the early 1770s,[71] when, according to an eminent Boston physician, Dr. Benjamin Waterhouse, Newport's merchants began to depend " 'more and more for emolument upon the slave trade.' "[72] In 1772 they sent at least 29 vessels to the African coast.[73]

Profit, of course, was the *raison d'être* of the triangular trade. Dealing in rum and slaves was a business, and it often yielded high returns.[74] By examining the 1772 tax list for Newport and comparing the taxpayers at the top of the list with a list of those merchants known to be involved in rum and slaves, some interesting patterns emerge. The merchants, of course, were assessed more than anyone else in the community. But those merchants who were most heavily involved in the slave and/or rum trade were assessed more—and theoretically had more taxable income or property—than those who dealt exclusively or primarily in other goods. Table I is constructed from the above-mentioned tax list. The table includes in descending order all taxpayers paying 2 or more pounds Rhode Island currency in taxes—135 in total. Merchants who can be established conclusively as owners (or part-owners) of slaving vessels are marked "MO" (merchant–owner).[75] Evidently an investment of this nature was a good one; the names of the 33 merchants who have been identified as slave traders are clustered toward the top of the list. Moreover, 34 of the merchants in the top half of the list either were involved in the slave trade or were extensive importers of rum or molasses, whereas only 14 of those in the bottom half of the list were involved with those commodities or with the slave trade.

Newport's participation in the slave trade made it relatively easy for the local population to acquire slaves. In 1774 the census takers reported 1,084 bond servants in a total population of 9,209—an unusually high proportion of blacks for a New England community.[76] Although slaveholding was widespread among the affluent, those trading in slaves monopolized the domestic market. In other words, the merchant–owners in Table I held more slaves than people engaged in other pursuits. Distillers also seem to have made good use of slave labor, as did people with large landholdings.

One should not infer from Table I that these merchants dealt exclusively in molasses, rum, and slaves. No merchant in Newport dealt with only one or two items; slaving and rum were only a part of their shipping business. For instance, Aaron Lopez was advised to send "Seven or Eight Hundred Barrels of Shads" to the consignee of a slave cargo, "that the Bitter and the Sweet may go together." And not all merchants made profits from every slaving venture: ". . . I note your being a Sufferer by your African trade at Kingston last year. I wish you better success for the future," commiserated one of Lopez' correspondents.[77] Yet, by and large, slaving seemed to offer a chance to make money on a large scale. Lopez' insurers talked of "the great success which the African vessels have had," and the Champlins wrote to Captain Samuel Snell from Newport, advising him that "Colo. Wanton's Brig . . . is arived here, cleared his owners £500 Stg." The Champlins' own ledgers showed a far greater profit. Between 1769 and 1775 their slaving ventures averaged a return of nearly £1,000 sterling per voyage. And to still other merchants, a £500 gain in the slave trade was "a Trifling Sum" when

TABLE I

Newport Taxpayers Assessed £2 or more, 1772.

Name	£	s.	d.	Occupation†	No. slaves owned 1774
Aaron Lopez	37	11	0	MO, MR	5
Joseph & Wm. Wanton*	18	12	0	MO, MR	6
George Rome	16	19	0	MO	13
Elisha Sheffield	16	10	0	farmer	5
Samuel Dyre	13	11	0	M, farmer	7
Jacob R. Rivera	13	11	0	MO	12
John Tillinghast	12	4	0	MO	1
Simon Pease	11	17	0	MO, MR, domestic slave trader	6
John Collins*	11	3	0	MO, MR	13
Evan Malbone	11	0	0	MO, MR, distiller	7
Francis Malbone	11	0	0	MO, MR, distiller	10
Edward Cole	10	3	0	tanner	6
James Honeyman	10	3	0	lawyer	6
Samuel & Wm. Vernon	10	3	0	MO, MR	10
John Scott	10	3	0	MO	x
Jacob Polock, est.	10	3	0	M	x
Nicholas Easton	9	10	0	landholder, farmer	6
Charles Wickham*	9	9	0	MO, MR	3
George Gibbs	8	9	0	MO	6
Benjamin Mason	8	9	0	MO, MR	7
Edward Wanton*	8	9	0	MO	x
Moses Levy	8	9	0	MO	1
Samuel Fowler	8	9	0	M	4
Charles Handy	8	3	0	M	4
George Irish	8	3	0	farmer, horse dealer	x
John Mawdsley	8	2	0	MO, MR	20
John Slocum	7	9	0	MR	3
Robert Stoddard*	7	9	0	MR	3
Caleb Gardner*	7	2	0	MO	2

Name	£	s.	d.	Occupation	No. slaves owned 1774
Samuel Johnson	7	2	0	MR, distiller	5
Thomas Richardson	7	2	0	MO, MR, distiller	4
John Fryers*	7	2	0	M	2
Thomas Robinson	7	2	0	M, spermaceti candles	x
Gideon Sisson	6	16	0	MR	2
Thomas Stelle	6	16	0	MR	4
Cahoone & Yeates	6	16	0	M	x
Henry Marchant	6	15	0	lawyer	2
Christopher Champlin*	6	2	0	MO	2
Elisha Coggeshall	6	2	0	landowner, innkeeper	3
Silas Cooke	6	2	0	MR, distiller	7
John Hadwen	6	2	0	M	1
Jonathan Otis	6	2	0	MO, silversmith	3
James Clarke	5	18	0	MO	5
Abraham Redwood	5	15	0	MO	3
Thomas Cranston	5	15	0	MO, MR, distiller	6
Ebenezer Richardson	5	15	0	MR, distiller	2
William Hunter	5	15	0	doctor	3
Samuel Holmes, est.	5	12	0	?	x
William Rogers	5	12	0	M, captain	x
John Tanner	5	6	0	M	1
John Bell	5	2	0	M	3
John Bours	5	2	0	MO	2
James Coggeshall	5	2	0	farmer	4
Jonathan Easton	5	2	0	landowner	7
Nap, Isaac, and Saml. Hart, est.	5	2	0	M	3
Henry Hunter	5	2	0	M	5
Josias Lyndon	5	2	0	M	4
H. John Overing	5	2	0	MR, distiller	8
Jonathan Thurston	5	2	0	distiller	4
David Chesebrough	5	1	0	MO	2
John Warren	5	1	0	M	2
Benjamin Brenton	4	18	0	farmer	4
Jahleel Brenton	4	18	0	farmer	3

Name	£	s.	d.	Occupation	No. slaves owned 1774
John Lawton	4	18	0	M	3
John Brown	4	15	0	farmer	4
William Gyles	4	15	0	M, timber	2
Joseph Jacob	4	15	0	?	3
David Moore	4	15	0	M	2
George Hazard	4	12	0	MO	2
Nathaniel Bird	4	8	0	M	1
Job Bennet	4	1	0	M	5
Peter Cooke	4	1	0	distiller	5
John Tweedy	4	1	0	doctor	3
Oliver R. Warner	4	1	0	M	4
Charles A. Wigneron	3	17	0	doctor	0
Benjamin Church	3	14	0	M, landowner	2
Isaac Lawton	3	14	0	MO, captain	0
Gideon Wanton	3	14	0	M	4
John G. Wanton	3	14	0	M	?
Francis Brinley	3	8	0	ropewalk	8
Nathaniel Coggeshall, Jr.	3	8	0	MR, distiller	x
Samuel Collins	3	8	0	M, landowner	4
Caleb Earl	3	8	0	M, building owner	1
Thomas Green	3	8	0	MR	1
John Halliburton	3	8	0	doctor	2
Samuel and Moses Hart	3	8	0	M	x
James Keith	3	8	0	MR	3
Robert Lillibridge, Jr.	3	8	0	M, innkeeper	1
Paul Mumford	3	8	0	M	0
Ichabod Potter	3	8	0	innkeeper	3
William Read	3	8	0	M, captain	4
Abraham Redwood, Jr.	3	8	0	M	1
Jonas L. Redwood	3	8	0	M	1
Wm. Redwood, Jr.	3	8	0	M	x
William Robinson	3	8	0	M, spermaceti candles	1
George Scott*	3	8	0	domestic slave trader	5

Name	£	s.	d.	Occupation	No. slaves owned 1774
Joseph Scott	3	8	0	domestic slave trader	x
Robert Stevens & Son	3	8	0	MO	5
James Tanner	3	8	0	M	x
William Tweedy	3	8	0	MR, apothecary	2
James Carpenter*	2	14	0	M	2
Samuel Carr	2	14	0	M	0
Samuel Freebody	2	14	0	M, distiller?	3
Joseph Hammond, Jr.	2	14	0	M	4
Giles Hosier	2	14	0	M	x
Robert Lawton*	2	14	0	M	0? 2?
Joseph Tillinghast	2	14	0	M, distiller, bakehouse	2
Joseph G. Wanton	2	11	0	M	3?
Simon Newton	2	9	0	distiller	3
Sheffield, tenant to Brenton	2	9	0	?	?
Philip Wanton	2	9	0	M	2
Jeremiah Clarke*	2	7	0	MR	1
John Fry	2	7	0	innkeeper	1
Jonathan Marsh	2	7	0	M, distiller	1
James Robinson	2	7	0	MO	2
James Taylor	2	7	0	M	0? 1?
John Thurston	2	7	0	distiller	1? 2?
Thomas Wickham, Jr.	2	7	0	captain?	3
Benjamin Wright	2	7	0	captain	4
Lemuel Wyatt	2	7	0	M, distiller	1
Matthew Cozzens	2	1	0	captain	4
Samuel Goldthwait	2	1	0	MR	2
Hyam & Simeon Levy	2	1	0	?	x
Solomon Littlefield	2	1	0	tavern	x
Peter Mumford	2	1	0	sugar importer	7
Thomas T. Taylor	2	1	0	MO, captain	x
John Townsend	2	1	0	furniture maker	3
Walter Chaloner	2	0	0	sheriff	6
George Champlin	2	0	0	MO, captain	2

Name	£	s.	d.	Occupation	No. slaves owned 1774
Nathaniel Coggeshall	2	0	0	MR, distiller	9
John Dupuy	2	0	0	?	3
Ebenezer Flagg	2	0	0	M?	x
Thomas Freebody	2	0	0	captain	3
Godfrey Wainwood	2	0	0	baker	1
Philip Wilkinson	2	0	0	MO	3

*Former slave captain
†M: Merchant
   MO: Merchant; owner of a slaving vessel
   MR: Merchant; extensive importer of rum/molasses
The number of slaves has been compiled from the MS census of 1774, Rhode Island State Archives, Providence. An "x" indicates that the merchant's name does not appear on the census.

The Newport tax assessment for 1772 may be found in manuscript form at the NHS. It is complete except for last names beginning with the letter "A." In 1775 there were four men whose last names began with "A" and who were assessed more than £2. Three were members of the Anthony family, Peleg, Joseph, and John. Peleg, assessed at £10 16s. 8d., and John at £2 6s. 1d., were landholders. Joseph, who was assessed at £4 12s. 2d., was a merchant, as was Stephen Ayrault (£7 2s. 10d.), who should be designated "MO."

The basis for the tax assessment was "An Act for taking a just Estimate of the Rateable Estates in this Colony in order that the Rates and Taxes may be equally assessed upon the Inhabitants," June 1767, Proceedings of the Rhode Island Assembly. According to the act, the following were ratable assets: real estate, including land, dwelling houses, distill houses, sugar houses, ropewalks, warehouses, wharves, mills, spermaceti works, lime kilns, tan yards, iron works, pot ash and pearl ash works, slaves, trading stock, money, wrought plate, and livestock. There was also a poll tax. Approximately 1,210 names appear on the list.

an £1,800 return on one voyage was at stake. The sloop *Adventure* yielded a 23% return after a voyage to Africa in 1773–1774. As news spread of one success after another, merchants from neighboring communities cast envious glances at the Newport traders whose wealth had "beene got in the Guiney trade."[78]

From his self-imposed exile in 1778, William Vernon, no stranger to the rum and slave trade, noted that the British had confiscated property valued at " 'not less than twelve thousand pounds sterling at least, besides my real estate at Newport. . . .' " This was no mean accumulation in the pre-Revolutionary era. The last word on profitability belongs to William Ellery, who wrote from firsthand knowledge that " 'an Ethiopian could as soon change his skin as a Newport merchant could be induced to change so lucrative a trade as that in slaves for the slow profits of any manufactory.' "[79] In their book on colonial shipping James F. Shepherd and Gary H. Walton estimate that colonial shippers as a whole earned an annual average of £20,000 sterling in the slave trade between 1768 and 1772. It is likely that Newport merchants claimed the lion's share of this money. As the most recent investigator of the trade suggests, "potential profits were sweet enough and predictable enough to tempt many otherwise prudent merchants."[80]

In Table I, a merchant positively identified as a rum/molasses dealer is labeled "MR" (merchant–rum). This designation signifies that no conclusive link has been established between that particular merchant and slaving, although that connection almost certainly exists in some cases. A merchant dealing in rum may or may not have been a distiller as well. Where he definitely can be labeled as such, Table I so indicates. The table implies that dealing in rum, that is to say, trading and/or distilling, was also a profitable business, but not as profitable as slave trading.[81]

The question that clouds the issue, of course, is whether these men were wealthy before they engaged in the slave trade and were able to participate in it only because of their affluence, or whether slaving added a more lucrative dimension to an otherwise ordinary commerce. That is to say, was slaving limited to the wealthiest merchants because of cost factors? Since account books and ledgers for most of the merchants are either missing or incomplete, the question must be answered circumstantially and only in part. In the 1760s and 1770s Newport merchants imported more molasses and rum than any other item. It was probably true that most, if not all, Newport merchants were involved with these commodities in one way or another. Rum distilling was the most important industry in pre-Revolutionary Newport. Since the "Guinea cargoes" were composed mainly of rum, it seems likely that any merchant who wanted to fit out a slaver would have had little difficulty obtaining and paying for cargo, except when a general shortage affected everyone. Before 1776, the slavers themselves were no larger than the vessels in the West India trade and thus only slightly more costly to build because of the modifications needed for the Guinea traffic. Crews on slavers were smaller and captains' wages lower than on other vessels.[82] Insurance was high, but only a small part of the total outlay. And to mitigate the cost (as well as the risk), many merchants went into partnership for a slaving venture. All things considered, it is reasonable to conclude that any fairly affluent merchant—and that includes those on the above list—could have traded in slaves if he so desired. Some merchants avoided the trade because the potential risks outweighed potential profits. For others, scruples stood between them and commercial slaving. In short, there is no reason to assume that anyone in Table I was shut out of the trade for financial reasons.

Newport's participation in the Atlantic slave trade became noticeable in the 1730s. There were few voyages in that decade, but the people who would take their place among the first families of slaving—the Scotts, Redwoods, Malbones, and Vernons—were the most active in the trade even then. They were joined in the 1740s and 1750s by the Wantons, Cheesebroughs, Ellerys, and Banisters. Within the next decade other merchants added slaving to their commercial activities, but almost all of them were from old Newport families. Except for George Rome, Newport's slaving community was limited to longtime residents. As to the wealth of these earlier slave merchants: their names were scattered throughout the first half of the 1760 tax assessment, but show no sign of clustering at the top as they did twelve years later in 1772 (see Table II).[83] This could imply that the tendency to cluster occurred between 1760 and 1772 as the number of slaving voyages increased and became more lucrative, and more merchants participated in the trade. It also suggests that even though it is not possible to establish precisely what proportion of each person's commerce was allotted to the slave trade, one need not have been among the wealthiest merchants to participate in it.

In order to maximize the potential profit of a slaving voyage very little was left to chance. Enterprising merchants sought and used vessels designed specifically for the African trade. They were swift because speed was vital. They were comparatively small because smaller ships proved just as advantageous in the African coastal trade as they did in America and the West Indies. A slaving captain could never be sure of his ability to purchase all his slaves at one location. More often than not he was forced to sail down the African coast from one port to another in search of cargo. Another benefit of a small ship was that it took less time to accumulate a sufficient number of slaves to make up a cargo. As one owner reminded his captain: "As your Cargo will be but small you'l the sooner get it off and if you can get Slaved

31

TABLE II
Newport Slave Traders, 1760

Name	First Documented Slave Venture	Position on 1760 Tax List	Amount Assessed
Peleg Thurston	1754	3	£46
John Malbone	1737	8	36
Abraham Redwood	1730s	10	30
Godfrey Malbone	1750s	13	27
Joseph Scott	1730s	23	21
William Ellery	1746	27	20
Stephen Ayrault	1740s	31	19
Philip Wilkinson	1740s	36	18
David Cheesebrough	1740s	42	16
Robert Crook	1754	43	16
Peter Bours	1733	63	12
Joseph Jacob	1750s	80	10
Jonas Redwood	1750s	81	10
Jacob Rodriguez Rivera	1750s	83	10
William Vernon	1730s	103	8
Thomas Teakle Taylor	1759	108	7
Robert Stevens	1756	126	6
James Carpenter	1750s	258 (approx.)	2
Samuel Vernon	1730s	312 (approx.)	2
Walter Chaloner	1754	382 (approx.)	1

This Table is compiled from the "Assessment List of £3110 Lawful Money made By Us the Assessors by Order of the General Assembly of the English colony of Rhode Island and Providence Plantations in New England—In America began and holden by adjournment at Newport in Said Colony, the Second Monday of June 1760." Rhode Island State Archives, Providence. There were 962 names on the assessment.

in time to get down to Jamaica in all the month of Jany. Will be a good Time for Sale of Slaves. . . ." It was commonly held that small cargoes were less likely to glut the market and depress the price of slaves.[84]

Notwithstanding these advantages, the British, who were the world's largest slave carriers at this time,[85] were skeptical about the size of Rhode Island slaving vessels. When Aaron Lopez tried to sell the American slaver

Deborah in London, it was rejected: "the smallness of her Hold in particular was a heavy objection. . . . though she was constructed in the manner usual for the Trade from Rhode Island to Africa, she would by no means suit for the Trade from Liverpool."[86] Newporters were satisfied, however, that less time spent in African waters was more lucrative in the long run. A quicker turn-around offered the possibility of a greater number of voyages. And, as William Vernon advised Captain John Duncan, "we have often found by experience that having slaves on board a length of Time, they become Sickly, and may dye befor they arrive at Market."[87] A shorter trip meant fewer pounds spent on food, and less time to worry about a slave insurrection on board. As crews averaged anywhere from six to eighteen in number, a general uprising could easily spell disaster. Unlike the hallucinations of southern planters, the threats of shipboard massacres were real enough for Newport traders. Newspaper articles and correspondence reported a number of actual insurrections. " 'We hear that Capt. Rogers [has] lately arrived in the West Indies from Africa, with a number of slaves. The Blacks made an attempt to overcome the Vessel's Company, but were subdued and twelve of them killed.' " Hearing of various uprisings, a nervous William Vernon was prompted to inquire of his insurers, "if an Insurrection of the slaves shou'd hapen, and a loss arise thereon more or less if your underwritters pay in that case. . . ."[88]

A number of healthy slaves brought quickly to market meant potential profits. Sick, injured, or rebellious slaves simply did not sell. This is probably the reason that Newport's merchants were so concerned with the health of the cargo. The Vernon brothers, always full of good advice, cautioned Captain Caleb Godfrey to "keep a watchful eye over 'em and give them no opportunity of making an Insurrection, and let them have a Sufficiency of good Diet, as you are sensible your voyage depends upon their health."[89]

33

REFLECTIONS

Newport's growth and prosperity were intimately bound up with the expansion and continuation of trade. Some people were connected with the maintenance of the ship itself; others, with the distribution and sale of cargo. Many Rhode Islanders earned their living by supplying produce for export; others became dependent on the importation of raw material which they turned into manufactured goods. In short, commerce created a ripple effect, whereby only a very few townspeople were disinterested in the outcome of a voyage.

Seafaring provided employment for 2,200 Rhode Island sailors in 1764 as well as for hundreds of caulkers, carpenters, sailmakers, ropewalk owners, and painters who contributed directly to the operation of the sailing vessels.[90] No less important were the stevedores and team drivers who could be assured of ships to load and unload or merchandise to haul away only if commerce was thriving. Coopers, too, prospered with every hogshead of molasses or rum that needed a barrel. Fishermen and farmers were dependent on the escalating shuttle trade between Newport and the West Indies for their economic well-being. White-collar employees of the merchants such as clerks, scribes, and warehouse overseers had a stake in the success of each ocean-going venture. So did the hundreds of vendors, hucksters, and shopkeepers who advertised in the *Newport Mercury*.

Newport was more than an entrepôt, however, and enterprising townspeople found it lucrative to produce manufactured goods from imported raw materials. Some of these goods were consumed locally; the surplus was exported wherever a demand arose. The rum distillers have been noted in this regard, but the spermaceti candle makers should not be forgotten. If it is true that Newport chandlers made more than one-half the number of candles produced in the English colonies, it is no less true that the vitality of this enterprise was dependent on the sea and the ships carrying the waxy headmatter.[91] At the same time, blacksmiths and ironworkers found merchants eager to buy their wares, as the demand for domestic cast-iron products increased. And by the early 1770s, merchants such as Aaron Lopez were supplying townspeople (primarily women) with thread or fabric which would be returned to the merchant in the form of cloth, garments, and shoes.[92]

Despite its eminence as a port, Newport never became a shipbuilding center because it lacked an immediate source of lumber. Nevertheless, ships from Jamaica brought mahogany, and that elegant wood combined with good New England maple, pine, and cherry allowed the firm of Goddard and Townsend to create desks, chests, and secretaries unparalleled anywhere in the colonies.

Newporters also provided services which were dependent on a flourishing trade. Ships were manned by itinerant sailors whose thirst was quenched by rum in Newport taverns, whose hunger was satisfied at boarding houses, and whose sexual desires were slaked by the prostitutes on Long Wharf.

In a word, the city of Newport depended on the sea. Any interruption of commerce would have sent shock waves throughout the entire community. There would have been no ships to unload, no tea to brew, no rum to distill (or to drink), no wood for the fireplaces, no candles to make, no accounts to copy, no slaves to trade, no broad cloths to tailor, no barrels to build. Even worse, no Rhode Island johnny cakes. By the second third of the eighteenth century, most Newporters relied very heavily on their silent partner—the Atlantic Ocean.

Although other New England communities shared some of Newport's characteristics, this does not mean that all eighteenth-century seaports were mirror images of each other. Even towns within short distances of each other had individual identities, different historical foundations and economic purposes. Boston and Newport, both mercantile communities, were separated by far more than miles. When one asks what gave Newport its particular flavor and identity, the answer must be molasses, rum, and slaves, "in which nearly all her merchants were interested."[93]

Vast quantities of these liquid commodities were shipped there, making rum distillation Newport's most important industry prior to the Revolution. In terms of volume, nothing exceeded molasses and rum as import commodities,[94] and Newport increasingly depended on these same items for export. The trade made it possible for more families in Newport to own slaves than families in any other New England urban center.[95] In terms of profit, evidence points to the triangular trade as a potential money-making venture. Rhode Island, along with the other northern colonies, had an unfavorable balance of trade with England. Unlike other colonies with major seaports, however, it had a favorable balance of trade with the West Indies. Since Rhode Island carried more slaves from Africa to the West Indies than did other colonies, it is also possible that this item swung the ledger sheet in Newport's favor, allowing specie to flow to England—and to Newport.

The merchants who were engaged in trading rum, molasses, and slaves among other merchandise had more taxable property than those not associated with the traffic. Pre-Revolutionary contemporaries attested to the profitability of the trade, as well as to the lavish standard of living its participants enjoyed. The war cut short Newport's golden era, but in the post-mortem following the Revolution more than one commentator remembered that in its heyday the town "owed a part of its prosperity to the slave trade." Others hoped for a restoration of those heady days, and drank a toast to the "Rhode Island African fleet."[96]

Although it is estimated that all the American colonies together were responsible for transporting only 6% of all slaves across the Atlantic in the mid-eighteenth century, this tells us nothing about the perspective that matters here: that is, the importance of the slave trade to Newport.[97] The British carried more slaves in the aggregate, but those the Newporters transported—no small number—were crucial to the town's economy. Similarly, knowing that Boston may have imported more molasses than Newport tells us nothing about the importance of molasses to the latter. The significance of these commodities lies in Newport's dependence on them.

But even more revealing is the importance given to Newport's peculiar trade by eighteenth-century observers. No one commenting on the town failed to note its existence, and many remarked on its dimensions. In 1768, a visitor to Newport, John Lees, described Newport as a place where "a vast quantity of molasses is distilled into Rum, and sent in large quantities to the Coast of Africa and all over the Continent of America. . . ." Lees went on to say that "they have severall Vessells in the Guinea Trade, most of their Dry-Goods they have from New York. . . ."[98] He commented on other particulars of trade, but it is clear that the traffic in rum and slaves caught his eye. Although the phrase "severall Vessells" cannot be quantified, the pervasiveness of slaving transcended the actual number of voyages to Africa, however many there were.

Although any eighteenth-century mercantile community encouraged subsidiary industries, it should be emphasized that rum and slaves spurred supporting industries in Newport to an extent unmatched in other urban areas.

In addition to providing jobs for so many seamen, Rhode Island vessels exported dried and pickled fish to feed the burgeoning West Indian slave population, and Rhode Island poultry, cheese, and sheep to nourish the planters.[99] Hoops, staves, and headings, supplied by Newporters to the West Indies, were hammered into casks and barrels to be filled with molasses and hurried back to Newport.[100] Local distillers also supplied rum to merchants from other American ports who sought to try their luck in the slave trade.[101]

It is all very well to acknowledge the economic importance of these commodities but in so doing one is left with a troubling question about Newport and the staples on which it relied: How did Newport's deep involvement in the slave trade affect its view of a Revolution allegedly fought for "freedom" and "liberty"? Even during the war a prominent visitor noted that Newporters "carry on the Guinea trade; they buy slaves there and carry them to the West Indies, where they take bills of exchange on old England. . . ."[102] For some Newporters, at least, profit took precedence over virtue. All that is known for certain is that the golden age of Newport neatly coincided with the town's spiraling participation in the trade of molasses, rum, and slaves. It is not too much to say that this "was the general employment of men of business, so as to be the source of the support and prosperity of the people."[103]

NOTES

1. Sailing orders for Captain Nathaniel Hammond, Newport, June 6, 1770, *Commerce*, I 333.

2. These comparisons refer to state size in 1790. Rhode Island was 1/44 the size of Pennsylvania and 1/30 the size of South Carolina, colonies with major urban centers. United States Bureau of the Census, *Historical Statistics of the United States: Colonial Times to 1970*, Bicentennial Edition, 2 vols. (Washington, D.C., 1975), I 39.

3. [William Hunter to a merchant in Glasgow], Newport, Jan. 26, 1762, Box 15, folder 1, NHS.

4. This was not always the case, however. In the seventeenth century, agricultural surplus was the motivating force behind expanding commerce. For the story of Rhode Island's commerce in the seventeenth century, see Bridenbaugh, *Fat Mutton*, passim. Governor Richard Ward's report to the Board of Trade gives ample evidence of its extent in 1741. See "Report of Governor Ward, to the Board of Trade, on paper money," Newport, Jan. 9, 1741, RICR, V 8–14.

5. Charles Dudley and John Nicoll to the Honorable Commissioners, Oct. 22, 1768, Customs Office Letters, 1767–1775, Book 90, NHS.

6. Unsigned letter (probably from William Vernon) to Richard Brew, Newport, Mar. 2[4], 1762, Slavery MSS, Box II, uncatalogued, NYHS.

7. "Report . . . on paper money," RICR, V 12–13. For a thorough discussion of the West Indies trade, see Bruce M. Bigelow, "The Commerce of Rhode Island with the West Indies, Before the American Revolution," Unpublished Ph.D. dissertation, Brown University, 1930.

8. "An Essay on the Trade of the Northern Colonies," *NM*, Jan. 30, 1764.

9. Samuel and William Vernon to Captain Caleb Godfrey, Newport, Nov. 8, 1755, Slavery MSS, Box II, V, #42, NYHS.

10. John Knowles to Samuel and William Vernon, Montego Bay, Dec. 24, 1774, Slavery MSS, Box I, K, #12, NYHS.

11. John Banister to Capt. John Thomlinson, May 28, 1739, Banister Copy Book, 1739, p. 174, NHS.

12. "An Essay on the Trade of the Northern Colonies," *NM*, Jan. 30, 1764; see also Richard Pares, *Yankees and Creoles: The Trade Between North America and the West Indies Before the American Revolution* (Cambridge, Mass., 1956), pp. 25–26.

13. Census Bureau, *Historical Statistics of the United States* (1975), II 1184, 1185, 1187. The intent of the 1750 Iron Act was to make sure that colonial iron was sent to England for processing. In order to discourage colonial manufacturing, Parliament forbade colonial rolling and slitting mills, tilt hammer forges, and steel furnaces. In addition, the act allowed pig- and bar iron to enter England duty free under special conditions (which were removed in 1757).

14. "Commerce of Rhode Island with the West Indies," Part I, chap. 7, p. 13.

15. The tonnage per capita was as follows: Massachusetts, .30; New York, .16; Pennsylvania, .21; Rhode Island, .36. See Census Bureau, *Historical Statistics of the United States* (1975), II 1168, 1179.

16. Charles Dudley and John Nicoll to the Honorable Commissioners, Oct. 22, 1768, Customs Office Letters, 1767–1775, Book 90, NHS.

17. According to Newport customs officials, wood was "chiefly supplied" by Connecticut and Long Island. Charles Dudley and John Nicoll to the Commissioners, Oct. 8, 1772, ibid.

18. Gov. Joseph Wanton to Earl of Hillsborough, June 16, 1772, in *Documents of the American Revolution*, ed. K. G. Davies, Colonial Office Series, 21 vols. (Dublin, 1972 ——), V 126.

19. *NM*, Mar. 12, 1764, and passim.

20. See Gilman M. Ostrander, "The Colonial Molasses Trade," *Agricultural History*, 30 (1956), 77–84; James F. Shepherd and Gary M. Walton, *Shipping, Maritime Trade, and the Economic Development of Colonial North America* (London, 1972), Appendix IV; Customs House Records of Charles Dudley, NHS.

21. Ezra Stiles noted that Newport had 16 distilleries in 1761. *Itineraries*, p. 23. Rhode Island had more than 30 distilleries in 1764, the majority of which were in Newport. There is a minor historical dispute concerning the number of distilleries in Newport in 1769–1770. Christopher Champlin claimed that there were " '10 distill houses which are employed the most part of the year and 3 more, that distill occasionally.' " Christopher Champlin to Colin Drummond, May 29, 1769, as quoted in George Mason, *Reminiscences of Newport*, inlaid edition (Newport, 1884), RIHS. Edward Field, *State of Rhode Island and Providence Plantations*, 3 vols. (Boston & Syracuse, 1902), II 401, states that "Newport in 1769, had 22 distilleries. . . ." "Bull's Memoirs of Rhode Island," 1636–1783, which appeared serially in the *Rhode Island Republican* between 1832 and 1839, agrees with the latter estimate: "The town contained 22 Rum Distilleries all said to have been in operation about this time [1769]. The places where 21 of them stood, and the names of their respective owners, we have ascertained, viz. . . ." The latter estimate is certainly more accurate than Champlin's, but it is strange that he would downgrade the actual number, unless Drummond was a tax collector.

22. "Report . . . on paper money." RICR, V 12–13.

23. Stephen Hopkins, "Remonstrance of the Colony of Rhode Island to the Lords Commissioners of Trade and Plantations" (1764), RICR, VI 381.

24. The Molasses Act of 1733 provided for duties on commodities from the foreign islands amounting to 9*d.* on rum per gallon, 6*d.* on molasses per gallon, 5 shillings on sugar per hundred weight. The Sugar Act of 1764 reduced the tax on molasses to 3*d.*, retained the duty on sugar, and prohibited foreign rum altogether. A further measure in 1766 reduced the duty on molasses to 1*d.*, but this was payable on all imported molasses.

25. "Remonstrance," RICR, VI 378–83.

26. Shepherd & Walton, *Shipping*, Tables, pp. 229–30. The middle and southern colonies, relying on this molasses from New England, reversed the New England pattern and imported much more rum from the West Indies than molasses. It was of some importance that in the case of Virginia, at least, the duty on West Indian rum was less

than on New England rum. James B. Hedges, *The Browns of Providence Plantations*, 2 vols. (Cambridge, Mass., 1952), I 73.

27. Hedges, *Browns of Providence Plantations*, I xvi. In a letter to Andrew Belcher dated Newport, Oct. 20, 1758, an unknown correspondent also referred to Newport as "the metropolis." NHS.

28. The most critical analysis of the triangular trade is Gilman M. Ostrander's "The Making of the Triangular Trade Myth," *William and Mary Quarterly*, 30 (1973), 635–44. Skepticism borders on dogmatism in John McCusker's study: "All statistical and economic indices unite to argue the minimal significance of the investment in African trade on the part of the merchants of the Continental Colonies." John James McCusker, Jr., "The Rum Trade and the Balance of Payments of the Thirteen Continental Colonies, 1650–1775," Unpublished Ph.D. dissertation, University of Pittsburgh, 1970, pp. 496–97. Other historians also claim that the African trade was an insignificant part of American commerce. See Shepherd & Walton, *Shipping*, p. 97, and the trade statistics in Appendix IV. Although this may be true of American commerce as a whole, it was not true of Newport, something Walton admits in an article which predates his larger study. Gary Walton, "New Evidence on Colonial Commerce," *Journal of Economic History*, 28 (1968), 369n.

29. [William Hunter to a merchant in Glasgow], Newport, Jan. 26, 1762, Box 15, folder 1, NHS.

30. Bridenbaugh, *Fat Mutton*, p. 24.

31. *Documents*, III 114n5. Spain was prohibited by papal arbitration from participating directly in the slave trade. In order to populate her colonies with slaves she was forced to engage other countries as carriers. The contract between Spain and the carrying country was the coveted assiento.

32. "Remonstrance," RICR, VI 380. Hopkins may have wanted Rhode Island to take sole credit for introducing rum to the African coast, but in fact Rhode Island shared this honor with West Indian merchants.

33. Jay Coughtry's excellent work on the trade is a welcome addition to the quantitative studies of this topic. Jay A. Coughtry, *The Notorious Triangle: Rhode Island and the African Slave Trade, 1700–1807* (Philadelphia, 1981). See also Tommy Todd Hamm, "The American Slave Trade with Africa, 1620–1807," Unpublished Ph.D. dissertation, Indiana University, 1975; Bigelow "Commerce of Rhode Island with the West Indies"; *Documents*, vol. III; *Commerce*, vol. I, passim.

34. *NM*, passim.

35. The most recent tally accounts for 18. Coughtry, *Notorious Triangle*, p. 27.

36. *NM*, Sept. 5, 1763.

37. *The Atlantic Slave Trade: A Census* (Madison, Wisc., 1969). For an extended discussion, see Roger Anstey, "The Volume of the North American Slave-Carrying Trade from Africa, 1761–1810," *Revue Française d'Histoire d'Outre-Mer*, 62 (1975), 47–66. Anstey argues for a higher volume of trade by the North American participants, and he is in turn upwardly revised by J. E. Inikori, "Measuring the Atlantic Slave Trade: An Assessment of Curtin and Anstey," *Journal of African History*, 17 (1976),

197–223. Anstey's eighteenth-century figures have been accepted by Seymour Drescher in *Econocide: British Slavery in the Era of Abolition* (Pittsburgh, 1977), p. 205.

38. C[hristopher] and G[eorge] C[hamplin] to Captain Samuel Snell, Newport, May 12, 1772, *Commerce*, I 398.

39. Correspondence between Stephen Ayrault and Captain John Stanton, and Ayrault and Capt. Nathaniel Whitting, Spring 1774, Haight Collection, NHS.

40. Charles Dudley and John Nicoll to the Honorable Commissioners, Feb. 20, 1772, Customs Office Letters, 1767–1775, Book 90, NHS.

41. James Clarke is referred to as a merchant and slave trader in correspondence collected in *Commerce*, I 343 and reprinted in *Documents*, III 245. A scribal notation on this correspondence places Clarke in Newport on Mar. 6, 1772.

42. How many returned to North Carolina is also conjectural since North Carolina's records are even less reliable than Rhode Island's. Slaves were often brought into North Carolina overland rather than by water, and there are no records for this importation comparable to customs entries or naval officers' lists. See *Documents*, IV 235.

43. Peleg Greene to Aaron Lopez, Newbern, N.C., Sept. 13, 1772, *Commerce*, I 413–14.

44. Lopez also participated in the inter-Caribbean trade, as demonstrated by the following comment from one of his captains: "I was resolved to dispose of our Cargo at Dominica . . . and invest it in New Negroes for Hispaniola. . . ." Captain William Taggart to Messrs. Aaron Lopez and John Cook, Jan. 1, 1774, Lopez Papers, Haight Collection, NHS. Between 1760 and 1775, 4,532 slaves were sent from Caribbean ports to South Carolina in 321 ships. Virginia imported 327 (in 26 ships) from the islands during the years 1760–1769. Since North American merchants played a more important role than English traders in the West Indian – North American trade, it is likely that Newporters cornered their share of this market. W. Robert Higgins, "The Geographical Origins of Negro Slaves in Colonial South Carolina," *South Atlantic Quarterly*, 70 (1971), 42; Herbert S. Klein, "Slaves and Shipping in Eighteenth-Century Virginia," *Journal of Interdisciplinary History*, 5 (1975), 386; Pares, *Yankees and Creoles*, p. 8.

45. For evidence of this trading pattern, see Bill of Lading of the *Little Beckey*, 1760, *Documents*, III 185; see also 198n, 194n, 209n, 210n.

46. Voyages following this geographical pattern were well known in the early-nineteenth century when, in an attempt to conceal their destination, slavers cleared " 'for the West Indies where they dispose of their out cargoes and proceed to Africa for slaves.' " Pennsylvania Abolition Society, Am. S. 01, Minutes of Apr. 7, 1800, as quoted in Anstey, "Volume of North American Slave-Carrying Trade," 48.

47. Hamm, "American Slave Trade with Africa," 128. One should not count on the absolute accuracy of existing clearance records: "P.S. . . . I find two ships which entered out for Europe are destind for Jamaica . . . ," noted one of Newport's merchants to his brother. George Champlin to Christopher Champlin, Charlestown, Dec. 8, 1768, *Commerce*, I 257. See also News Items Relating to Slave Trade, Newport, Sept. 5 [1763], *Documents*, III 187, and the route of the *Beginning* noted above.

48. Anstey, "Volume of North American Slave-Carrying Trade," 50, quotes an African merchant who maintained that " 'there go annually from North America and the West Indies at least 60 or 70 [ships] and they are yearly increasing.' "

49. According to Ostrander, "Making of the Triangular Trade Myth," 625, "this famous triangular trade is, in fact, a myth, for no such pattern of trade existed as a major factor in colonial commerce."

50. G. and J. Malbone to Messrs. Trecothick and Thomlinson, Newport, July 28, 1764, Malbone Papers, Box 174, folder 12, NHS. In the pre-Revolutionary era, the vast majority of Newport-owned ships headed toward the West Indies to sell their cargoes, with occasional deliveries to South Carolina and Virginia.

51. In 1768 Rhode Island sent 18 ships to Africa, Boston, 0; in 1770, Rhode Island showed 18 slaving ventures, Boston, 6; in 1771, Rhode Island had 11, Boston, 4. "An Account of the vessels cleared outward at the several ports in North America," PRO, Customs 16/1, Great Britain; transcript, Library of Congress. See also *Documents*, III 70n2, 71n, 72 and note, 73n, 75n, 76, 189, 202, 209, 213, 217; and Coughtry, *Notorious Triangle*, p. 25. Coughtry does not appear to take into account the fact that Newport-owned vessels cleared from other ports, thus giving Newport, in fact, more than 70% of the trade.

52. Oliver Ransford, *The Slave Trade: The Story of Transatlantic Slavery* (London, 1971), p. 123. Bristol was one of England's leading slave-trading ports.

53. "A Dialogue Concerning the Slavery of the Africans Showing it to be a Duty and Interest of the American Colonies to Emancipate all the African slaves with an Address to the owners of such Slaves" (1776), *Timely Articles on Slavery* (Miami, 1969), p. 590n.

54. "Commerce of Rhode Island with the West Indies," Part I, chap. 7, p. 12.

55. *Notorious Triangle*, p. 28. Elizabeth Donnan shows 14 African clearances for 1763 and 22 in 1764, but does not distinguish between outward entries and clearances for departure. See Newport Custom-House Entries, *Documents*, III 189, 202, 209, 213, 217. A contemporary, Granville Sharp, estimated that British Americans shipped 6,300 slaves from the coast of Africa in 1768 alone. Even on the assumption that Sharp, as an abolitionist, inflated his figures to make his point, Newport merchants were undoubtedly transporting far more than customs records indicated. St. George Tucker, *A Dissertation on Slavery, With a Proposal for the Gradual Abolition of It, in the State of Virginia* (Philadelphia, 1796; repr. Westport, Conn., 1970), pp. 27–28.

56. For instance, during April and June 1774, the coastal clearances for Newport break down this way:

APRIL: Halifax, 2; Connecticut, 9; Maryland, 3; Virginia, 2; Newfoundland, 2; Penobscot, 1; New York, 9; Egg Harbour, 2; North Carolina, 5; Martha's Vineyard, 1; fishing, 6; Falmouth, 1; Nantucket, 1; South Carolina, 1; Philadelphia, 1; Pleasant River, 1.

JUNE: Quebec, 1; Pleasant River, 2; New York, 7; Penobscot, 1; Connecticut, 7; Egg Harbour, 1; Virginia, 3; Philadelphia, 2; Nova Scotia, 2; North Carolina, 1; South Carolina, 1; New Jersey, 1; Piscataqua, 1; Nantucket, 1; Kennebeck, 2; Yarmouth, 1; St. Johns, 1; Halifax, 1; fishing, 5; Maryland, 3; Falmouth, 2. *NM*, outward clearances, April and June, 1774.

57. Samuel Hopkins, *The Works of Samuel Hopkins*, 3 vols. (Boston, 1854), II 615.

58. For examples of the use of this term, see Peleg Greene to Aaron Lopez, Annamaboe, Dec. 25, 1774, *Commerce*, I 524, and Captain Peleg Clarke to John Fletcher, July 25, 1772, *Documents*, III 259, as well as Hopkins, "Remonstrance," RICR, VI 380.

59. Hopkins, "Remonstrance," RICR, VI 380, and Ostrander, "Colonial Molasses Trade," 78, 79.

60. They were also inclined to tamper with what imported rum they had on hand to make it stretch farther: "our method is to take very Black Sugar and Boil it untill as hard as Pitch and as Black which we add water to while boiling to make it thin, and put as much of this liquor to a hogshead as will please the Eye. . . ." William Vernon to Capt. J. Sleight, Apr. 29, 1772, Vernon Letter Book #77, NHS.

61. This may or may not represent full distilling capacity. No reliable statistics exist on the rum output of various distilleries. Estimates range anywhere from one hogshead per day to one hogshead per week. On April 4, 1774, the *NM* advertised a distill house for rent which would "work off about 100 gallons a day." In 1749 a hogshead of molasses was fixed at 100 gallons.

62. In February 1765, a prime male slave sold for 130 gallons of rum in Annamaboe. Thos. Rogers to William Vernon, Feb. 26, 1765, Slavery MSS, Box II, R, #3, NYHS. For evidence that female slaves were less expensive than males, see Christopher and George Champlin to Captain Samuel Tuell, Newport, May 12, 1772; Captain Tuell to Christopher Champlin, Annamaboe, Sept. 26, 1772; and Thomas Dolbeare to Rivera and Lopez, Kingston, Jamaica, Nov. 20, 1773; all in *Documents*, III 258, 261, 275.

63. Hamm, "American Slave Trade with Africa," 375.

64. *Documents*, III 189n3. See also Hamm, "American Slave Trade with Africa," 278–79 for support of this proposition. Hamm estimates that the average cargo carried by American slavers was 106 slaves. Anstey calculates on the basis of 110 and 130, depending on the year. "Volume of the North American Slave-Carrying Trade," 52. Coughtry's figures average out to 118 per ship between 1760 and 1775. *Notorious Triangle*, pp. 27–28.

65. For an interesting discussion of foreign competition and its effect on Bristol merchants, see David Richardson, "West African Consumption Patterns and Their Influence on the Eighteenth-Century English Slave Trade," in *The Uncommon Market: Essays in the Economic History of the Atlantic Slave Trade*, edd. Henry A. Gemery and Jan S. Hogendorn (New York, 1979), pp. 324–27.

66. Shepherd & Walton, *Shipping*, pp. 50n4, 100, 227.

67. Coughtry's figures are based on British and American sources only. *Notorious Triangle*, p. 28. See also Anstey, "Volume of the North American Slave-Carrying Trade," 65.

68. Virginia Bever Platt, " 'And Don't Forget the Guinea Voyage': The Slave Trade of Aaron Lopez of Newport," *William and Mary Quarterly*, 32 (1975), 618;

Ostrander, "Making of the Triangular Trade Myth," 635; Hamm, "American Slave Trade with Africa," 282–84.

69. United States Bureau of the Census, *Historical Statistics of the United States: Colonial Times to 1957* (Washington, D.C., 1960), p. 758. This is the only year for which comparable statistics are available.

70. "Remonstrance," RICR, VI 380.

71. *Documents*, III 217n1, suggests that pirate activity on the African coast may have dampened the Rhode Island slaving spirit. Equally restricting was the prohibition on slaves imported into South Carolina in 1766, 1767, and 1768. Census Bureau, *Historical Statistics of the United States* (1960), p. 770.

72. Quoted in Hedges, *Browns of Providence Plantations*, I xvi.

73. Coughtry, *Notorious Triangle*, pp. 27–28.

74. Not all historians would agree with this assertion. See, for instance, R. P. Thomas and R. N. Bean, "Fishers of Men: The Profits of the Slave Trade," *Journal of Economic History*, 34 (1974), 885–914. The authors conclude that there was little or no profit to the slave trade. A position more compatible with my own is taken by Robert Stein, "The Profitability of the Nantes Slave Trade, 1783–1792," ibid., 35 (1975), 779–93.

75. The list of merchants involved in the slave and rum trade was compiled from the following sources: Volume III of *Documents*, Volume I of *Commerce, NM*, and the many letters, bills of lading, shipping orders, and customs records of the NHS and NYHS.

76. "An Account of the number of Families and Inhabitants of the Town of Newport, 1774," Rhode Island State Archives, Providence; hereafter referred to as MS Census, 1774.

77. Benj. Wright to Aaron Lopez, Nov. 16, 1766, and Feb. 21–29, 1772, Lopez Papers, Haight Collection, NHS; Abraham Lopez to Aaron Lopez, Savanna La Mar, Jamaica, Nov. 16, 1766, *Commerce*, I 175.

78. Hayley and Hopkins to Aaron Lopez [London], Apr. 29, 1774, *Commerce*, I 494; C[hristopher] and G[eorge] C[hamplin] to Captain Samuel Snell, Newport, May 12, 1772, *Commerce*, I 398. George J. Lough, "The Champlins of Newport: A Commercial History," Unpublished Ph.D. dissertation, The University of Connecticut, 1977, p. 125. Messrs. William and Samuel Vernon to ———, [1766], *Documents*, III 201; Bigelow, "Commerce of Rhode Island with the West Indies," Part I, chap. 7, p. 58; John Brown to Moses Brown, Nov. 27, 1786, Peck Collection, Box 8, 1786–1792, RIHS.

79. William Vernon to Josiah Hewes, Oct. 10, 1778, as quoted in *New England Historical and Genealogical Register*, 33 (1879), 317–18. £1 sterling in 1774 was equal to $37.86 in 1973. Census Bureau, *Historical Statistics of the United States* (1975), II 1175; William Ellery to Dr. Samuel Hopkins, 1791, as quoted in Elizabeth Donnan, "The New England Slave Trade After the Revolution," *The New England Quarterly*, 3 (1930), 255.

80. Shepherd & Walton, *Shipping*, p. 144. Coughtry, *Notorious Triangle*, p. 19.

81. According to one source, distillers earned an average profit of approximately 2*d*. sterling per gallon, "suggesting a gross profit per year of £250 or some 25% on the original investment." *Atlas of Early American History: The Revolutionary Era, 1760–1790*, edd. Lester Cappon et al. (Princeton, N.J., 1976), p. 103.

82. James Lucena to Aaron Lopez, Savannah, Georgia, June 28, 1768, *Commerce*, I 242; Platt, " 'And Don't Forget the Guinea Voyage,' " 606.

83. "Assessment List of £3110 Lawful Money Made By Us the Assessors by Order of the General Assembly of the English Colony of Rhode Island and Providence Plantations in New England—In America began and holden by adjournment at Newport in Said Colony, the Second Monday of June, 1760." Rhode Island State Archives, Providence. There were 962 names on the 1760 assessment, approximately 1,210 in 1772.

84. The most detailed study of ships used in the Newport slave trade will be found in George C. Mason, "The African Slave Trade in Colonial Times," *American Historical Record*, I (July–August 1872), 311–19, 338–45. John Fletcher to Captain Peleg Clarke, London, Feb. 24, 1772, *Documents*, III 255. Threlfal and Anderson to Christopher and George Champlin, Grenada, Apr. 22, 1771, *Documents*, III 249.

85. Curtin, *Atlantic Slave Trade*, p. 212.

86. Hayley and Hopkins to Aaron Lopez, [London], July 20, 1774, *Commerce*, I 500.

87. William Vernon to Captain John Duncan, Newport, Mar. 13, 1770, Slavery MSS, Box I, D, #14, NYHS. Virginia Platt states in her article about Aaron Lopez that because of the smaller size of Newport vessels "it is doubtful that the Newport traders of the 1760s and 1770s could have competed effectively with the Liverpool slavers." " 'And Don't Forget the Guinea Voyage,' " 617. My own feeling is that the smaller ships were used precisely because they did compete effectively. "It was found that [slave] vessels between 60 and 100 feet in length paid the best. . . ." Howard I. Chapelle, *The History of American Sailing Ships* (New York, 1935), p. 158.

88. Mason, "African Slave Trade," 314; Newport Entries and Manifests, 1786–1790, *Documents*, III 337–40, and passim. *Massachusetts Gazette and News Letter*, Nov. 28, 1765; S & W Vernon to Hayley and Hopkins, Aug. 11, 1774, Vernon Papers, Box 45, folder 1. NHS.

89. Samuel and William Vernon to Captain Caleb Godfrey, Newport, Nov. 8, 1755, Slavery MSS, Box II, V, #42, NYHS.

90. Hopkins, "Remonstrance," RICR, VI 379–80.

91. Richard Rudolph, "The Merchants of Newport, Rhode Island, 1763–1786," Unpublished Ph.D. dissertation, The University of Connecticut, 1975, pp. 8off.; Spermaceti Candle Agreement, Nov. 5, 1761, *Commerce*, I 88–92, and Spermaceti Candle Agreement, Apr. 13, 1763, *Commerce*, I 97–100.

92. Lopez Account Book, pp. 767 and 715, NHS.

93. Field, *State of Rhode Island*, II 401.

94. Shepherd & Walton, *Shipping*, p. 229.

95. MS Census, 1774.

96. Jacques Pierre Brissot de Warville, *New Travels in the United States of America*

Performed in 1788 (London, 1792), p. 144*n*; *Newport Herald*, Aug. 19, 1790.

97. Curtin, *Atlantic Slave Trade*, pp. 212–13.

98. "Rhode Island in 1768," *Rhode Island Historical Society Collections*, 14 (1921), 123.

99. Hopkins, "Remonstrance," RICR, VI 379.

100. Pares, *Yankees and Creoles*, pp. 25–26; Shepherd & Walton, *Shipping*, Table 5, pp. 223–24.

101. James Lucena to Aaron Lopez, Savannah, Georgia, June 28, 1768, *Commerce*, I 242.

102. *Travels in North America in the Years 1780, 1781, and 1782 by the Marquis de Chastellux*, trans. Howard C. Rice, 2 vols. (Chapel Hill, N.C., 1963), I 67.

103. William Patten, D.D., *Reminiscences of the Late Rev. Samuel Hopkins, D.D.* (Boston & New York, 1843), p. 80.

II

An Interdependent People

From the beginning, Newport's relationship with the sea molded its form and substance. The town's link to commerce shaped its pattern and growth, and created the society that emerged in the pre-Revolutionary era. Confined to an island and forced to import the necessities of life, Newport became a community completely dependent on the sea for sustenance and livelihood. And because of this single-minded commitment to commerce, it was also a community where people were overwhelmingly dependent on each other for their mutual prosperity. The merchants who most enjoyed the fruits of commerce knew full well that their empires rested on unskilled seamen, spermaceti candlewick spinners, distillers, coopers, and dock workers—to mention only a few indispensable participants. In turn, the larger Newport community relied on the merchants for their well-being, which meant employment in good times and support in bad. From this dependency, symbiotic relationships developed—like that between a merchant and his captain. The employer–employee relationship notwithstanding, a shrewd merchant realized that in the end he had to trust the "discretion, Fidelity and Candour"[1] of his captain in order to maximize the potential success of a voyage.

Over a period of time the sea affected the people of Newport in other ways. It was more generous to some than to others, and because of this disparity, an economic hierarchy developed. Wealth was created, displayed, and sometimes lost. Conversely, while the sea enriched some, it denied anything more than a meager existence to others. To many it denied existence altogether, and Newport's census showed a disproportionate number of women—some widows, others single—the result of an unending number of ocean tragedies. At the same time, an ocean tragedy of Newport's own making—the slave trade—encouraged the expansion of the town's black community and the institution of slavery. Meanwhile, Britain's halfhearted attempts to restrict Newport's essential commerce—and the merchants' routine evasion of the navigation laws—created an atmosphere of lawlessness which affected the community more than anyone might have suspected.

All the developments mentioned above—and several that were not—evolved from some aspect of Newport's mercantile roots. This in itself would be reason enough to explore them more fully, but their importance transcends that background. They are the threads from which the fabric of revolution was woven. Left to mature on its own, Newport saw its unique evolution come to an abrupt halt with Britain's decision to reorganize her empire in the 1760s and 1770s. Merchants and mariners alike were affected by the new policies, which, at the very least, called for an entirely new lifestyle. In short, Newport was expected to be more responsive to Britain's needs than to its own. In this crisis the people of Newport were forced to decide how best to preserve their institutions—that is to say, their way of life. It thus becomes essential to know what that way of life was in order to understand the impact of Britain's challenge.

3

A Mercantile Metropolis

I F THE AERIAL BALLOON had been invented a generation earlier than it was, and if someone had been wafting in one over Newport harbor on a fine spring day—say in the early 1760s—he (or she) might have noticed that Newport's spatial patterns reflected a thriving commercial center. This did not necessarily mean that the town was crowded—even by eighteenth-century standards. Tiny in comparison to the great cities of London and Paris (each of which had over half-a-million people), Newport at the height of its pre-Revolutionary population could not claim even 10,000 people.[2] It was urban, nonetheless. Newport was large and bustling by American criteria, even though the congested alleyways that were beginning to dot Philadelphia were still alien to it. The word "compact" describes Newport best; the town did not sprawl very far from the waterfront, which was the hub of activity. Wharves stretched for about a mile along the marvelously protected harbor. Sometimes, if the warehouses or wharves were filled to capacity, the tall ships, their billowy sails now semi-furled, would wend their way in and out of the old wooden piers searching for a likely spot to unload merchandise. The sea gulls, attracted by the smell of fish and spilled rum, screeched their delight, adding to the cacophony of the waterfront. Most of the ongoing conversations concerned trade, because in Newport everyone (or nearly everyone) had something to sell. Almost every Newporter was a merchant to some extent. The great merchants had their docks and warehouses and stores on Thames Street next to the water; the petty tradesmen cornered an extra counter in someone's shop. Shalloon and ozenbrig were sold at homes and in stores added on to homes. Gimblets and rattinet were bartered off a ship before it fully tied up. Kitterns changed hands on the dock after a round of serious bargaining, and hawkers and hucksters went from street to street haggling with their customers over a few pence worth of calamanco.[3]

If further evidence of commercial activity (and prosperity) should be needed, it would be found in the impressive homes built on Water and

Thames streets, both of which ran parallel to the harbor for about a mile. These softly colored mansions faced west to the wharves and water, allowing their merchant-owners to keep a constant vigil over their sources of income. Built on the east side of Thames Street, the large houses often looked across the main thoroughfare to a row of beautiful gardens. Since the occupants of the houses on Thames and Water streets were the most prominent merchants of Newport, it is clear that they preferred each other as neighbors to middle- or lower-class artisans, mechanics, and seamen. Indeed, there was an area on the southern end of Thames Street known as the "court end of town" where several of the most prosperous merchants built their grand residences next door to each other.[4]

A glance along the streets would show that it was not only the merchants who lived close to or at their place of business. Where occupation and residence can be traced for middle-class tradesmen and artisans, more often than not they are similarly located. Furthermore, a number of commerce-related occupations were clustered in particular areas. The distillers usually produced their liquid gold at the southern end of town, about Brewer Street close to the molasses-carrying ships. Another popular location for distilleries was the cove area. The shipwrights and carpenters also worked close to the waterfront, on or about Shipwright Street, for the simple reason that lumber was more easily carried one block than ten. Similar inducements caused food markets to locate near the harbor where produce could be unloaded quickly and sold before it spoiled. Ropewalks needed open space, and at least two of their owners, Francis Brinley and William Tilley, were undoubtedly delighted to find houses combining proximity to work and the right kind of neighbors.

Vendors and storekeepers lived along Thames and Spring streets in considerable numbers. Cordwainers, butchers, bakers, tailors, and other tradesmen apparently set up shop wherever the need arose, and lucky the man who acquired two skills and who could benefit from both. When Benjamin Marshall was not somewhere at sea as a mariner, he worked as a miller, and if the dry goods trade was slow, William Gardner turned to his butcher's shop—or vice versa. If Timothy Allen's customers could not afford his hand-wrought jewelry, perhaps they would purchase his choice Philadelphia flour.[5] If Robert Proud found no watches to repair, he might pull someone's tooth—with the same instruments. A number of Newporters doubled their occupations in the hope of doubling their incomes.

Inns and taverns were scattered throughout the town, although there seems to have been a disproportionate number—not surprisingly—in the southern part of Thames, near the distilleries. Laborers who could afford a choice probably lived close to their place of employment; those who could not clustered together on the outskirts of town in the poorer neighborhoods. A list of property owners and the location of their property is deceiving in terms of residential patterns because a person very often would own a house for the purpose of collecting rents and live elsewhere. From all indications people frequently changed their place of residence, particularly single men.

Single women or female heads of households, oddly enough, formed a distinct residential pattern. Although women were located on every street, they appear to have clustered together on some of them, forming little enclaves within the block. It is probably more than just accident that three, four, or five households in a row were headed by women, rather than randomly separated on the street census. This was particularly prevalent in the poor neighborhoods and was most striking among black female heads of households.[6]

Actually, in a town like Newport, this kind of residential pattern made sense. By 1774 there were 500 more adult women than men in Newport. Moreover, at any given time a great many men were away at sea, and this *de facto* drain of men left the community with a greater female : male ratio than even the census indicated. Thus it is not surprising that, forced to rely on each other, the women might want to live in close proximity, to be available perhaps during emergencies and to have fewer streets to walk on dark nights. Sarah Osborn hinted that such was the case when she noted that her female friends were available to " 'Help me in any wise.' "[7] In light of the female friendship network of the nineteenth century, this seems like a plausible explanation.[8]

No observant visitor to Newport could have failed to notice an unusual congestion at the southern end of Thames Street. This, and the accompanying commotion, may have meant that a cargo of newly arrived slaves from Africa or the West Indies was being led to a holding pen at that location.[9] Or it may have heralded a slave sale, most of which were conveniently held at the corner of Mill and Spring streets, and at the juncture of North Baptist and Thames. The most respected businessmen in the community engaged in the pursuit of profit by bringing slave and master together, an enterprise which made Newport the slave market of New England.[10]

51

Newport's extensive participation in the slave trade also made it possible for nearly 30% of the families in the community to own slaves. Although households with slaves were found in every part of Newport, an increase in number was noticeable near the waterfront where the wealthiest families congregated. Manumitted blacks also made up part of the city's population, but these families congregated in the Easton's Point area and more toward the periphery of town. There were no streets completely occupied by black families, although many claimed only white families. Most streets were integrated by both black and white residents. It was class, not color, that divided the people of Newport into residential patterns.

Nor were there any religious ghettos in eighteenth-century Newport.[11] People of every denomination could be found everywhere, but certain neighborhoods seemed to attract particular groups in greater proportion than others. For instance, the Quaker proprietors who originally owned all the land in the Easton's Point section and sold land subject to a quitrent found members of their own persuasion eager to take advantage of one or more lots. The area was laid out in a gridiron pattern about 1725, and is a striking contrast to other parts of Newport, which followed no pattern at all.[12] There was also a slight tendency for the merchants who happened to be Anglicans or Episcopalians to settle in the neighborhood of Trinity Church, an area of fine homes which reflected the affluence of their owners.

4

The World of the Wealthy

THE ABUNDANT EVIDENCE pointing to a mercantile community bound together in common interest also suggests that this economic interdependence took place within a structured society: a society in which one was identified by rank. Much like other eighteenth-century communities, the town of Newport was host to four basic groups: "the genteeler sort," the middling group, the "poor part of the Inhabitants," and, at the bottom of the ladder, indentured servants and slaves.[13] Distinct classes were perpetuated in part because, according to newspaper announcements and church records, marriages did not ordinarily cut across class lines.[14] Caty Malbone discouraged a young man "not possest with riches and honnours" because, as she sadly admitted to her brother, "my Friends didn't think him a proper match for me."[15]

Commerce created opportunities for great wealth, and the merchants were recognized as "the Support of this Sea-port Town," a belief that evolved from fact.[16] Furthermore, the merchants were becoming more supportive as the years went by. Although the total number of taxpayers continued to increase through the early 1770s, wealth was becoming concentrated in the hands of fewer people.[17]

The rest of the community may not have realized that they were accumulating a smaller share of taxable assets, but they surely were aware that the great merchants enjoyed a disproportionate prosperity. Their splendid town houses were matched by magnificent country seats a few miles away from Newport. Indeed, the ghosts of New England's Puritan ancestors must have stood aghast at this show of opulence unparalleled—according to contemporary accounts—anywhere in the colonies.

Godfrey Malbone, for example, who in 1740 was recognized as "the most considerable Trader of any here to the Coast of Guinea,"[18] epitomized the lavish lifestyle of eighteenth-century Newport merchants. Known for his scintillating soirees as well as his fabulously furnished home, he—so

TABLE III

Concentration of Wealth in Highest Taxpayers, 1760, 1772, 1775*

33 highest taxpayers

year	% of tax paid	% of total taxpayers
1760	27	3.4
1772	30	2.7
1775	34	3.3

86 highest taxpayers

year	% of tax paid	% of total taxpayers
1760	50	8.9
1772	51	7.1
1775	57.5	8.7

Source: "Assessment List of . . . June 1760," Rhode Island State Archives, Providence;
Tax assessments for 1772, 1775, NHS.
*Total number of taxpayers:
    1760: 962
    1772: approximately 1210
    1775: 985

legend has it—once moved his guests to the garden of Malbone Hall while his house burned to the ground rather than break up a good party.[19] Less likely to be apocryphal is the description of Malbone's country house by Dr. Alexander Hamilton, a prosperous Annapolis physician, who recorded various impressions of Newport during a stay there in 1744. Hamilton maintained that Malbone's mansion was the largest and most magnificent dwelling house I have seen in America. It is built intirely with hewn stone of reddish colour; the sides of the windows and corner stones of the house being painted like white marble. It is three stories high and the rooms are spacious and magnificent. . . . Round it are pretty gardens and canals and basins for water, from whence you have a delightful view of the town and harbour of Newport. . . .[20]

If Malbone's country estate merited comment, Abraham Redwood's garden in Portsmouth could hardly escape notice. An enthusiastic botanist, Redwood took time from his mercantile activities (which included slaving) to pursue his hobby. "We saw Mr. Redwood's garden," noted Dr. Solomon Drowne from Providence, "one of the finest I . . . ever saw in my life. . . . it grows all sorts of West India Fruit. . . . It has also West India flowers . . . and a fine summer house." Drowne seemed particularly impressed by the rumor that the garden was worth £40,000 (probably Rhode Island currency), and that the gardener "has above one hundred dollars per annum."[21] That one hundred dollars was a considerable salary in 1767, and Charles Dunham, the recipient, was probably Newport's first professional gardener.

The community at large had few doubts about where the money came from to "acquire" these "great estates." As one commentator noted, "It is owing to the great trade these Gentlemen have had with those Savages"— the "savages" in this case being Africans.[22]

It is somewhat fitting that the affluent had large homes because the number of people in a household increased in proportion to the affluence of that household. In other words, by weaving together tax and census figures it appears that wealthier people had larger households than those with smaller tax assessments.[23] Not only did the wealthy own more slaves, but there was a greater number of white members in the household. In some of these cases elderly parents may have shared a large house with their children and their children's family. It is also possible that the more opulent with a better standard of living had a greater number of surviving children than the poor. Another explanation may be that larger households reflected a responsibility of the well-to-do to educate, apprentice, or support the less affluent members of the community, as well as members of their own class. Artisans such as blacksmiths, carpenters, or cordwainers also had households of greater size because they were expected to train others. If, in fact, the less affluent depended on merchants and tradesmen for instruction in this way, their constant proximity would give impressionable adolescents an opportunity to view at close range the aspirations and values of the middle and upper classes —and perhaps the desire to emulate them. In other words, merchants and artisans may have acted as role models, and thus created an atmosphere in which both rich and poor shared some common interests and values.

If, in fact, many of Newport's merchants "were growing wealthy on the spectacular triangular trade,"[24] there were ample opportunities to diffuse this wealth throughout the community as well as to enjoy its benefits personally. Though Newport's streets were not paved in gold, they were indeed paved with the money raised from the impost levied on the importation of slaves into the colony. From 1715, when the Rhode Island General Assembly, "taking into consideration that Newport is the metropolitan town in this colony . . . and that it hath very miry streets," saw fit to use these duties to remedy the situation, a succession of acts provided for subsequent road paving and bridge building from the same source of funds.[25]

Individual merchants, as well as governments, found it easy to spend the profits derived from molasses, rum, and slaves, and a splendid house was only the beginning. Reinvestment of earnings was one course open to a successful merchant. A rum dealer might open his own distillery instead of farming out the imported molasses for processing. A merchant might expand his ventures or invest in a boat-building concern. A trader with excess capital and no hard feelings toward Massachusetts might take advantage of the 6% interest that colony paid on borrowed money. Ezra Stiles was privy to the information that "Simon Peas, Esqr of Newport . . . has A.D. 1764 Eighteen Thousand Dollars in the Massach. Treasury lent to the Province. . . . Mr. Jacobs of Newport has four thousand Sterling in that Treasury. . . ."[26] A few years earlier, assessors took a valuation of all the towns in Rhode Island, and Stiles noted that cumulatively Newport had £709,527 "money at Interest [probably old tenor]."[27] The English merchants to whom the Newport traders were indebted might have been interested in that information.

Land, of course, was always an attractive investment, but according to a 1767 ratables list, Newport merchants held few large parcels in the immediate area.[28] The largest landholdings were those of fulltime planters and farmers—and there was only a handful of such people. Isolated advertisements in the newspapers hint that Newport merchants sought country homes and farms with substantial acreage in the neighboring communities of Portsmouth and Middletown, as well as in North and South Kingston.[29] In addition, town lots in Woodstock, Connecticut (some 60 miles away), were eagerly sought after by both well-to-do and middle-class Newporters. The "First Division of the Township of Woodstock," laid out in 1762, indicates that Newport residents quickly bought up all 60 lots.[30] Most of the lots were probably held for investment and rented out by the owners since the Newport census of 1774 shows that few owners removed to Connecticut. Although the list of owners contains a number of prosperous Rhode Islanders, a number of the middling sort, including several women, also invested.

Another list, this one of the "Proprietors of the township of Killington," also shows that Newporters with a little extra cash were not at all reluctant to put their money to work for them farther away in what was then New Hampshire, now Vermont.[31] Again, it is both middle class and well-to-do who sought an investment of this nature. Three people bought shares in both Connecticut and New Hampshire (Vermont); and in Woodstock, Connecticut, several different members of the same families were listed as owners of lots. There were undoubtedly others who owned land outside of Newport, but they defy systematic investigation since the Newport tax lists give no indication of how much land people owned elsewhere.

Newport residents were also inclined to buy structures in town either for their own residential and commercial use or to rent out to others. That approximately 85% of those on the ratable list owned at least one structure, and some owned anywhere from two to twenty-one buildings, suggests that the business of being a landlord was both lucrative and popular.[32]

What else attracted these eighteenth-century shipping magnates with surplus capital to spend? Investment in slaves was common, which is hardly surprising since access to them was relatively easy. In 1755 there were 1,234 blacks in Newport out of a total population of 6,753 (18.2%). Of the colonial urban centers only Charleston had a higher percentage of blacks in the community.[33] According to the 1774 census of Rhode Island, there were 1,084 slaves in Newport (11.7% of the total population). This was a larger proportion of slaves than in either Philadelphia or Boston at this time, and slightly less than in New York.[34]

Although any ratables list has certain drawbacks, it probably reflects accurately the patterns of taste and the living standards of the community. Of particular interest is the frequency with which silver plate—apparently a

TABLE IV

Number of Slaves Owned by Families in Newport, 1774*

No. of Slaves Owned:	1	2	3	4	5	6	7	8	9	10	11	12	13	14	15	16	17	18	19	20	Total
No. of Families Owning Slaves:	222	89	55	44	18	14	8	3	1	2	0	1	2	0	0	0	0	0	0	1	460
Male head of household:	185	75	46	36	16	13	8	3	1	2	0	1	2	0	0	0	0	0	0	1	389
Female head of household:	37	14	9	8	2	1	0	0	0	0	0	0	0	0	0	0	0	0	0	0	71

Source: MS Census of Newport, 1774, Rhode Island State Archives, Providence.

* There were 1590 families in Newport in 1774, of which 1538 were white.

much sought-after commodity—appeared on the 1767 list which tabulated the property of 860 Newport residents. Three-quarters of the people on the list (whose property is broken down into categories) owned silver plate in greater or lesser quantity. A successful merchant—someone with a substantial amount of money and trading stock—usually owned more "wrought plate," as the General Assembly defined it, than a farmer with a good many acres, but the ownership of silver plate was extremely widespread. George Berkeley noticed as early as 1729 that even the "sly Quakers," austere in outward appearance, succumbed to the rage for finery by lining their sideboards with "plate."[35]

Newport, alone among the major ports, had a favorable balance of trade with the West Indies at this time. Did this happy situation supply the coin which was ultimately converted into plate?[36] Clearly, collecting silver was a hedge against inflation, and with Rhode Island's bout with paper money still fresh in the memory of most Newporters in 1767, it is scarcely odd that they found wrought plate appealing.[37]

It seems that there was still some cash left over after building a grand house, filling it with furniture by Goddard and Townsend, and setting the table with gleaming silver, because the Newport merchants supported the arts to a degree surprising for their small community. It is surely no coincidence that at various times during the eighteenth century John Smibert, Robert Feke, Samuel King, and Gilbert Stuart converged on Newport and set up studios. Evidence suggests that local families patronized these artists.

Success could also be measured in terms of religious affiliation. Although Newport claimed a bewildering variety of persuasions, membership in the Church of England (Trinity Church) was tacit acknowledgment of both wealth and status. According to Ezra Stiles, the Anglicans (or Episcopalians) cornered a disproportionate share of the wealth of the community, and the tax assessors corroborated his assertion. In 1772 at least 27 of the top 50 taxpayers were members of Trinity Church.[38] Many had not been born into this faith since most of Newport's founding families embraced the Quaker religion in the seventeenth century. Growing prosperity and an increasing ability to purchase luxuries must have tempted many of these plain people toward churches which did not disparage worldly possessions. By the 1760s and 1770s, the roster of the Church of England included a variety of people whose families had originally been Friends—among them Coggeshalls, Clarkes, Coddingtons, and Wantons.

Whether these people remained friends with the dissenters is a story best left to a later chapter. For the time being suffice it to say that in the pre-Revolutionary era a tolerant attitude best served the needs of this seaport town where, since the time of George Berkeley, Anglican merchants had been conducting business with "four sorts of Anabaptists besides Presbyterians, Quakers, Independents, and many of no profession at all."[39]

Newport merchants enjoyed the profits from their mercantile activities, seemingly untroubled by the thought that money earned in the slave trade might somehow be tainted. They entertained lavishly, lived on a grand scale, cheered at horse races on Easton's Beach, and ate the losers at the turtle races on Goat Island.[40] They indulged in all the comforts the eighteenth century could provide. Indeed, it is possible that some Newporters had running water—through pipes—at home.[41]

But as one affluent merchant, Godfrey Malbone, found out, money would not buy everything. This gentleman, a slaving captain and subsequent slave trader and merchant, was reputed to have asked a friend "What will not money buy?" According to the story, a man standing nearby and overhearing the remark, penned the following reply and placed it where Malbone could not help but see it:

"All the money in the place
Won't buy old Malbone a handsome face."[42]

The number of wealthy inhabitants in Newport swelled by several hundred each summer as out-of-towners took advantage of the town's cooling sea breezes. From all accounts, Newport was blessed with an extraordinarily favorable climate which made the seaport the most desirable of colonial resorts. "Since my return to this place," exulted one happy visitor after a prolonged stay in Newport, "I have Experienced a more agreeable state of health, than I enjoy'd for a long time before; to that Friendly, healthy and delightful climate (Dear Newport) I owe under God, this great advantage."[43]

At the height of Newport's prosperity as many as 400–600 vacationers might have spent the season, which ran from May through October.[44] These long-term tourists added to the prosperity of the community by paying for lodging, food, and entertainment with silver coin. In return, those who could afford to exchange the sweltering humidity of Charleston, Philadelphia, Georgia, or Jamaica for the cool air of Newport would find compatible company and pleasant diversions up north. Whether business relationships followed personal friendships or vice versa, no matter; the exchange of ideas on a long summer evening no doubt encouraged further communication and economic interdependence. It also went a long way toward making Americans out of Rhode Islanders and elite Pennsylvanians, Georgians, and South Carolinians, as they realized how much they had in common. Indeed, several families found they had so much in common that intermarriage became a common phenomenon. Once having spent a few months in Newport, a vacationing merchant might want to make Newport his permanent headquarters: "I am pained to think my business should tie me so fast to this Spot as not to allow me the freedom of passing the remainder of my life at Dear, Dear New-port," wrote one enchanted visitor.[45]

Since life was undeniably pleasant for the merchants of Newport, there was good reason to keep a tight grip on the reins of power—in the hope of preserving their lifestyle through the political process. Economic prestige, therefore, ran hand in hand with political control. By statute, a man who possessed realty worth £40 or which rented for 40 shillings annually qualified as a voter, as did his eldest son at age 21. Women, blacks, Jews, and Catholics were excluded. There is no indication that voting rights could be purchased as in New York, and, in fact, men who qualified by virtue of a profitable marriage were excluded from the voters' roll.[46] From the extent and restrictive nature of the voting statutes, one would almost think there was a conscious attempt to limit the franchise. Although it is likely that more than half the adult male population could vote, a list of voters indicates that merchants, doctors, lawyers, and well-to-do tradespeople such as butchers, carpenters, silversmiths, and tavern keepers exercised this privilege more frequently than the rest of the eligible voters. It is hardly surprising, then, that between 1764 and 1794 the vast majority of elective and appointive offices were filled by men who were merchants, shipmasters, or professionals.[47]

What all this means is that voting and officeholding were controlled by the upper 10%–15% of the population and that Newport hardly represented a participatory democracy—even in eighteenth-century terms.[48] More accurately described: it was a society in which an exclusive club managed the larger community. There is no evidence to suggest, however, that the franchise—or lack of it—produced tensions within the society. Those who were excluded may have felt that voting for the sake of voting was not important, or that having the franchise was not necessary to enhance their well-being.

In theory, at least, those who exercised the franchise did so in pursuit of the "common good" rather than in the interest of self-advancement. Although theory and reality may have been far apart in Newport, since the ruling clique and the less fortunate were motivated toward common goals, it is likely that the town leaders did not try to use their power to establish inequitable burdens upon those who had no say.

5

Dependent People,
Helping Hands

I F THIS HUMMING, COMMERCIAL SEAPORT provided the atmosphere in
which an elite merchant class could thrive, it also made room for a
growing number of poor. Most of the people at this end of the economic
spectrum were either sailors or dependents of sailors. Others were unmarried
women from lower-class families or simply tradespeople who had fallen on
hard times. The urban poor are not easy to locate in the surviving records.
They are rarely, if ever, taxed, and thus defy identification from the assessment
lists. By boarding with a family or renting a room, they escape the census as
well, becoming invisible members of the community. Paradoxically, they are
rescued from obscurity in death because, even if they died intestate, inventories were usually made of their meager belongings. Although estate inventories are at best only a rough index of personal wealth, enough of them exist
to reconstruct an approximate lifestyle of people whose poverty stands in
sharp contrast to the easy affluence of those for whom they toiled.

The poor had few of life's amenities, even by eighteenth-century standards. At the extreme, a mariner might have died with no more property
than his "sea cloths" and a few pounds in back wages.[49] With no furniture,
he may have lived aboard ship, or in a furnished room when in port. His
possessions might have included "an old sea chest" and "1 gun or small
arm." If a sailor had permanent quarters on shore, he might also have owned
a bedstead, some "old chairs," andirons, and a "pot and kettle." Slightly
more prosperity meant that an ordinary seaman's widow could inherit a few
earthenware plates, a table, a couple of pillows, a quilt, and perhaps even a
looking glass. With luck and bargaining skill, some could have acquired even
table linens and a chest of drawers. The rare mention of such items as a
razor, silver buckle, or curtains and the brevity of the inventories only serve
to accentuate a dearth of worldly effects.

These people had few expectations and little control over their lives. It is not likely that any of them could vote or hold office, and they therefore were completely excluded from the decision-making process of the community. In terms of proportions, they may have made up as much as one-third of the population at any given time.[50]

Although the percentage of poor remained unchanged throughout the 1760s and early 1770s, the actual number of poor increased during these years.[51] The implication of this growth did not escape the Town Council, which announced late in 1763 that "there are now in this town a number of able-bodied men, women and children, who are poor persons, that have no Employ, and who are likely to be a Town Charge. . . ." By 1765, likelihood had become reality: "There are sundry men, women and children, who have been chargeable to the Town, and many more who are likely to do so." If this distress can be ascribed to the dull post-war economic situation, it is more difficult to explain the complaint from "Americus" which appeared in the *Newport Mercury* in March 1771 during a period of prosperity. "The town of Newport is at an immense charge to support their poor; the truth of which appears by the present town tax."[52] "Americus" apparently had access to the town records, because the Council authorized more expenditure for support of the poor than for any other single item in the 1760s and 1770s.[53]

Newport, like any other economy-minded New England community, did everything in its power to avoid adding to its number of unproductive citizens. First on the list of precautionary measures was an attempt to guard against the itinerant poor. Any non-resident could be "warned out" and shipped home for a variety of reasons.[54] Indeed, non-residents had to provide evidence of a "legal settlement" to which they could be deported if necessary before they were allowed even to catch their breaths in Newport.[55]

In spite of these efforts to limit newcomers, the town fathers were only partly successful. Between 1736 and 1772, men, particularly those with families, were coming into Newport in greater numbers than they were leaving town.[56]

Given to occasional introspection, the people of Newport found it easy to explain poverty in the midst of plenty. Just as they linked great wealth to the slave trade, so they were ready to accuse it of creating privation: "It has long been . . . the complaint of poor laboring white men, that there are so many Negroes in this colony, and particularly in this town, they [poor white

men] can scarcely find half labour enough to support their families com-
fortably."[57] This accusation may have had a basis in fact. Because Newport
was the center of the slave trade in the North, the community had the largest
proportion of blacks in New England. This demographic development created a substantial labor pool.[58] Distillers, for instance, owned a disproportionate number of slaves, and it is likely that some distilleries were run by
slaves.[59]

The anonymous but "True Son of Liberty" who brought the excess labor
supply problem to the attention of the public also had a solution: importers of
slaves should pay an import tax to discourage the importation of competitive
black labor. This proposed remedy was not received enthusiastically by
slave-trading merchants, but the argument had some effect on the anti-
importation legislation of 1774, discussed below. Increasing hostility to
competitive slave labor may even have helped slavery to wither away in the
North.

The reality of the labor market seems to have had little effect on the per-
ceptions of those who relocated, however, because in the few cases in which
a person gave reasons for moving to Newport, it invariably was "for the
better support of himself (or herself) and family."[60] Perhaps people were
drawn to Newport by false prospects, or perhaps the job market contracted
and competition increased in the 1760s and 1770s. In an expanding economy,
a large unskilled class acted as a labor pool, but during a recession they became dependent on the town for sustenance.

Another reason for the growing number of poor may have been related
to seamen's wages, which appear to have followed the Philadelphia pattern
between 1763 and 1776, and according to various accounts were, on the
whole, even lower than wages in Philadelphia. Prices in Newport were
cyclical in the decade following the Stamp Act, and with non-importation,
impressment, and seizures, ordinary seamen were losing ground in terms of
what they could buy. They were dependent on imports, which became more
costly with each crisis, and they were unemployed more frequently.[61]

Another cause for poverty as seen by more than one eighteenth-century
Newporter was overindulgence in spiritous beverages. Even the Rev. Samuel
Hopkins occasionally digressed from his tirade on the slave trade to acknowledge the "incredible quantities of rum, and molasses which has been distilled into rum among ourselves, have been imported, the most of which is
consumed in intemperance and drunkenness, in such a dreadful degree as to

exceed anything of the kind in any part of the world."[62] If easy access to rum contributed to this sad situation, Newport's heavy traffic in this commodity must be held at least partly responsible.

According to the most knowledgeable, those who imbibed too heavily were prone to "neglect their business, and families, and become a town charge." Apparently the Town Council was concerned less with the issues of health and morality than with the distinct possibility that the town treasury might have to part with funds to support an increasing number of drunkards. After publicly naming nine people who "make a frequent Practice of getting DRUNK," the Town Council prohibited all "Retailers of strong drink" from selling to those particular tipplers because of the probability that "they will become chargeable to the town." In a curious placement of responsibility, it was the retailers who were fined for disobeying the edict rather than the purchasers. If the miscreants persisted in their drinking habits, however, the Overseers of the Poor informed the public that "they will put out at service any of the aforementioned persons. . . ."

These weak attempts to eliminate poverty notwithstanding, the town fathers realized that as long as it existed they had to cope with it. Indeed, a rather modern-sounding argument appeared in a newspaper article, as one Newport resident concluded that not only was a society responsible for the care of its indigent, but it was "the indispensible duty of every society to find employment for its own poor. . . ."

The Town Council of Newport subscribed to this sentiment and took responsibility (along with the Overseers of the Poor, Work House, and Alms House) for binding out the less fortunate "for a number of years to any good person or persons." The overseers were no less eager to bind out "a number of poor children, boys and girls, . . . to any credible Persons." In this situation, then, the needy were dependent on the community, and the administrative leaders of the community were dependent on the wealthier citizens to come forth to provide employment for the poor. There is little evidence that the government directly employed the poor to any great extent. In 1774, Jacob Richardson, collector of rates, recommended that poor men who owed back taxes be employed by those who set the town watch. Richardson's proposal was an exceptional case, but it served two purposes: the town would collect in work what it would otherwise be unable to collect in cash, and an unpopular job would not want for takers.[63]

The city of Newport had a Work House, Alms House, and out relief, but employment, not charity, was the basis for help. As late as 1767 the town did not give the impoverished a regular supply of firewood for the winter, the lack of which was a perpetual problem in Newport during the colder months.[64] It was private employment that offered the greatest hope for lifting the less fortunate from their distressed circumstances. As the British noose tightened in the late 1760s, and colonial manufacturing increased, so did employment opportunities—at least temporarily. In 1768, the *Newport Mercury* noted that one Caleb Earle had manufactured 400 yards of cloth over the prior few years, and that the spinning was "partly performed by poor People, whom he supplied with wool, and who, by being thus employed, and punctually paid for their work, were greatly assisted in supporting themselves and Families."[65]

A letter to the editor in the same paper a year later pursued much the same idea. Showing the profitability of woolen manufacture in Newport, the author hoped it would "stimulate people to employ the poor in carding, spinning and weaving (which may be done without incommoding the common Family business . . .)."[66]

Although the more affluent were clearly willing to share ideas for the useful employment of Newport's poor, it is more difficult to assess their generosity in terms of actual charity. There is little mention of philanthropy during the 1760s and 1770s in Newport, and one cannot be sure of who or how many were willing to make donations to the economically distressed.[67] Churches distributed collections among the poor, and the Quakers paid rent for their less fortunate brethren, but how systematically this was done, and what effect it had is hard to say.[68]

Even though some people left money to the poor in their wills and others assisted on a sporadic basis, a commentator in the *Mercury* argued that most eighteenth-century Newporters were unwilling to lend or give. Whether this accusation had any substance or not, it is clear that some Newporters did give generously of their time and skill. Two doctors advertised that they would give "advice to the poor, gratis every day," and one dentist (undoubtedly mindful of the vast quantities of molasses consumed in Newport) offered to treat without charge "the poor afflicted with the Tooth ache . . . every morning from eight to ten." The Rev. Mr. Wheeler, who opened a school in 1772, advertised that "ten poor Boys will be instructed gratis," while Henry Hymes raised money for the benefit of the poor by giving a "musical entertainment."[69]

Deciding there might be something to the adage that God helps those who help themselves, a number of seafaring Newporters instituted the Fellowship Club in 1752. Composed mainly of ship captains, the society, according to their charter, was designed to "relieve such of their Fellow Members, as, by Misfortune and Losses, shall become proper objects of their Charity." The mutual aid society was much like an insurance company today. A member paid his premiums (called dues), and if he died or was captured by an enemy, the society would "refund all the money that such member has paid into the Treasury" to the widow or children of the deceased—if, and this was in small print, "the Society shall think them proper objects of their charity."[70] In addition there were sickness and old age benefits for the member himself. The society carried on above and beyond the call of duty in 1769 when certain members, whose staggering financial losses put them in debtors' prison, were feted—behind bars—by those more fortunate. From all accounts, the wine flowed freely.[71]

6

The Cruel Sea

I T IS HARDLY SURPRISING in a community where men earned their living from the sea that the sea extracted a heavy toll in return. Seafaring was a dangerous occupation and a mixed blessing. If it provided employment for a large number of skilled and unskilled mariners, it was also a risky means of earning a living. A single ship going down could leave at least half a dozen widows. The *Newport Mercury* constantly reported heavy mortalities on the coast of Africa.[72] Captain Croswell died on a voyage there, leaving a wife and five children. Casualties often occurred much closer to home: the *Mercury* described how a ship commanded by Captain John Malbone was consumed by fire off Point Judith when a boy dropped a candle in a cask of rum. Before the boats could be lowered, many passengers perished in the flames. John Coddington left a widow with six children to support when his vessel was hit by lightning. Captain Joseph Gardner wrote his owners that both his mate and another seaman were washed overboard in a storm.[73] Dr. Stiles reported that in Newport "from January 1, 1760 to January 1, 1761 . . . there died 210 Persons, of which 24 died at sea."[74]

These "Persons" who died at sea were usually men, and this is one reason why by 1774 white adult women drastically outnumbered white adult men.[75] This demographic imbalance came late in Newport's history, however; less than twenty years earlier men had outnumbered women by a small margin.[76] Historians have argued that this inequitable ratio resulted from a flight of males away from the older seacoast towns as available land and economic opportunity dwindled.[77] But this was clearly not the case in Newport, for the men were not fleeing. A better explanation for the sexual imbalance is the one suggested by Ezra Stiles's computations. If his figures are correct, this number multiplied over a period of fourteen years could easily contribute to the disparity between the number of men and the number of women in Newport by 1774.[78] Moreover, the drop in the number of adult males occurred during the war years. Newport gave men to the war effort in great numbers, and the town suffered from their loss. Ezra Stiles noted in 1764 that

> Doctor Hunter of Newport was Surgeon to the Rhode Island Regiment of Provincials the last war for several campaigns. . . . He tells me that of raw troops new raised there returned at End of the Campaign but *thirty nine out of a hundred* . . . and that few died in a second campaign. So perish in a Campaign 600 out of 1000 and 6,000 out of 10,000.[79]

By 1774, 20% of the households in Newport were headed by women.

The excess number of women in this New England seaport was one more element molding the shape of the community. Although the town itself may have been only vaguely aware of the implications, its disproportionate sex ratio portended an unsettled future. With men of marriageable age not so readily available, the potential and mobility of the many young women remaining in Newport were seriously affected.[80] Fewer marriages heralded a declining birth rate as did the great number of women widowed by the war. This, in turn, would lead to smaller families. An entry in Ezra Stiles's diary reinforces this supposition. He noted that "In 1775 in the Spring a numeration was made, 9200 Souls in Town. At 6 to a family this would be 1500 Families, but truely there were 1800." The implication of his remark is that families usually averaged five members.[81] If Stiles's word is not enough, more support for this conclusion comes from recent studies of household size and composition in various British colonies.[82] These studies concluded that in 1774 the mean household size in Newport was 5.8, which was reduced to 5.0 when the white members of the household were isolated.[83] Although the mean size of a family in Rhode Island was 6.3 persons,[84] the greater number of *childless* households in Newport than in the rest of Rhode Island diminished the size of the immediate family in that town.[85] Moreover, households headed by women were clearly smaller than those headed by males, averaging 3–4 people including blacks.

A lower birth rate also led to a proportionately older population, and, in fact, Newport had a larger percentage of older people generally than the colony as a whole. Despite a shorter life expectancy in the eighteenth century, a number of people survived childbirth and infancy, and by avoiding smallpox, storms at sea, and other hazardous activities, lived to a ripe old age. But for those lacking the resources to put together a nest egg, retirement or sickness or the infirmities of the elderly could be a frightening prospect, particularly if one did not have any children on whom one could lean. The justices of the peace could determine the amount of responsibility a child had for the support of a parent, but the court could not force a son or daughter to provide what he or she did not have; nor could a judge create a son or daughter out of thin air.[86] In cases in which the younger generation was unable to offer support, the elderly would be forced to depend on other relatives or on the town itself for help. By creating this situation, the sea must be held at least partly responsible for breaking down the traditional means of intergenerational support.

The subject of family size also raises the question of housing availability. Stiles noted in his diary that in October 1775 there were 1,100 houses in Newport. Whether there were 1,500 or 1,800 families in the community, there clearly were a great many more families than houses. Under these circumstances, house sharing must have been a common phenomenon. Related families could share the same roof, and any number of families could take in paying boarders. It is also likely that unrelated families shared a dwelling. How this infringed on privacy—indeed, what attitude Newporters took toward personal privacy—is not recorded. It would not be surprising, however, if this situation, caused in part by a dwindling supply of building wood, created tensions which were exacerbated as Newport's population increased.[87]

Women as a group were considerably less affluent than men and often dependent on them and the community for assistance. Newporters may not have realized that, given eighteenth-century social codes, a geographic area "with a male surplus had a greater potential for labor and economic productivity than one in which women predominated," but the very few female names on the published tax lists should have hinted at the problem.[88]

To say, as one correspondent did in the *Newport Mercury*, that "we do not greatly abound in female fortunes" was to understate the case.[89] In 1760 only 35 women paid taxes (3.6% of the taxpayers), and the 1772 list showed only 44 female names (3.7% of the total).[90] The economic imbalance is striking enough when adult white men outnumbered adult white women in 1755, but when in 1774 the reverse is true, and adult women outnumbered adult men, the comparative earning power as suggested by the tax assessments stands out even more sharply. A woman's upward mobility was inextricably linked to a husband. Women may have married for love, but they also married for security.[91] Their lives revolved around the home, in housewife-related occupations, or in working alongside their husbands in whatever trade he happened to be employed. Running a tavern or boarding house—both of which were common enough in a seaport—was also an appropriate occupation for women since it was an extension of their duties as housewives.[92] In addition, single women or widows with property often collected rent to help support themselves.[93] Women might also add a little to their meager incomes by acting as midwives or by taking care of the sick or elderly and receiving pay for this from the town itself.[94]

As members of a seaport community, married women were dependent not only on their husbands, but when their husbands were away at sea, on the merchants for whom their husbands sailed. An arrangement might be made whereby a merchant would dole out a sailor's accrued salary to his wife periodically.[95] The money was rarely much, and there must have been many women like Marther Mackloud who found themselves "in great want." Mrs. Mackloud begged Aaron Lopez for money and food, hoping that her husband who was in Lopez' "Service" had "wages a nuff Due" to cover the cost.[96] If a mariner sailed from another port (or if his wife lived elsewhere), he might have lodged money in the hands of the merchant for whom he worked, perhaps in the form of a salary advance. This money could be sent on to his wife immediately or held to be dispersed at her request. In any case, evidence suggests that women who were married to sailors often turned to the merchants for money to see them through the long months when their husbands were on a voyage.[97] As Lydia Bissell reminded Aaron Lopez, "all my Dependance is upon you."[98]

In the eighteenth century, one could never predict the exact length of a voyage. Nevertheless, long absences clearly suggested the possibility of some disaster, and as a voyage stretched from months to years, it became increasingly difficult for a wife (or widow) to support herself and her children. Widows whose husbands were members of the local Marine Society might receive aid from that group if the Society concluded they were "proper objects of their Charity," but two-thirds of the society's membership was limited to ship captains, and thus their benevolence was similarly limited.[99]

Without confirmation, one could never be certain of a catastrophe at sea which would release a woman from her legal restrictions as a feme covert. At the same time, the Rhode Island General Assembly recognized that those left behind were entitled to a "comfortable subsistance." For this reason, the General Assembly passed a law as early as 1711 which stated that wives whose husbands had been absent for three years could apply to the Town Council for power to "demand, sue for, recover, possess, and improve all lands and houses or other real estate and personal property" as if the husband had left a power of attorney.[100] To safeguard the estate, however, the act did not give the wife the power to sell property, and, indeed, she was accountable to two freeholders who had posted bond in her behalf. This law fell far short of the feme sole trader acts of the other colonies which gave married women whose husbands were away immediate access to courts and immediate contractual ability. In Rhode Island, women were forced to wait three years for qualified powers, and the powers were not automatically conferred at that time. It was still necessary to go, bonnet in hand, to the Town Council to request permission to act.

The presumption in the above law is that the husband was still alive, although after seven years of continual absence a husband could be considered away "without just cause." If, at the end of this period, the wife was convinced that she had been deserted, she could apply for a divorce. Rhode Island law permitted absolute divorce in such cases, allowing the wife (who might very well be a widow by this time, anyway) the opportunity of remarrying, which was rare under the common law, but necessary in Rhode Island.[101]

The laws described above, as well as other statutes which addressed insolvency and intestacy, suggest that legislators acted paternalistically to enhance women's economic status—without giving women too much power. In other words, the legislation reinforced female dependency by substituting governmental agencies for absent husbands and giving the agencies control over women's economic well-being. A good example of this attitude is in the powers delegated to the Overseers of the Poor. It was the responsibility of this committee to bind out any male person who might become a town charge and "to receive his wages and deal the same out for the use of his family. . . ."[102] Rather than give the wives direct responsibility for the money, the wages were allotted to them through the agency, and in such amounts as the Overseers deemed proper.

Many poor women could find no way of supporting themselves at all. Recognizing this problem, the *Newport Mercury* called for the rich to distribute 50–100 spinning wheels among those poor women of town "almost starving for want of employ."[103] These figures suggest that women as a group were particularly dependent on the community for support, and there is some curious evidence that this reliance was not misplaced. While a "True Son of Liberty" was calling for a tax on slaves to be paid by all importers and owners, he specifically exempted widows, allowing them to keep "two Negroes untaxed." Sometime later, a letter to the newspaper raised the problem of hucksters: "If hucksters are to be tolerated, it is my opinion poor helpless women and destitute widows are the only objects to escape with Impunity."[104] These comments suggest that the economic plight of poor women without families was recognized and that there might have been a number of informal arrangements designed to make life financially easier for them.

Indeed, the 1767 List of Polls and Estates offers the best clue to the relationship of women to the rest of the Newport community. Toward the end of this calculation of ratables are two lists. The first is a list of 129 persons who "were at sea or sick at the Time of receiving lists in Newport therefore not to be fourfolded." In other words it is a list of people not to be penalized for submitting a late accounting. On this list are an extraordinary number of women's names—49 (38%) to be exact. Clearly, these women, mostly widows, were not at sea; nor could they all have been sick at the time of the original assessment. The second list enumerated 140 people who *were* to be fourfolded (taxed quadruple the ordinary amount) for their delinquency in presenting their ratable estates. This list contained only male names. The possibility exists that by common consent the assessors "overlooked" the female delinquencies in an attempt to soften the economic blow to women as best they could. Supporting this conclusion is a notation in the Newport Town Meeting Records that delinquent freeholders were not to be excused from their tax obligations, "women excepted."[105]

The whole question of an eighteenth-century mercantile community where women predominated numerically for so much of the time has never been studied adequately, despite the paradoxes which present themselves. For example, women were brought up to be dependent, yet circumstances thrust independence upon them. Home, church, and law taught women to defer to men, but when hundreds of men were continually away at sea, important day-to-day decisions were made by women. One might even speculate that

74

this independence carried over into the Revolutionary era when some women were strong enough to part company with their husbands on the great political issue of the day.

Furthermore, there are many social issues which remain unexamined. Sex ratios not only determined marriage and child-bearing patterns but may have affected extra-marital relationships as well. Given an excess of females, what happened when shiploads of sailors came in from other domestic and foreign ports? Would the adultery rate increase in this situation? [106] Because of the sexual imbalance, there were a number of unmarried females in the community whose chances of marriage decreased as the imbalance became more severe. Is there a possible connection between this ratio and what was considered a growing promiscuity? Although prostitution was illegal by virtue of the laws governing fornication, brothels flourished. Citing an encounter with the madam of one such establishment, a British officer noted that

> "She keeps a house of pleasure and has done so for a good many years past in a more decent and reputable manner than common, and is Spoke of by everybody in Town in a favourable manner for one of her Profession. . . . This place must have arrived to a tollerable degree of modern luxury when houses of that kind were publickly allowed of, and the Manners of the People by no means rigid when subjects of that sort become family conversation." [107]

Apparently the houses were not only tolerated, but well frequented, because "Deborah Meanwell" complained to the *Newport Mercury* that all the "young gentlemen" of Newport went "whoring all night," and "Americus," practical to the end, cautioned against spending excessive amounts of pocket money on "wh--ing." [108]

7

The Black Community

NEWPORT'S UNIQUE INTEREST IN SLAVING earned it a dubious
reputation as "the main port of the New England slave trade."[109]
At the same time, this traffic in humans gave the townspeople easy
access to slaves for their personal use, and since the town found its growth
and prosperity quite compatible with slaveholding, the number of bondsmen
grew steadily until after mid-century. Although the white population continued to increase until the Revolution, the 1774 census indicates that the
black population had remained remarkably stable over the preceding twenty
years.[110] The percentage of blacks in the total population, therefore, had declined over two decades.[111] Despite this decline, slaveholding was more per-
vasive in Newport than one might have expected in a northern city on the eve
of the Revolution.

TABLE V

Growth of White, Black, and Indian Population
in Newport, 1730–1774

	WHITE		BLACK		INDIAN		
Year	Number	% of pop.	Number	% of pop.	Number	% of pop.	Total pop.
1730	3843	82.82	649	13.98	148	3.18	4640
1748	5335	81.97	1105	16.97	68	1.04	6508
1755	5519	81.72	1234	18.27	—	—	6753
1774	7917	85.97	1246	13.53	46	.49	9209

Source: *Valuation of the Cities and Towns in the State of Rhode Island from 1860–1869
for Purposes of Taxation. Together with the Census of the Colony in 1730 and 1775
and Other Statistics*, ed. Elisha Dyer (Providence, 1871); Account of the People of the
Colony of Rhode Island, Whites and Blacks Together with the Quantity of Arms and

According to the letter of the law, Roger Williams' descendants never did have the right to own slaves. In 1652 Rhode Island passed a statute designed to prevent "the common course practised amongst Englishmen to buy Negers."[112] No one could hold either white or black persons in bondage for more than ten years, and for a while the colony enforced this statute. At the turn of the century, however, Newporters were already treating this law with their usual disregard for inconvenient legislation, and by 1708 perpetual slavery was recognized in Rhode Island. In that year the legislators laid an impost of £3 on each slave imported into the colony, a source of revenue Great Britain disallowed some twenty-five years later on the grounds that it hampered trade.[113] While it may be said that England encouraged both colonial slavery and the slave trade, it is equally true that Rhode Islanders in the eighteenth century needed little encouragement.

Of the slaveholding families, nearly one-half claimed only one slave, and two-thirds held no more than two servants for life.[114] Crowding, therefore, was not a serious problem, although privacy must have been a precious commodity. One wonders where John Mawdsley put his twenty slaves, or how Jacob Rivera kept his twelve slaves and the six white members of his family from intruding upon each other. Occasionally the number of slaves exceeded the capacity of a household. In that case, an owner might try to reduce his "family" by selling what he called a Negro wench, "on account of her too frequent breeding."[115] This happened often enough to raise the possibility that what would have been the delight of the southern planter was a gadfly to the northern urban merchant.

Merchants might also have sold off slaves to avoid a concentration of blacks in one small area of the city. Since ideas can be bred as easily as babies, perhaps the slaveowners realized that their chattels might take the words "liberty" and "independence" seriously if heard often enough. With slaves successfully ensconced in all trades and industries in colonial Newport, what may have been unsuccessful in the long run—and here one can only speculate—is the accommodation of slavery to increasingly crowded urban living.

There can be little doubt that the blacks were among the most dependent

---

Ammunition in the Hands of Private Persons (1755), NHS; *Census of the Inhabitants of the Colony of Rhode Island in 1774*, ed. John Russell Bartlett (Providence, 1858); MS Census of Newport, 1774, Rhode Island State Archives, Providence.

Percentages have been rounded off to the nearest hundredth; totals, therefore, do not equal 100 per cent.

members of the Newport community. Whether slave, indentured servant, or free, nearly all were at the mercy of their white brethren for support. Slaves were permitted a certain latitude, however, and functioned as a community within a community. Amidst a general revelry they held annual elections, at which time they elected a "governor" or "king" who exercised a certain amount of control over them. This, apparently, was less a New England practice than a fusion of West African culture and American conditions since similar elections were held throughout the Caribbean and South America.[116] The "government" also incorporated a "court system" where during the year a variety of petty cases were brought by master against slave and slave against slave. Slaves were therefore tried, condemned, and punished by their peers.

According to various accounts, the black election day was an extremely popular occasion which began with political haggling and ended with festivities as the new "governor" hosted a banquet for the black community. With the financial encouragement of their owners, the slaves emulated the white upper class as closely as possible in appearance on this occasion, each slave having tried to outdo the other in fashion and style.[117] Eyewitnesses to the events testified that the outcome of the election was determined in no small measure by the opulent appearance of the candidate. If the accounts are correct, it might suggest that there was a subtle competition among masters as well as slaves and that what was really at stake was the white leadership of the black community. Given the nature of slavery in the colonies, it seems highly unlikely that the whites would have allowed complete self-government among the blacks. In other words, although the electoral contest was nominally between slaves, it may have been the owners of the successful black candidates who really "won" the election. This means not so much that the black governor and courts did not exert authority as that their actions were carefully monitored by those whites closest to the black leaders. Given the comparatively large number of slaves in this New England town, it was a matter of some importance to the white community to know just who the black leaders were. Although there is no record of black uprisings in Newport, the possibility of a conspiracy always existed, and it was to the advantage of the white community to know in advance which blacks might take command. In some parts of Rhode Island these elections continued well into the nineteenth century, but the most detailed account of the practice in Newport indicates that it may have been abandoned there when the British took possession of the town in 1776.

It is not likely that Newporters were overly concerned about a potential black rebellion. Slaves were permitted to attend weekly services at the home of Sarah Osborn in 1766–1767, and by her own admission, the townspeople supported her efforts to guide these " 'poor creatures' " both spiritually and academically. Since Mrs. Osborn preached submissiveness, the possible benefits of the lesson evidently outweighed the inherent danger in having large numbers of slaves congregate in one location. Moreover, warning the blacks that " 'any disturbance or disorder' " would end the sessions " '*at once*' " insured both " 'decency and quietness' " for the larger gain of education.[118]

Although Mrs. Osborn indicated that the black community appeared eager to further their learning, Mary Brett did not meet with so enthusiastic a response when she opened a free school for "Negro children" in August 1772. So few parents sent their children (or, more likely, so few owners permitted the children to go) that Mrs. Brett threatened to give up the project entirely.[119]

Historians have taken the position that slaves were treated much like apprentices or white indentured servants in Newport. If this view is meant to imply a favorable comparison—that is to say, that slaves were treated *as well* as white indentured servants—one could take issue with it, since by most standards white indentured servants in Newport were treated as poorly as, well, slaves. The best evidence of this was the substantial runaway record by both classes of servants. Slaves were more easily tempted by freedom than indentured servants, although indentured servants were known to flee as well. According to newspaper advertisements, approximately 77 slaves vanished from Newport and its vicinity in the period from 1760 to 1766. A great many were described as scarred, but whether this disfigurement was the result of punishment, accident, or a former tribal rite must be left to conjecture. Two curious footnotes to the runaways: almost all appeared well dressed, according to their descriptions, and although white female indentured servants took to their heels nearly as often as males, it appears from the advertisements that female slaves either were satisfied with their lot or had decided that the chances of successful flight were slim. In either case advertisements for black female runaways are almost non-existent.[120]

The black mortality rate in Newport also gives evidence of a lower living standard than that enjoyed by whites. The only year for which comparable statistics exist is 1774, but it would be surprising if the figures were not indicative of a general pattern. In that year, 186 (2.3%) of the 7,917 whites in Newport died. At the same time, 47 (3.7%) blacks died out of a total black population of 1,246.[121] How many were "kill'd by hard usage" is impossible to know, but the dates engraved on the tombstones in the segregated burying ground attest to a short lifespan for many of Newport's servants for life.[122]

That Newport slaves were determined to take out their resentments on society in much the same way as their brethren on southern plantations did is not to be doubted. The following letter from John Malbone is a good example of what must have been a widespread practice:

> I have not been master of a Dollar in cash since I saw you, except on occasion of Theft repeatedly committed by my Fathers Negroes, Jos, Jack, James and Master Primus. . . . These fellows have broken open the Mills near the Farm three times, stole from thence forty odd Bushels Corn and meal at different times, broken open Downers shop stole Eleven pairs of Shoes . . . three pair of which was recovered, your locked cellar was broken open. . . . They say they took from thence only one of the long bottles of rum, these things they confessed by the Dint of Stripes in the prison House Yard and some others not so considerable. . . . The goods principally disposed of to Naphs the Crimp and Rud the Miller the principle complainant, but did not find this out 'till after making him restitution for his loss. . . . Primus will Relate the whole as whipping and imprisonment has made him put on the Appearance of Honesty at Present.[123]

Punishments for restless slaves became more stringent as the eighteenth century wore on. In 1770, for instance, any Indian or colored servants found abroad after 9 P.M. were to be confined in a cage, instead of jail, until morning, and to be whipped ten strokes unless redeemed for a small sum by their masters.[124]

It is one of the ironies of Newport that it was both dominated by slave traders and populated by Quakers. This unique combination was one more ingredient that flavored the town since the Quakers were the first Americans to condemn the traffic. At the same time, their official stand created tensions in a community where Quaker merchants were as eager as anyone else to reap the profits of the trade. As early as 1717 the issue had become a "weighty concern," and the Meeting in Newport in that year hoped that merchants would "write their correspondents in the islands and elsewhere to discourage their sending any more (slaves) in order to be sold by Friends here."[125] Ten years later the practice was censured and from that time on more and more pressure was applied to discourage trade and ownership by members of the Society of Friends. The Quaker elder John Woolman visited Newport at least twice in his life. His second trip in 1760 was devoted to speaking out against slavery and the slave trade: "The great number of slaves in these parts and the continuance of a Trade . . . made deep impressions on me . . . ," he wrote in May 1760. Woolman saw the trade as "a great evil," which tended "to multiply troubles and bring distresses." He did not, however, convince his audience, who listened politely, expressed "concern," and sent the good preacher on his way. Woolman was not deceived: "I am aware that it is a tender point to speak to."[126] When the Friends finally prohibited slavery among themselves in the 1770s, Abraham Redwood chose to retain his slaves rather than his membership in the Society.[127]

If Woolman used gentle persuasion to convince his fellow-Quakers of the iniquity of the slave trade, another Newport clergyman, Samuel Hopkins, was more vigorous—or at least louder. Hopkins was named pastor of the First Congregational Church in 1770, and he lost no opportunity to denounce from his pulpit Newport's slave owners and the town's role in the slave trade. There were many members of Hopkins' congregation who must have squirmed to hear him excoriate "the more than savage slave merchant."[128] But the sound of clinking coins was probably more persuasive than Hopkins' rhetoric since Rhode Island did not give up the slave trade until long after the Revolution. One other clergyman, however, joined Hopkins' crusade. The Baptist minister, Gardiner Thurston, who was a cooper by trade, refused to make casks for use in the shipment of rum to the African coast.[129]

As the Revolution drew near, the merchants of Newport, like Americans elsewhere, were discomfited by the incongruity of demanding liberty for themselves while denying it to others. Surely, one correspondent argued, if Newporters had the right to enslave Negroes, then Great Britain had the right to enslave the colonists.[130] Torn between their consciences and their pocketbooks, the merchant-legislators passed a halfhearted act "prohibiting the importation of Negroes into this Colony," in June 1774.[131] The lofty preamble acknowledged that "those who are desirous of enjoying all the Advantages of Liberty themselves, should be willing to extend personal Liberty to others." Toward that end, the legislation proposed that "for the future, no Negro or mulatto slave shall be brought into this colony." Following this sweeping prohibition were several paragraphs of exemptions which nullified the act to a large degree. Furthermore, these subsequent modifications clearly safeguarded the existing rights and privileges of Rhode Island's slave traders who, not surprisingly, were heavily represented in the Rhode Island Assembly. For example, slaves not disposed of in the West Indies could be brought to Rhode Island as long as their owners posted a bond.

But the most visible evidence of the ambivalence with which most Newporters viewed the problem of slavery was their reluctance to extend full "personal liberty" to those slaves imported in violation of the act. True, the legislation guaranteed their emancipation and "enjoyment of private property"—but only on the same terms as the "native Indians." In other words, personal freedom for blacks meant a great deal less freedom than for whites. No connection was made between the ideas in the preamble and those people already enslaved in Newport, except to reassure slaveholders that they could take their servants in and out of the colony without penalty.

Yet despite a less than overwhelming mandate for abolition and curtailment of the slave trade, Quaker agitation may have had at least some effect. The 1774 census, which listed households by color, indicates there were 52 black families—or 162 free black people—in Newport at that time. This would have been 1.7% of the total population or 13% of the black population. It assumes, moreover, that slaves lived with their owners and free blacks established their own residences. It is possible that some slaves maintained separate residences, and that some free blacks or indentured servants lived in white households, but the number is probably so small as to make no appreciable statistical difference. Free black households were even smaller than households headed by women, averaging 2–3 people per unit.

Although manumissions probably accounted for the greatest number of free blacks in the community, there is evidence that good business sense rather than good will prompted the release from bondage. Slaveowners appear to have manumitted old and helpless servants in disproportionate numbers. Fearing a drain on the town treasury for the support of these people, the legislature as early as 1728–1729 passed a law requiring former owners to deposit a sum of not less than £100 with the town treasurer. The evidence is scanty, but it is likely that the number of manumissions dropped sharply as a result of this legislation. Nevertheless, the problem of unsupported blacks probably did not disappear entirely, since the legislature passed another act in 1770 which provided that any owner freeing a slave had to be prepared to support him or her for life, should the necessity arise.[132] These enactments may explain why the few Quakers who did manumit their slaves stipulated a period of service or apprenticeship prior to granting complete freedom. When Sara Thurston manumitted Phyllis in 1775, she insisted on keeping Phyllis for seven years "at which time she will be 18." In the meantime, "she will be clothed, victualed and Educated in a manner suitable for an apprentice of her age, station, and capacity."[133] In other words, by the time Phyllis reached 18 she should have been able to provide for herself.

The possession of marketable skills should have resulted in an adequate standard of living for free blacks. As a matter of fact, historians have argued that many free blacks left sizable estates before the Revolution.[134] In reality, however, the ability to function as a painter, distiller, sailor, cooper, spinner, blacksmith, barber, peruke maker and hairdresser, baker, or dairymaid did not ensure a comfortable existence as a free person.[135] If it had, there would have been no need for legislation absolving the town from responsibility for the support of manumitted slaves. More concretely, if free blacks with skills were able to earn a living in Newport, it would have shown up in the tax assessments. There were no black names on the tax lists. It is conceivable, therefore, that the community was not short of labor and that preference was given to white workers. Since the black codes restricted almost every kind of trade between slaves and whites, these same restraints may have influenced business relations between free blacks and whites as well.[136] It is also likely that Newport's slaveowners simply did not want to shoulder the burden of unproductive, elderly slaves, and, in sporadic bursts of altruism, freed them. Thus, as Samuel Freebody calculated his estate, he noted "One old Negro woman, I have offered her Freedom, I do not value her at anything."[137]

Not all the blacks were either slaves or free; there is some evidence that they existed side by side with indentured servants.[138] While it is impossible to estimate the number of black indentured servants living in Newport, it is likely that in some cases, at least, this kind of servitude resulted from certain civil or criminal convictions.[139]

8

A Lawless Rabble

I F Newport's merchants had not been so dependent on a steady supply of cheap molasses, the inhabitants of the town—indeed, the entire colony—probably would not have been condemned as "a set of lawless piratical people . . . whose whole business is that of smuggling and defrauding the king of his duties. . . ."[140] If merchants from all the American seaports evaded the navigation laws to some extent, those from Newport stood alone as the greatest offenders. And just as the wheels of commerce spun out patterns of wealth, poverty, family structure, and ethnic composition, so too they created a lawless atmosphere which pervaded the community at large.

It is a testament to the crucial importance of molasses and rum to Newport that merchants were willing to go to such lengths to carry on the trade. Moreover, merchants showed an incredible creativity in their various methods of evading the navigation laws. There were many ways of falsifying shipping papers, and, as a result, customs officers constantly complained that "masters and seamen [were] not making true reports of their cargoes. . . ."[141]

In a letter to their ship captain Thomas Rodman, Newport merchants Godfrey and John Malbone explained their particular method of avoiding customs payments on a shipment of French molasses. Rodman was told to proceed to Jamaica and

> if it can be done without Risque, to get a clearance from the Custom House there for as much molasses as you shall judge your vessel will stow, and proceed with your casks filled with water for Ballast to Port au Prince . . . and address yourself to our Friend John Baptist La Barthe who will deliver you a cargo of molasses which you are to load with the greatest Expedition Lest the Date of your Jamaica Clearance should discover the Transaction. You are to endeavour as much as possible to keep your going to Hispaniola a profound secret, as a Discovery thereof might be attended with bad consequences.[142]

In other words, they would *pretend* to buy Jamaican molasses (which was duty free at this time), collect the necessary clearance papers for it, fill their casks with water, and sail off to buy from the French at Hispaniola with utmost speed so the date on the clearance papers would not give the game away. Was it economically worth the risk? Apparently so.

In addition, illegal cargoes were often entered with the connivance of the customs inspectors, whose reputations for corruption were widespread. "The officers of the Customs under the Crown were not very conscientious; and it has been said that a guinea, being placed over one eye, had a considerable effect, while another guinea rendered them blind to what was going on."[143] By 1773, Rhode Island's detractors spoke derisively of "this noble smuggling colony."[144] In a word, official documents reflect no more than a portion of Newport's vast trade in sugar, molasses, and rum.

Similarly, private correspondence indicates that merchants regularly used their ingenuity to avoid customs payments. The matter could be settled with a simple "present to the Wa[i]ter . . . to save the Duty," even though on occasion "the damned Custom house officers put one allmost mad with there extravigent demands."[145] The demands seemed excessive, perhaps, because they were far above the official fees to which the customs agents were entitled. The General Assembly had officially—but no less arbitrarily—reduced the schedule of customs fees in 1764, possibly as an expression of displeasure over the Sugar Act. Since the new rates were "much lower than the ordinary and usual Fees which the officers had been accustomed to receive," it is hardly surprising that the agents were receptive to a little extra money under the table.

By late 1769, however, the customs officials had become so greedy that 51 Newport merchants signed what must have been America's first (and possibly only) anti-bribery agreement.[146] The officials claimed in rebuttal that these payments were "Lawfull Fees" and that by withholding them the merchants only hoped to intimidate the agents and thus prevent them from interfering with the "iniquitous Practice of Smuggling." To make matters worse (at least from the standpoint of the agents), the General Assembly created a special court of common pleas to prosecute—and thus persecute—the "faithfull servants of the Crown" who insisted on an extra emolument to enter and clear ships. In defense, the king's men maintained that their only crime was suppressing "a Body of Smugglers."[147] The customs officers had good reason to be wary of such a court from which there was no appeal. With a packed jury, hostile counsel, and an unfriendly judge, there was every possibility that they would be "sacrificed to the rage and resentment" of the local rum runners.[148]

If a Newport merchant wanted to circumvent both duties and bribes, he might have given his captain sailing orders such as the following:

> Proceed here, go in the Backside of the Island . . . and Give us Intelligence there of as soon and privately as Possible, if you Meet with any Man of Warr or Cutters . . . you must say you Put in in Distress, . . . and that you are bound to Fyal one of the Western Islands, for Which Place your Invoices and Bills Lading must Absolutely be made out for and . . . for which Purpose we have Given you Orders to Proceed There, . . . which you are to Produce . . . , concealing Every Paper that may give the Least Intimation of your stopping here. . . .[149]

Francis Malbone, merchant, slave trader, and gentleman of the first rank, went to the most elaborate lengths to conceal illegal cargo. He built subterranean passages in his cellar which led to a subway ending at the water's edge. Presumably these tunnels were used to smuggle dutiable goods into the house.[150]

Goods were smuggled not only into Newport, but out of Newport and into the Caribbean as well. A captain in the employ of Aaron Lopez described a close call on Nevis: "The officers there had Seized two vessels which had more goods on board then was Cleared, which alarmed me very much, when I retrospected our Situation and probably might meet the Same fate."[151] Caribbean customs officers often stood in the way of cheaply purchased goods, a situation which sometimes occasioned a word of advice from ship owner to captain:

> At St. Jago you will doubtless purchase as many St Jago cloths as you possibly can to advantage, but be very cautious that you do not Indanger your vessel, we are Inform'd that this article is formed and sold only by the King's officers, yet you may Inform yourself of the Priests how this matter is circumstanced.[152]

Illicit trade was not confined to sugar, molasses, and rum. "St. Jago cloths" were apparently worth some risk, as was the sale of hats. "There is many hatters in this place," noted John Lees on his trip to Newport in 1768, "as they Carry on a good deal of Counterband trade in that branch to the West Indies." As an afterthought, Lees added that he believed "much Counterband is carried on here, indeed the Kings officers dust not venture to do their duty with strictness. . . ."[153]

Individual acts of smuggling or bribery give little indication of its pervasiveness, but repeated references in the merchants' correspondence imply that it was widespread. Many of the first families of Newport could claim members who were skilled in the art of smuggling. A list would include such prominent names as Vernon, Champlin, Malbone, and Lopez. As unimpeachable a source as Ezra Stiles suggests that the practice reached staggering proportions:

> Mr. Robinson, Collector of Customs at Newport, came there May, 1764. It is said he gives his Salary of £100 ster. for his office and more. Mr. William Vernon, Mercht, tells me he well knows the Collector makes Six thousand Dollars a year, and that the other officers of the Customs make Three Thousand Dollars per Ann. and that the merchants would gladly compound for Seventy Thousand O.T. [old tenor] per Ann. with the Customhouse.[154]

"We all pay them," commented a business associate acting on orders from Newport merchant William Vernon, "and are glad to get of[f] in that manner. . . ."[155]

One of the graver problems, however, was that not everyone was able "to get off in that manner." Smuggling, bribery, and connivance were only a few of the bad habits acquired by Newport's merchants over the years. Violence, to achieve the same ends, was both common and expected. In February 1772 the crown officers reported to the commissioners in Boston that

> A few Days ago we Caused Seizure to be made of a Quantity of Molasses . . . because the . . . Master had willfully omitted to Comprise the same in his Report Inwards. We have the disaggreeable Account to give you, that in this Case we have met with our usual Fate. The goods have been Wrested out of our Hands while our Officers were forcibly confin'd by that Outrageous Violence we have so often experienc'd.[156]

Both the customs letter book and Treasury Office Documents describe similar and more serious incidents. Jesse Saville, a tidewaiter at Rhode Island, was tarred, feathered, beaten, and threatened with death for trying to enforce the navigation laws. Saville's assailants accused him of trying to influence other tidesmen who were, according to Saville, "more favorable to the merchants than . . . trusty to their King." Saville was warned that "to see everything that passed" would cost him a broken neck. Although Saville may have exaggerated the danger to his person, he was clearly frightened enough to request a change of assignment in his report.[157]

Some merchants engaged in illegal activities harbored no second thoughts; others were uneasy and sought to justify their actions. As William Vernon explained while directing one such operation: "I am persuaded my self that our restrictions in America on Trade etc. are oppressive and unjust, therefore to evade them is no crime."[158] Unjust, perhaps, for William Vernon, unjust even for the majority of Newport's merchants, but were the laws unjust in terms of Britain's entire commercial scheme? And who was to judge? There were few laws Parliament could pass which would placate the West Indian planter and the New England merchant at the same time. Detente existed until 1763 because smuggling was overlooked. But no one overlooked the fact that Newport's development and prosperity rested to some extent on this illegal traffic.

To ensure the success of such ventures, the merchants were dependent on the cooperation of many people: the willing dock workers unloading hogsheads of molasses in the dead of night who surely knew they were employed to break the law; the law enforcement officers whose deliberate lack of visibility furthered the interests of those breaking the law; and the civil authorities, often merchants themselves, who lacked the requisite enthusiasm to apply sanctions against their friends, associates, and employees.

This cooperative spirit (which bordered on conspiracy) is best illustrated by the delaying tactics employed by Governor Wanton in 1768 to thwart the efforts of the customs collectors. Having good reason to suspect that illegal cargo had been unloaded from the *Rhoda*, customs agents applied to the governor for a writ of assistance at ten o'clock on the morning of December 7, in order to examine the contents of a warehouse. Although the urgency of the situation dictated immediate action, the governor decided he could not proceed without advice from the Judge Advocate who was not available for consultation until noon of that day. The Judge Advocate subsequently advised Wanton that he was legally entitled to draw up the writ, which the governor proceeded to do. This procedure was completed by 1 P.M., but as the governor was concerned about the form of the document, another hour elapsed before the paper was in the hands of the customs officials. Law dictated that the writ be presented to the civil officer named therein, who in this case was the sheriff. Unfortunately, on this particular day the sheriff was confined by sickness. The document, therefore, was presented to his deputy who denied the ability to act without instructions from the sheriff himself. It was now 3 P.M. Instructions having been received from the sick bed, the group made its way to the warehouse, where, presumably, the smuggled goods rested. The keys to the warehouse had disappeared by this time, and although someone made a "weak effort to force open the Doors" the whole effort was ineffectual. A sudden recovery brought the sheriff to the scene, who after taking a quick look at the writ announced that he could no longer act since "the Sun was set, and consequently his Power for that Day at an End."

This was not an isolated incident, but one that saw frequent repetition. After another particularly violent confrontation, customs officials who should have known better reported that although they made "immediate application to the Civil Authority for Aid and Assistance . . . we were disappointed in our Expectations. We could obtain no Assistance at all."[159] The circle of illegality widened with each person's involvement, as the better and lesser sorts joined together as partners in crime.

But William Vernon argued that it was no crime at all. Did this mean that *any* law Newporters decided was unjust could be ignored? Evidence suggests that the borderline between unjust and disadvantageous was somewhat wavy, and that evasion of British navigation laws was perhaps only the most flagrant example of the way in which the people of Newport bent the law when it suited them. For instance, in 1767, assessors requested an accounting of the number of slaves in each person's possession for purposes of taxation. The final tally showed one-third the number of slaves as reported by both the 1755 and 1774 censuses. One cannot help wondering if Newporters were not a little reticent about reporting the number of slaves they actually owned when they were about to be taxed at whole value.

For those who might argue that smuggling and tax evasion were unconnected, it should be noted that both were in the self-interest of the merchant, and both indicated a disrespect for the law. And in a deferential society, where the motions of the upper class were carefully monitored, unlawful behavior may have become acceptable, if not respectable. In short, other townspeople may have been influenced by this indifference to the rule of law. Since the mobs were well aware of merchant smuggling activities, breaking and entering to retrieve the same cargoes may have seemed less criminal than it actually was. By setting the pace and sanctioning the illegal importation of merchandise, merchants had put their stamp of approval on related activities. Although one cannot argue with assurance that there was a disproportionate number of felonies in Newport in the 1760s and 1770s, the number of burglaries reported in the newspapers leaves little doubt that these crimes took place frequently. Just as William Vernon felt that he was entitled to the fruits of his trade—by whatever means—other Newporters may have felt that they too were justified in appropriating the material goods to which they were clearly not entitled by law.

Bypassing the law could take the form of humane gestures as well as acts of defiance or self-interest. For example, part of the same pattern may have been the willingness of the town fathers to excuse the town mothers from taxes. The assessment was on the books, but in recognition of their special plight, women were not pressed for their share. Whatever position one takes on this issue, it is safe to say that Newporters were not His Majesty's most lawabiding citizens.

REFLECTIONS

With its endless web of personal relationships, and intertwining network of economic interests, pre-Revolutionary Newport was a society where rank and status mattered—and was likely to remain so for what to Newporters was the foreseeable future. The rich perpetuated themselves by intermarriage and by clinging tenaciously to the seats of power through the electoral process. By the eve of the Revolution they had cornered an increasingly disproportionate share of the city's wealth, and there was no sign that this would change soon. The growing number of poor might aspire to the perquisites and pleasures of the upper class, but it was unlikely that many would join that select group. Although upward movement was possible, downward movement was not unknown. Since the poor were more likely to leave the community than the affluent in the Revolutionary era, it may have appeared to those who did remain that the ladder of success was an easy climb.

What is perhaps most striking about Newport is the close dependence of one group of people on another. Despite the consuming interest in profit—or perhaps because of it—one senses a degree of cooperative effort that somehow would evaporate in the complexities of modern industrialized society.

The picture that emerges from the depths of two hundred years is of a small group of people, self-seeking and self-perpetuating, to whom the rest of the community turned for sustenance and direction. Not only did the merchants provide jobs both directly and indirectly for the rest of the townspeople, but it was their tax contribution—far out of proportion to their numbers—which provided support for the growing number of people unable to support themselves. It was in their homes that youngsters from outside the immediate family were educated and it was to them that the Town Council looked for assistance in providing for the needy. Merchants may also have influenced the behavior of other members of the community.

In turn, the merchants depended on Newport's skilled and unskilled laborers to provide those services without which no merchant could carry on business. Merchants may have supplied shopkeepers with laces, apothecaries with medicines, and teachers with books, but every merchant who owned a vessel needed people to build, load, and sail it. Moreover, he needed merchandise to ship out of Newport. The merchants may have imported the amber liquid that tavern keepers sold in such quantities, but without coopers to build barrels, tavern mugs would have been empty. If the merchants were the support of the town, they in turn were supported by other Newporters who answered their needs.

If merchants depended on slave labor in a wide variety of jobs, the slaves themselves had nowhere to turn but to their owners for the necessities of life.

Women, because of their meager earning power, were also among the most dependent members of the community. A married woman was under the protection of her husband and relied on him for support. Single women and widows depended on each other. Those who still could not eke out a living turned to the town to extend the protection that a husband would ordinarily provide. In addition to traditional means of support, relief took the unusual form of an unwritten code whereby women received favored status in terms of taxation and privileges. This dependency network extended beyond the boundaries of Newport, as the town acknowledged its responsibility for all its inhabitants should they become burdens to other communities. But the interdependent network was fragile. It was dependent on outside markets and susceptible to disintegration by outside forces. In the last analysis everyone in Newport was dependent on the sea. The *ability* to trade insured Newport's continuance as a viable community. Whatever threatened mercantile activities threatened the life of the town. Inadvertently, the British—after 1763—did exactly that.

1. William Vernon & Co. to William Pinniger, Feb. 10, 1768, Vernon Letter Book #77, NHS.

2. The population of Newport in 1774 was 9,209. MS Census, 1774. This census was published in alphabetical order by J. R. Bartlett, *Census of the Inhabitants of the Colony of Rhode Island and Providence Plantations, 1774* (Providence, 1858). The census was taken street by street, although the streets were neither named nor divided one from the other. However, by matching the names of people with the information in Antoinette F. Downing and Vincent J. Scully, Jr., *The Architectural Heritage of Newport, Rhode Island, 1640–1915* (Cambridge, Mass., 1952; repr. New York, 1967) and the "List of Occupants of Houses in Newport, Rhode Island During the Revolution," NHS, it is possible to determine the route of the census takers.

3. Shalloon, ozenbrig, rattinet, and calamanco are fabrics. A gimblet is either a boring tool or a large shallow tub used for salting bacon or other purposes. A kittern was probably a kitereen or covered vehicle, possibly from the West Indies.

4. The only time this residential pattern appears to break down is if a merchant was involved in a business requiring space. Thus Edward Cole, a very wealthy merchant—but also a tan yard owner—chose to live on Broadway in a less than prosperous neighborhood. His tan yard was one block away, near the edge of town where there was open space, a necessity for a tannery. Cole's workers undoubtedly lived nearby—close enough, at least, to be frequently under his scrutiny. Much of the preceding and following information has been acquired through matching occupation and tax assessments on the MS census of 1774 (compiled street by street) and a 1777 map. "A Plan of the Town of Newport, in Rhode Island, surveyed by Charles Blaskowitz, Engraved and Published by William Faden, Charing Cross, September 1, 1777." NHS. The map is reproduced on the endpapers. This comparison gives a very clear picture of the neighborhoods and of who lived where. See also Downing & Scully, *Architectural Heritage*, p. 9.

5. *NM*, Feb. 13, 1764.

6. MS Census, 1774.

7. Mary Beth Norton, " 'My Resting Reaping Times': Sarah Osborn's Defense of Her 'Unfeminine' Activities, 1767," *Signs: Journal of Women in Culture and Society*, 2 (1976), 528.

8. See Caroll Smith-Rosenberg, "The Female World of Love and Ritual: Relations Between Women in Nineteenth-Century America," ibid., 1 (1975), 1–30.

9. Downing & Scully, *Architectural Heritage*, p. 513.

10. See *NM*, June 6, 1763, for an advertisement of a newly arrived cargo from Africa; Irving Bartlett, *From Slave to Citizen: The Story of the Negro in Rhode Island* (Providence, 1964), p. 9; William D. Johnston, "Slavery in Rhode Island, 1755–1776," in *Slavery in the United States* (New York, 1969), p. 127.

11. The Jewish members of the community were scattered around town, despite the reference to "Jew Street" on the 1777 map. The street was probably so called because the Jewish cemetery was located there.

12. Downing & Scully, *Architectural Heritage*, p. 485.

13. *NM*, June 10, 1765, July 14, 1766.

14. See the various issues of *NM* for the years 1758–1776 for marriage announcements; *Vital Records of Rhode Island, 1636–1850*. IV. *Newport County*, ed. James M. Arnold (Providence, 1901). But marriages *did* cut across religious lines; the Quakers, in particular, despaired over this.

15. Caty Malbone to her brother, undated, uncatalogued Malbone Papers, NHS.

16. *NM*, Feb. 28, 1763.

17. The Newport assessment list of 1760 shows 86 people, all men and nearly all merchants, paying £10 or more in taxes for that year. Those men represent only 9% of the 962 taxpayers, but they were expected to contribute 50% of the taxes. Indeed, those people assessed £20 or more in 1760 (33 in total) represent only 3.4% of the taxpaying population, yet they paid 27% of the tax. A list of 1,210 Newport taxpayers also exists for the year 1772. A comparison of the two lists suggests that during the intervening years wealth had become even more concentrated. In 1772, the 33 people assessed the highest taxes (2.7% of the total) paid nearly 30% of the tax, while the first 86 men (7.1% of the total) paid 51% of the entire assessment. Though the same pattern emerges in New York, Philadelphia, and Boston, this change is less dramatic in Newport than in those cities in the decade immediately following the French and Indian War. Although it is true that during these years slightly fewer people were paying a slightly greater share of the tax in Newport, the most dramatic change occurred between 1772 and 1775. In the latter year, the top 33 men (3.3% of the taxpayers) paid 34.3% of the total bill for that year, and the first 86 men on the list (8.7% of the taxpayers) paid 57.5% of the tax. This information is summarized in Table III.

The Rev. Ezra Stiles confirmed this implicitly unequal distribution of wealth in his *Itineraries* written some months after the 1760 tax assessment. He estimated that there were 1,200 families in Newport (which was probably very close to the actual number), of which 5/6 or 1,000 were worth "at a mean" £2,000 old tenor (o.t.) each. Stiles maintained that the remaining 1/6 or 200 families were worth, again "at a mean," £40,000 each but that of those 200 "there may be 20 families worth £100,000 apiece; and 2 of £500,000 or £20,000 sterling apiece; several of 150 & 200,000 Old Tenor." Emissions of paper caused Rhode Island "old tenor" currency to depreciate. Stiles implied that in 1760 old tenor and sterling were in a ratio of 25:1. *Itineraries*, p. 90.

The 1772 and 1775 tax assessments may be found in MS form at the NHS. A word about using the tax lists: The 1760 assessment seems complete in all respects. The others are not, but are still usable despite this drawback. The 1772 tax list is complete except for the names beginning with "A." From the number of missing pages it is likely that there were about 40 names beginning with "A." In 1760 the "A's" paid 2.3% of the entire assessment; in 1772, 5%, and in 1775, 4.6%. By 1775, a great many Newporters had fled to safer environs and though the tax report is accurate for that year, it is necessary to keep in mind that Newport was no longer the same prosperous community it had been in 1772. So many, in fact, left Newport in 1774–1775 that when the *NM* reprinted the 1775 list of taxpayers in February and March, 1853, it also printed the names of those "persons of considerable importance who left the island on the breaking out of the war," with the amount of tax paid by them in 1772, a useful list in itself.

For comparisons with Boston and Philadelphia, where statistics indicate that wealth was becoming concentrated in much the same way, see James Henretta, "Economic Development and Social Structure in Colonial Boston," *William and Mary Quarterly*, 22 (1965), 75–92; Gary Nash, "Urban Wealth and Poverty in Pre-Revolutionary America," *Journal of Interdisciplinary History*, 6 (1976), 545–84; G. B. Warden, "Inequality and Instability in Eighteenth-Century Boston: A Reappraisal," ibid., 585–620. For thoughts on the use of eighteenth-century quantitative data in general, see Jacob M. Price, "Quantifying Colonial America: A Comment on Nash and Warden," ibid., 701–709.

18. Abraham Redwood to James Woodcock, Apr. 4, 1740, Redwood Letter Book, p. 644, NHS.

19. See "Bull's Memoirs of Rhode Island," under 1766, NHS. The story of the fire was reported in *NM*, June 9, 1766, with a note that the furniture had been saved.

20. *Gentleman's Progress: The Itinerarium of Dr. Alexander Hamilton, 1744*, ed. Carl Bridenbaugh (Chapel Hill, N.C., 1948), p. 103. On this particular trip Hamilton covered 1,600 miles from Maryland to Maine, over a four-month period.

21. "Solomon Drowne's Journal," *The Newport Historical Magazine*, 1 (July 1880 – April 1881), 67–68.

22. *NM*, Feb. 21, 1763.

23. Although only a small percentage of the community was exceedingly wealthy, the best estimates indicate that approximately two-thirds of the people in Newport could be considered middle or upper class. See below, note 50.

24. Bigelow, "Commerce of Rhode Island with the West Indies," Part II, chap. 2, p. 22.

25. Act of the General Assembly, July 15, 1715, *Documents*, III 113, 115*n*6; RICR, IV 191–93, 208, 225, 330, 424.

26. *Itineraries*, p. 217. Simon Pease was a slave trader.

27. Ibid., p. 23.

28. "A List of the Polls and Estates Real and Personal of the Proprietors and Inhabitants of the town of Newport in the Colony of Rhode Island taken pursuant to an Act of the Rhode Island General Assembly passed in June 1767" is deposited at the NHS. The list is obviously undervalued for three important reasons. (*a*) The names of several very prominent people are omitted. (*b*) It acknowledges only 352 slaves for the town of Newport, a ridiculous number, since there were about 1,100 slaves in both 1755 and 1774 according to the census figures. This casts doubt on the veracity of the other figures in the report. (*c*) The General Assembly itself sent the commissioners back for a recount and subsequently (in February 1769) revised Newport's total value of ratables upward.

29. Real property held outside Newport would not appear on the 1767 ratables list; nor would Newport residents be taxed on it by the Newport tax assessors. This makes it difficult to ascertain how many town residents bought property outside Newport since wills and probate records are sparse. See *NM*, Mar. 16, 1762; Apr. 25 and June 20, 1763; May 13, 1765; Feb. 17 and Sept. 1, 1766; and Mar. 6, 1771.

30. "First Division of the Township of Woodstock," new acquisition, NHS. Ezra Stiles made an earlier entry in his *Itineraries* indicating that the formation of this township had been in the thinking stages for several years. *Itineraries*, p. 81. See also pp. 86–87 for references to the formation of other towns and the prices of lots.

31. Killington, Vermont, plot of lots, 1764, NHS. In December 1782, when Vermont was rebuked by the Continental Congress for disregarding its recommendations, only New Jersey and Rhode Island supported Vermont. New Jersey's delegates were "under instructions," but rumor had it that Rhode Island was "interested in lands in Vermont." *Journals of the Continental Congress, 1774–1789*, edd. Worthington C. Ford et al., 34 vols. (Washington D.C., 1904–1937), XXIII 859.

32. The 1767 "List of Polls . . . of the Town of Newport. . . ." Advertisements in *NM* indicate that there was frequent tenant turnover in rental property.

33. "Account of the People in the Colony of Rhode Island, Whites and Blacks, Together with the Quantity of Arms and Ammunition in the hands of private persons" (1755), Box 121, folder 10, NHS; Lorenzo Greene, *The Negro in Colonial New England* (New York, 1969), p. 88; United States Bureau of the Census, *A Century of Population Growth* (Washington, D.C., 1909), p. 183.

34. Gary Nash, "Slaves and Slaveowners in Colonial Philadelphia," *William and Mary Quarterly*, 30 (1973), 223–56; Greene, *Negro in Colonial New England*, pp. 84–85; Winthrop D. Jordan, *White Over Black: American Attitudes Toward the Negro, 1550–1812* (Baltimore, 1968), p. 103; Gary Nash, *The Urban Crucible: Social Change, Political Consciousness, and the Origins of the American Revolution* (Cambridge, Mass., 1979), pp. 107, 320.

35. *The Works of George Berkeley*, ed. Alexander C. Fraser, 4 vols. (Oxford, 1901), IV 157*n*.

36. Historians have had little to say on the matter, but antique experts assert that it was common practice for a silversmith to melt down coin in order to create a coffee pot, candlestick, or bowl. "Plate," in the eighteenth century, was derived from the Spanish word *plata*, meaning "silver," and should not be confused with the twentieth-century definition of silver plate. Eighteenth-century wrought plate was 92.5% silver with 7.5% copper added for hardness. See Graham Hood, *American Silver* (New York, 1971), pp. 11–20; Census Bureau, *Historical Statistics of the United States* (1960), p. 758.

37. For a synopsis of Rhode Island's attempts to control its currency in the 1750s and early 1760s, see James, *Colonial Rhode Island*, pp. 275–83, 303–304.

38. *Itineraries*, p. 17; 1772 Newport tax assessment, NHS.

39. *Works*, IV 160. See also William Weeden, "Ideal Newport in the Eighteenth Century," *Proceedings of the American Antiquarian Society*, 18 N.S. (1906), 108.

40. The only entertainment universally condemned was the theater. Outlawed in a town meeting in 1761 and by statute in 1762 on the grounds that theatergoing discouraged frugality, acting companies were notified that any thespian daring to perform in Rhode Island would be fined £100. Given Newport's attitude toward the law, however, it will not surprise anyone to learn that a month after the town meeting vote, a "Company of Comedians" acted out *The Comedy of the Provok'd Husband*. It was apparently justified on the grounds that it was a benefit performance. Town Meeting Records, 1679–1779, Book 2007, p. 710, NHS; *Acts and Laws of the English Colony of Rhode-Island and Providence Plantations, in New England, in America*, revised codification (Newport, 1767), p. 242; *The New Hampshire Gazette*, Sept. 25, 1761.

41. The Field's Fountain Society received a charter in 1772 for the purpose of conveying water in pipes to certain residents of Providence. It is possible that experiments along the same lines were being conducted in Newport. RICR, VII 54. In addition, when John Bartlett advertised his home for sale in Charleston, he added as a selling point that "it is accommodated with an excellent Rivulet of the best Water, running in such a Manner, that it may, with the Greatest Ease, be conducted by a Trough or Pipe, into either [the] First or Second Story of the House." *NM*, Mar. 6, 1771.

42. Quoted in Edward Peterson, *History of Rhode Island* (New York, 1853), p. 135.

43. John Francis Williams to John Malbone, Augusta, Georgia, Dec. 18, 1769, Malbone Papers, Box 174, folder 15, NHS.

44. Carl Bridenbaugh, "Colonial Newport as a Summer Resort," *Rhode Island Historical Society Collections*, 26 (1933), 23.

45. John Francis Williams to John Malbone, Augusta, Georgia, Dec. 18, 1769, Malbone Papers, Box 174, folder 15, NHS. In a happy ending to the story, Williams sold his business and moved to Newport.

46. *Acts and Laws of the English Colony of Rhode-Island* ... (1767), pp. 78ff. See also Rudolph, "Merchants of Newport," p. 36.

47. "A List of the Names of the Persons who Proxed for General Officers of the Government for the ensuing year [April 15, 1767]," Rhode Island State Archives, Providence. Occupations have been matched to this list. Rudolph, "Merchants of Newport," p. 42. See also the Town Meeting Records, 1679–1779, Book 2007, passim, NHS, for names of council and committee members.

48. Both David Lovejoy and Irwin Polishook argue that the overwhelming majority of adult white men could vote in Rhode Island. They do not isolate Newport, however, which had a proportionately larger property-less population. Richard Rudolph insists that no more than 60% of the white male population could vote. My own position is that Rudolph is probably closer to the truth. See Lovejoy's *Rhode Island Politics and the American Revolution, 1760–1776* (Providence, 1958), pp. 16–17; Polishook's *Rhode Island and the Union* (Evanston, Ill., 1969), pp. 28–30; and Rudolph's "Merchants of Newport," pp. 36–40. See also Robert E. Brown, *Middle Class Democracy and the Revolution in Massachusetts, 1691–1780* (Ithaca, N.Y., 1955).

In a letter written in 1767, Ezra Stiles implied that in the other charter colony,

Connecticut, only 11% of the people were eligible to vote. Ezra Stiles to Benjamin Gale, Oct. 1, 1767, Stiles Papers, Yale University.

49. This inventory and those mentioned below will be found in the Town Council Records, 1768–1771, vol. 15, pp. 51, 68, 179, 187, and passim, NHS.

50. It is difficult to calculate the number of poor. I have arrived at the one-third figure after evaluating the following factors:

(a) The number of adult white male taxpayers in both 1760 and 1772. In 1760 this group numbered 927 out of an approximate total of 1,610 white adult males. This means that 57.5% of the white adult men paid taxes in that year. The 1772 assessment indicates that there were approximately 1,166 taxable adult white males in Newport at that time. Since there were roughly 2,050 white males above age 16 in the community, calculations show that slightly less than 57% of the adult white males in Newport paid taxes (a percentage remarkably close to the 1760 figure). That there were more taxpayers in 1772 (1,210) than in 1760 (962) is interesting in itself. According to the most recent studies, the number of taxpayers declined in both Boston and Philadelphia in the quarter century before the Revolution. These figures may be deceiving, however, to the extent that the 1772 assessment appears to have included a far greater proportion of unratable polls than the earlier list. See below, and Gary Nash, "Social Change and the Growth of Pre-Revolutionary Urban Radicalism," in *The American Revolution*, ed. Alfred F. Young (DeKalb, Ill., 1976), pp. 9–10.

(b) The ripple effect of those paying taxes. Although only slightly more than 3% of the taxpayers on both the 1760 and the 1772 tax assessments were women, many women in the community were married to men who *were* taxed, on their own property and on that acquired through marriage. Presumably these married women still enjoyed this property after marriage (e.g., silver candlesticks or a vegetable garden) although their names did not appear on the tax assessment. Therefore, if the tax lists are the basis on which to divide the poor from the rest of society, not only the taxpayers themselves but their immediate households must be taken into consideration. This would include wives, dependent children, and elderly parents, who presumably shared the same lifestyle. If each of these taxpayers supported a household of five members, this would mean that about two-thirds of the community enjoyed the benefits of a middle- or upper-class lifestyle. One should keep in mind, however, that people at the lower end of the tax scale (those paying merely a poll tax) did not enjoy the same lifestyle as people paying more, and may have been only on the fringes of the middle class. The 1767 "List of Polls . . . of the Town of Newport . . ." indicates that of 1,118 ratable polls 350 (31%) paid only a poll tax. This list is the one on which the 1772 assessment was based.

(c) The variable of expectancy. Even on the assumption that those on the lower end of the tax assessment were only marginally middle class at best, these people are compensated for by others whose names do not appear on the tax list at all but who were in a temporarily dependent position. A merchant's son, living in a household other than his father's, could expect to inherit a business. Perhaps he had no taxable real or personal property of his own at the time of the tax assessment, but his situation was hardly comparable to that of a 45-year-old laborer who had climbed as high as he could on the economic ladder. The same is true of the cordwainer's apprentice who lived in back of the shop. He was a young man with no current taxable property, but his immediate needs were provided for by his master, and he had a comfortable future in prospect. He cannot be equated with a retired seaman who had never been able to make ends meet. Neither the merchant's son nor the apprentice had ratables at the time of the assessment, but the variable of expectancy cannot be ignored, even though the percentage of people not paying taxes appears to remain constant, at least during the period under consideration.

51. Although in 1761 Ezra Stiles noted there were only 6 unratable polls out of a total of 1,250 polls, six years later nearly one-third of those assessed were declared unratable—that is to say, they paid merely a poll tax. *Itineraries*, p. 23.

52. *NM*, Dec. 12, 1763, Jan. 7, 1765, Mar. 6, 1771.

53. Treasurer's Account Book B, 1761–1796, NHS.

54. Besides "warning out" potential charges, the best Rhode Island could do before 1774 in an effort to avoid further drain on the government treasury by an influx of poor whites was to pass "An Act preventing foreigners coming into this colony from any parts whatsoever, by sea, excepting Great Britain, Ireland, Jersey and Guernsey, from being chargeable to any Town in this government, where they shall be landed." *NM*, Aug. 17, 1767.

55. New England towns had reciprocal agreements to provide for the support of their own residents. Someone from South Kingston, for instance, would arrive in Newport with the following certificate in his pocket: "To the Town Council of Newport in the colony of Rhode Island. Gentlemen. If you will allow [name], wife and children to live in your town we will receive them at any time when you may think proper to order them back (we allowing them to be inhabitants of the Town of South Kingston) except they or any of them gain a legal settlement elsewhere."

In turn, someone removing from Newport would be provided with the following: "To the Selectmen of any of the Towns of the Province of Massachusetts Bay or Elsewhere Greeting: Gentlemen, [name] and her two children . . . being inhabitants of this Town, if you will allow them to live in your town the Town Council of Newport hereby certify that they will receive them back here at any time whenever you may think fit to order them back (except they gain a legal settlement elsewhere) given under my hand by order and in behalf of Town Council of Newport in the Colony of Rhode Island [date]."

Sometimes a person's legal settlement would agree to pay all the charges that might accrue from allowing him or her to reside in another town. Miscellaneous Records, Newport, R.I. (1 vol.), NHS. See also *Acts and Laws of the English Colony of Rhode-Island* . . . (1767), pp. 228–32.

56. The records show 109 married men with families and 12 single men opting to take up residence in Newport during this time. Between 1750 and 1776, 66 men with families and 25 men without families chose to leave Newport. Miscellaneous Records, Newport, R.I. (1 vol.), NHS.

57. *NM*, Jan. 11, 1768.

58. An Account of the People in the Colony of Rhode Island . . . (1755), NHS; *Census . . . 1774*, ed. Bartlett.

59. The census of 1774 lists the number of blacks in each white household. Though this list may include some free black servants who lived in, it is probable that most were slaves. By comparing a list of distillers with the census, it is possible to count the number of blacks (slaves) each distiller owned.

60. Miscellaneous Records, Newport, R.I. (1 vol.), NHS.

61. According to Billy G. Smith, seamen's wages in Philadelphia declined at the end of the Seven Years' War, and for most of the 1760s, real wages hovered between 81% and 90% of their 1762 value. "The Material Lives of Laboring Philadelphians, 1750 to 1800," *William and Mary Quarterly*, 38 (1981), 192; *Commerce*, I 472.

62. Hopkins, "Dialogue Concerning the Slavery of the Africans," p. 554.

63. *NM*, Mar. 6, 1771, Jan. 16, 1769, Jan. 11, 1768, Dec. 12, 1763, July 8, 1765, Nov. 14, 1774.

64. *NM*, Nov. 30, 1767. Carl Bridenbaugh notes that the Town Council supplied one or two cords of wood to each of four Newport widows in 1747, but apparently such generosity occurred sporadically rather than on a regular basis. Town Council records confirm this. *Cities in Revolt: Urban Life in America, 1743–1776* (London & New York, 1971), p. 124.

65. *NM*, Jan. 25, 1768. Two years later a correspondent called woolen manufacturing "the most profitable of any business now carried on in America." *NM*, Oct. 8, 1770.

66. *NM*, Feb. 6, 1769.

67. In 1747 Abraham Redwood donated £500 to buy books for an as yet unbuilt library. After Redwood's death, Benjamin Waterhouse wrote to Christopher Champlin that Redwood was " 'the greatest public and private benefactor of any man I ever knew on Rhode Island.' " This does not say very much for Rhode Island. Quoted in George C. Mason, *Reminiscences of Newport*, enlarged edition, #241 D, p. 260, NHS.

68. Twice during the Christmas season the Congregation of Trinity Church collected for "the poor of all denominations," but neither time did the amount exceed £100; *NM*, June 5, 1769, Apr. 25, 1763, July 9, 1770, Dec. 28, 1772, Dec. 27, 1773.

69. *NM*, Sept. 24, 1764, Apr. 18, 1774, July 24, 1769, June 22, 1772, Aug. 17, 1767.

70. Charter of the Marine Society, NHS. The Fellowship Club evolved into the Marine Society.

71. George C. Mason, *Reminiscences of Newport* (Newport, 1884), p. 98.

72. For example, the issue of June 17, 1765, reported that Capt. Spear of Boston and Capt. Hopkins of Providence lost "near . . . all their men." The paper also noted that John Bennett and Edward Belcher, both of Newport, died on the coast.

73. *NM*, July 13 and Aug. 31, 1767, Oct. 3, 1768, June 7, 1773.

74. *Itineraries*, p. 13.

75. In that year there were 2,624 white adult women and 2,100 white adult men.

76. In 1755 Newport claimed 1,696 adult white men and 1,633 adult white women.

77. See, in particular, Kenneth Lockridge, "Land, Population, and the Evolution of New England Society, 1630–1790; and an Afterthought," in *Colonial America*, ed. Stanley Katz (Boston, 1971), pp. 466–91.

78. For support of this proposition, see Susan Grigg, "Toward a Theory of Remarriage: A Case Study of Newburyport at the Beginning of the Nineteenth Century," *Journal of Interdisciplinary History*, 8 (1977), 198–200.

79. *Itineraries*, p. 213.

80. This may be the reason why more women than men were voluntarily leaving Newport. Between 1736 and 1772, 76 single women and 48 women with children decided to make their homes somewhere else in New England. Only 23 women (one-half of whom had children) emigrated to Newport during those years. Miscellaneous Records, Newport, R.I. (1 vol.), NHS.

81. Stiles meant 1774, but his figures are accurate. *Diary*, II 105, I 623.

82. Robert V. Wells, "Household Size and Composition in the British Colonies in America, 1675–1775," *Journal of Interdisciplinary History*, 4 (1974), 543–70; and idem, *The Population of the British Colonies in America Before 1776: A Survey of Census Data* (Princeton, N.J., 1975). See Lynne E. Withey, "Household Structure in Urban and Rural Areas: The Case of Rhode Island, 1774–1800," *Journal of Family History*, 3 (1978), 37–50.

83. Wells, *Population of the British Colonies*, p. 104.

84. Wells, "Household Size and Composition," 554.

85. In Newport in 1774, 28.2% of the households were childless. In both 1755 and 1774 only 40% of the population in Newport was under 16 while the proportion of children under 16 in the colony as a whole was 46%–49% during those same years. Wells, *Population of the British Colonies*, p. 102; idem, "Household Size and Composition," 557.

86. *Acts and Laws of the English Colony of Rhode-Island* . . . (1767), p. 210. If the court found that a child was unable to support a parent, the town of Newport might dig into its pocket to help out. This would seem to be the case when the Town Council authorized payment to Ralph Stanhope "for 5 weeks support of his father— £10." Child support was also common. Town Council Records, 1768–1771, vol. 16, p. 164, NHS.

87. *Diary*, I 623; David H. Flaherty, *Privacy in Colonial New England* (Charlottesville, Va., 1967), pp. 51ff.

88. Wells, *Population of the British Colonies*, p. 289.

89. *NM*, Dec. 28, 1767.

90. The women who had enough income to pay taxes were, for the most part, merchants, shopkeepers, merchants' widows, or tavern keepers.

91. Women also married because they became pregnant. Robert Gross, *The Minutemen and Their World* (New York, 1976), p. 100, argued that in Concord, Massachusetts, "in the 20 years before the Revolution, more than one out of every three firstborn children had been conceived out of wedlock." Comparable statistics are not

available for Newport, but a reading of the Friends' Minutes suggests that the same situation occurred there. The Friends were constantly reproving members for having children "too soon after marriage."

92. Somewhat unsure of how to describe one of Newport's most successful tavern operators in her marriage announcement, Solomon Southwick, the *NM* printer, compromised and reported the marriage of "Sir John Treville, Knight of Malta, Capt. of the Cavalry to Mrs. Abigail Stoneman, . . . a lady descended from a reputable family, of a good genius, a very polite and genteel address, and extremely well accomplished in every branch of family economy." *NM*, Sept. 5, 1774.

93. See *NM*, passim, especially the advertisements.

94. Town Council Records, 1768–1771, vol. 16, NHS.

95. In July 1775 Mary Rogers noted that she had received £103 (old tenor) "for two months and 2 days wages, due my husband John Rogers on Board the Brig Royal Charlotte." Slavery Papers, Box VII, NYHS.

96. Marther Mackloud to Aaron Lopez, May 25, 1776, Lopez Papers, Haight Collection, NHS.

97. See Gracy Walch [Watch] to Mr. [Lotrop], Mar. 25, 1776; Mary Forrester to Aaron Lopez, Oct. 22, 1776; and Martha Finley to——, Jan. 21, 1775; ibid.

98. Lydia Bissell to Aaron Lopez, Mar. 18, 1776, ibid.

99. Articles of the Marine Society (1754), NHS.

100. "An Act for Granting Administration to the Wives of Persons Three Years Absent and Unheard of," *Acts and Laws of His Majesty's Colony of Rhode-Island, and Providence-Plantation. In America* (Newport, 1730), p. 69; *Acts and Laws of the English Colony of Rhode-Island* . . . (1767), pp. 217–18; "An Act for the Probate of Wills, and Granting Administration," ibid., pp. 214–17.

101. "An Act Empowering justices . . . to give Sentence of Divorce for the relief of such persons as are injured by the Breach of the Marriage Covenant," *Acts and Laws of the English Colony of Rhode-Island* . . . (1767), p. 74.

102. "An Act Empowering Overseers of the Poor of Newport to Commit persons to work house" and "An Act Empowering Overseers of the Workhouse to Secure the Town from Costs arising from idle and disorderly persons," ibid., pp. 197–99.

103. *NM*, June 5, 1769.

104. *NM*, Jan. 11, 1768, Oct. 9, 1769.

105. Town Meeting Records, 1679–1779, Book 2007, pp. 890–92, NHS.

106. Adultery and desertion were the only legal grounds for divorce in colonial Rhode Island.

107. Diary of Lt. John Peebles, Dec. 31, 1776, microfilm Library of Congress, as quoted in *William and Mary Quarterly*, 26 (1969), 441.

108. *NM*, May 29, 1769, Mar. 6, 1771.

109. William B. Weeden, *Economic and Social History of New England*, 2 vols. (Boston, 1890), II 453.

110. *Valuation of the Cities and Towns in the State of Rhode Island from 1860–1869 for Purposes of Taxation. Together with the Census of the Colony in 1730 and*

1775 and Other Statistics, ed. Elisha Dyer (Providence, 1871). The census for 1748–1749 is included in this publication, having been copied from *Douglass' Summary, etc. of the first planting, progressive improvements and present state of the British settlements in North America* (London, 1754). The number of blacks in Newport in 1748–1749 has been the source of confusion because when the figures were reproduced in RICR, v 250 (from the same source) the last digit was omitted. This error makes it appear as though there were only 110 blacks in town.

111. It is likely that the black population continued to increase for some years after 1755, but with the growing anti-slavery sentiment which led to the non-importation legislation of 1774, it is not surprising that the blacks account for a smaller proportion of the population just before the war. But Newport's slave population did not decrease as rapidly as Philadelphia's, where an estimated 1,392 slaves in 1767 had dwindled to 672 by 1775. This meant that slaves made up only 3.4% of Penn's city in 1775. Boston's black population was already declining by 1755, and by 1765 there were only 811 slaves in a population of approximately 15,000 (5%). New York, as heterogeneous a northern city as Newport, could boast of many more slaves than either Philadelphia or Boston (about 14% in the 1750s and 1760s), but we do not know whether slaveholders there held as tenaciously to their property in the pre-Revolutionary era as their countrymen in Newport. Nash, "Slaves and Slaveowners in Colonial Philadelphia," 223–56; Jordan, *White Over Black*, p. 103; Greene, *Negro in Colonial New England*, pp. 84–85.

112. RICR, I 243. Representatives from only two of the four towns were present when this law was passed (Providence and Warwick), and one might make the argument that it rested on shaky legal ground to begin with.

113. W. E. B. DuBois, *The Suppression of the African Slave Trade to the United States of America, 1638–1870* (New York, 1954; repr. 1965), pp. 33–35.

114. The 1774 census lists households and members of households by color.

115. *NM*, Jan. 7, 1765, Jan. 1, 1760, Feb. 20, 1764.

116. See Herbert G. Gutman, *The Black Family in Slavery and Freedom, 1750–1925* (New York, 1976), pp. 332–33.

117. For an account of this election practice in Newport, see Orville H. Platt, "Negro Governors," *New Haven Historical Society Papers*, 6 (1900), 322–24. See also Wilkins Updike, *History of the Narragansett Church*, 3 vols. (Boston, 1907), I 213–15; Peterson, *History of Rhode Island*, p. 104; William B. Weeden, *Early Rhode Island: A Social History of the People* (New York, 1910), p. 306; Greene, *Negro in Colonial New England*, p. 250.

118. Norton, " 'My Resting Reaping Times,' " 523.

119. *NM*, Aug. 3, 1772, Mar. 29, 1773.

120. See Gerald W. Mullin, *Flight and Rebellion: Slave Resistance in Eighteenth-Century Virginia* (New York, 1972). The author found a similar pattern in the upper South.

121. Bill of Mortality, 1774, *NM*, Jan. 9, 1775.

122. John Manly's Account Book, p. 51, NHS.

123. John Malbone to Godfrey Malbone, Newport, May 6, 1767, Malbone Papers, Box 22, folder 8, NHS.

124. *Acts and Laws of His Majesty's Colony of Rhode-Island and Providence Plantations, Made and Passed Since the Revision in June, 1767* (Newport, 1772), pp. 56–59.

125. A Minute of the Society of Friends, 1717, *Documents*, III 115–16.

126. *The Journal and Essays of John Woolman*, ed. Amelia M. Gummere (New York, 1922), pp. 233–34.

127. Friends Records, Book 810, Monthly Meetings, 1773–1790, 26th 9th Month, 1775, p. 67, NHS; cited in Gladys E. Bolhouse, "Abraham Redwood, Reluctant Quaker, Philanthropist, Botanist," *Newport History*, 45, Part 2, No. 146 (Spring 1972), 31. The Quaker ex-governor of the colony Stephen Hopkins also parted company with the Society of Friends on this issue. What makes his intransigency the more interesting is that he was reputed to be the author of the anti-slave trade legislation of June 1774. See below, and William Foster, *Stephen Hopkins, Rhode Island Statesman: A Study in the Political History of the Eighteenth Century*, Rhode Island Historical Tracts No. 19, 2 vols. (Providence, 1884), II 246–49.

128. "Dialogue Concerning the Slavery of the Africans," p. 554.

129. George R. Channing, *Early Recollections of Newport, Rhode Island* (Newport, 1868), p. 105.

130. *NM*, Jan. 11, 1768.

131. "An Act prohibiting the importation of Negroes into this Colony," RICR, VII 251–53.

132. *Acts and Laws of His Majesty's Colony of Rhode-Island . . . Passed Since the Revision in June, 1767*, pp. 56–59.

133. Friends Records, Book 821, Quaker Manumissions, passim, NHS.

134. Bartlett, *From Slave to Citizen*, p. 9.

135. *NM* mentioned these trades in the following issues: Feb. 11, 1765; Jan. 24, 1763; Mar. 3, 1766; June 15, 1767; Apr. 17, Nov. 13, 1769; May 20, 1771.

136. *Acts and Laws of the English Colony of Rhode-Island . . .* (1767), pp. 151–53.

137. An Estimate of Samuel Freebody's Estate taken September 16, 1795, Freebody Papers, Box 42, folder 2, NHS.

138. The *NM* occasionally advertised for Negro or mulatto runaway indentured servants. For examples see the issues for Sept. 30, 1771, and Oct. 24, 1774. In addition, the tax assessor, at least, distinguished "Negroes" from "servants for life," taxing their owners at different rates. *NM*, May 11, 1767.

139. In 1770 an act was passed "For breaking up disorderly Houses kept by free Negroes and Mulattoes, and for putting out such Negroes and Mulattoes to service." Johnston, "Slavery in Rhode Island," 129–30.

140. Gov. Thomas Hutchinson to the Earl of Hillsborough, Boston, June 12, 1772, in *Documents of the American Revolution*, ed. Davies, V 119.

141. *NM*, June 19, 1769. See as well the issue of Jan. 23, 1764, for a notice signed by the customs officers that all cargoes must be entered.

142. Godfrey and John Malbone to Capt. Thom. Rodman, Newport, Dec. 20, 1763, Malbone Papers, Box 14, folder 4, NHS.

143. Quoted in Peterson, *History of Rhode Island*, p. 86. This was not always the case, however. In 1768, Captain Zeb Grinnell recorded the importation of 20 hogsheads of molasses. Collector of Customs Charles Dudley checked on Grinnell and charged him with filing a false report. Grinnell was tried in Vice Admiralty Court. Customs Report, Quarter ending September 1768, NHS.

144. Chief Justice Frederick Smyth of New Jersey to Lord Dartmouth, Feb. 8, 1773, Chalmers Papers, p. 75, NYPL.

145. The tidewaiter was a customs officer who boarded boats to prevent the evasion of customs duties. Simeon Potter to Aaron Lopez, Bristol, R.I., Mar. 1, 1770, *Commerce*, I 312; Benjamin Wright to Aaron Lopez, Savana la Marr, June 2, 1770, *Commerce*, I 331.

146. John Robinson, Hen. [Hulton], William Burch, Charles Pastor to the Right Honorable the Lords Commissioners of His Majestys Treasury, Nov. 14, 1769, PRO, Treasury I, Vol. 471, Part 2; *NM*, Oct. 9, 1769.

147. Charles Dudley and John Nicoll to the Commissioners in Boston, June 13, 19, 1769, Customs Office Letters, 1767–1775, Book 90, NHS. The General Assembly agreed to a special court after lending a sympathetic ear to the following petition: "Whereas divers Merchants in this Colony preferred a Petition, and represented unto this Assembly, That although there are good and wholesome Laws provided for regulating the Fees of the Officers of his Majesty's Customs within this Colony, and suitable Penalties inflicted upon any Officer of the Customs who shall take greater Fees than is prescribed by the Laws of this Colony, or who shall delay to clear out or enter any Vessel, or who shall neglect to have the Table of Fees hanging up in his Office; yet that the Merchants, especially Strangers, having Trade and Navigation in the Colony, will labour under great Inconveniences, if the Suits and Prosecutions for Breaches of the Laws against any Custom House Officer must be brought to the Inferior Courts of Common Pleas at their stated Terms: And thereupon they prayed that in such cases, Trials may be had in a more summary way." The General Assembly considered the petition and agreed to "a special Inferior Court of Common Pleas within the county where the offence shall be committed . . . and that the Judgment entered up by the Justices of the Inferior Court, so specially called and held, shall be final." Rhode Island General Assembly Sessions, June 1769, Evans Microcard Series No. 11440, pp. 33–34.

148. Charles Dudley and John Nicoll to the Commissioners in Boston, June 19, 1769, Customs Office Letters, 1767–1775, Book 90, NHS. See also the documents on this subject in PRO, Treasury I, Vol. 471, Parts 2, 4, 6, 7.

149. William Vernon & Co. to William Pinniger, Newport, Feb. 10, 1768, Vernon Letter Book #77, NHS; *Documents*, III 243.

150. Downing & Scully, *Architectural Heritage*, p. 188.

151. Captain William Taggart to Messrs. Aaron Lopez and John Cook, Jan. 1, 1774, Lopez Papers, Haight Collection, NHS.

152. St. Jago is probably St. Jago de la Vega, more commonly known as Spanish

Town, Jamaica. Samuel and William Vernon to Thomas Rogers, Newport, May ——, 1764, Slavery MSS, Box II, V, #43, NYHS.

153. "Rhode Island in 1768," 123–24.

154. *Itineraries*, p. 204. In approximate terms, $6,000 was worth £1,500 sterling, and £70,000 o.t. (old tenor) equaled £2,300 sterling.

155. William Richards to William Vernon, Mar. 9, 1769, Slavery MSS, Box II, R, #3, NYHS. Despite irrefutable evidence branding William and Samuel Vernon first-rate smugglers, the brothers recoiled at the suggestion that they were involved in such activities, insisting that the "accusation alone justly deserves death." Thomas Moffat to [J.] Harrison, Oct. 16, 1765, Chalmers Papers, p. 101, NYPL.

156. Charles Dudley and John Nicoll to the Commissioners in Boston, Feb. 20, 1772, Customs Office Letters, 1767–1775, Book 90, NHS.

157. See, for example, customs book letters dated Aug. 3, 1770, and April 11, 1771. Customs Office Letters, 1767–1775, Book 90, NHS. Jesse Saville to the Commissioners of Customs in America, Newport, May 25, 1769, PRO, Treasury I, Vol. 471, Part 7.

158. William Vernon to Messrs. John [Turner] & Son, July 9, 1765, Vernon Business Papers, Box 154, NHS.

159. Extract of a letter from the Collector and Comptroller of Rhode Island [Charles Dudley and John Nicoll] to the Commissioners of Customs at Boston, Dec. 9, 1768, PRO, Treasury I, Vol. 471, Part 7; Charles Dudley and John Nicoll to the Commissioners at Boston, Feb. 20, 1772, Customs Office Letters, 1767–1775, Book 90, NHS.

III

A Dependent People

I know not why we should blush to confess that molasses was an
essential ingredient in American independence. Many great events
have proceeded from much smaller causes.[1]

JOHN ADAMS

If Newport was marked by an underlying harmony of interests, this does not mean
that the community was without fracture lines. If Newport's network of inte-
grating relationships was central to its character, this does not deny that certain
tensions and stresses were often present. Some of these were of long standing;
others can be attributed more directly to the agitations and recurrent crises that
marked the Revolutionary era. The last chapters will show that unrestricted trade
provided the only setting in which interdependence and harmony could flourish.
They will also explain how British policy ultimately determined Newport's fate
as the community was forced to resist both imperial policy and the people who
spoke for that policy.

As a heterogeneous community, Newport hosted a variety of religious and political
viewpoints. Up to a point, the town coped remarkably well with the conflicting
opinions and dissenting ideas these factions spawned. But this toleration was not
necessarily a positive force. It bordered on indifference and was, perhaps, an extension of an apathy toward community life in general. Newporters were as willing
to tolerate lawlessness as ethnic or religious diversity. They were apathetic toward
voting, unresponsive to appeals for charity. Cooperation was in their self-interest
only as long as ships sailed and profits mounted. In a different economic environment, both religious and political differences could produce tensions which, although usually submerged, lay close enough to the surface to break the calm from
time to time. Because the pre-Revolutionary decade was a time of growing strain,
tension was expressed more often in episodes of religious and political strife.

The ultimate challenge to the community was the new set of British commercial
restrictions and taxes. Enforcement of the measures meant inevitable conflict because the people of Newport recognized their dependence on the sea and unre-

stricted trade. In short, the larger part of the community, having evaded British laws with relative impunity for so many years, refused to submit to the new regulations, which would have destroyed commercial prosperity. As the rebels grew in number and power, the law-evading community of the 1750s became in the 1760s and 1770s a town ruled by mobs determined to resist British imperialist policy at all costs. In one sense, then, the conflict of the Revolutionary era was merely an extension of a pattern set decades earlier. Both militant and non-militant protest was used interchangeably throughout the 1760s and 1770s, widening in scope and intensity as the years wore on. Newporters responded to the British challenge with smuggling, non-importation, and home manufacturing as well as with more violent expressions of dissatisfaction such as mob rioting and destruction of British property.

With an escalation of British provocations, the people in Newport became increasingly frustrated, and with each succeeding crisis, the town's division widened. Those who challenged the rebels by speaking for empire and order appeared to threaten an entire way of life. Since numbers were in their favor, the rebels were able to suppress those who supported the crown and the rule of law. The tragedy was that the loyalists saw themselves as the patriots of the Revolution. They loved Newport no less than the rebels, but felt the town was best served by a way of life based on order and stability.

Each upheaval strained the fragile chain of interdependency until it disintegrated completely as the last link failed. The merchants were unable to trade and therefore could neither buy goods nor hire seamen. Out of work, seamen turned to the town for help only to find that the coffers were empty—because the merchants were unable to meet the tax assessments. Finally, caught between the narrow alternatives of violent resistance to British laws and reluctant compliance with the demands of the Continental Association,[2] the townspeople could only despair as they watched "poor Newport"[3] decline.

9

Economic Arguments
and Mob Rule

SUBTERFUGE WAS A WAY OF LIFE in Newport, and until the last year of the French and Indian War, there was a *modus vivendi* between the community and Britain's program of trade regulations. The laws were on the books, the customs duties were calculated, and both were evaded. If His Majesty's customs officers were foolish enough to confiscate an illegally imported cargo, they might find themselves facing a hastily organized mob bent on retrieving the merchandise. As early as 1719 complaints reached the Board of Trade in England about mobs in Newport which made a habit of repossessing confiscated cargo in a "riotous and tumultous manner."[4] As long as the customs officers closed their eyes and opened their palms, they and the people of Newport got along amicably. But once the restrictions were enforced, and new regulations promulgated, there was no hope of an alliance, however uneasy. Newport's survival, no less its prosperity, depended on trade. The townspeople were, they readily admitted, "a dependent people,"[5] forced to import the necessities of life, and to export in order to pay for those necessities.

With merchants relying on the West India trade, the Molasses Act of 1733, supported by the British sugar planters, caused a flurry of excitement in Newport. Rhode Island's agent in London, Richard Partridge, vigorously opposed the bill, but to no avail as Parliament held strong for its favorites, the sugar colonies. As one British pamphleteer put it: "The least sugar island we have is of ten times more consequence to Great Britain than all of Rhode Island and New England put together."[6] In terms of profit he was right, and it was in Britain's interest to keep the Caribbean merchants happy.

Those merchants had several objectives in mind which could be achieved by the passage and enforcement of the Molasses Act. First, if the British

Caribbean colonies held a monopoly and acted as the sole suppliers of molasses to the mainland colonies, the price of that commodity could be inflated. Secondly, since the West Indians did a little smuggling on the side, they could buy the inexpensive French molasses themselves and resell it under their own auspices—and at their prices. Thirdly, if the mainland colonists cooperated, the whole empire would benefit since French trade would be thwarted.

Fortunately for Newport, the British made only halfhearted attempts to enforce the 1733 Molasses Act, which put heavy duties on all *foreign* sugar, molasses, and rum. For the next three decades the British sugar planters were happy because they received favored-colony status, and the Newport merchants were happy because there was only an occasional crackdown on the practice of smuggling French molasses.

By 1763, however, there were signs of discontent. In a long article in the *Newport Mercury*, worried merchants recited a list of economic grievances against Great Britain—the most important of which was England's hampering of Newport's trade.[7] At the same time, Parliament made no secret of the fact that it was becoming increasingly dissatisfied with the colonies' and especially Rhode Island's total disregard for imperial trade regulations.[8] The result was the Revenue Act of 1764, commonly known as the Sugar Act.

Of the more than forty commandments handed down in this comprehensive revenue measure, only those relating to molasses, sugar, and rum caught the eye (and ire) of the Rhode Islanders. The act reduced the tax on foreign molasses from 6 to 3 pence per gallon, retained the tax on foreign sugar, and for the first time put an outright prohibition on foreign rum. The biggest difference, however, was that Britain actually tried to collect the duties. Rhode Island's governor, Stephen Hopkins, realized the potential effect on commerce: "a duty of three pence per gallon on foreign molasses is . . . much higher than that article can possibly bear, and therefore must operate as an absolute prohibition." He went on to calculate the ripple effects of such a duty. Not only would it "cramp the trade and ruin the interests of many of the colonies," but it would "put a total stop to our exportation of lumber, horses, flour, and fish to the French and Dutch sugar colonies. . . ." If this happened, Hopkins asserted, there would be no way for Newport to pay for costly English manufactured goods.[9]

The *Newport Mercury* took up the argument.[10] One anonymous writer explained that the English sugar islands could not absorb the surplus goods Newport ships carried. Very simply, Newport needed markets, and the French and Dutch islands not only provided those markets but offered the molasses necessary for Newport's growing number of distilleries. Furthermore, the British West Indies, Hopkins charged, could not keep up with Newport's insatiable demand for molasses.[11]

Specifically referring to the Sugar Act, the *Mercury* echoed its merchant readers by asserting unequivocally that "Duties as high as are laid by this act cannot by any means whatsoever be collected being vastly greater than the Trade itself can bear. . . ."[12]

Individual merchants, such as the Malbones, penned angry letters to their English business associates:

> It is certainly unnatural for us to Suppose that [the Ministry] have premeditateingly [laid] these schemes to effect our Ruin . . . but . . . in general we do think so . . . it being impossible for us to pay the Duties on foreign molasses. . . . Had the Duties been fixed at a Penny instead of Three Pence, some few of us who have a good correspondence at Hispaniola might have been able to have retrieved the losses which we have suffered by the late war at the same time have benefitted the Revenue; But as matters now stand our Trade is [knocked] up [and] the Revenue will not be benefitted one Copper. . . .[13]

The Malbones' explanation makes it quite clear that their argument is based on profit rather than on principle. They might be willing to pay a one-penny duty; they were not willing—or able—to pay 3*d*. When Parliament considered reducing the duty to 1*d*. in 1765, the reaction from Newport was favorable.[14] When Parliament's compromise was actually confirmed the next year, and a 1*d*. duty placed on *all* imported molasses, the clamor from Newport died down. Rhode Island traders could live with a 1*d*. impost, even though it had become, for all intents and purposes, a revenue measure rather than a regulation of trade.

At the height of the protest over the Sugar Act, Newport received word that the British ministry was about to launch the Stamp Act and create Vice Admiralty Courts which would try the offenders without juries far from the scene of their alleged offenses. Newport merchants, who could be fairly sure of a favorable decision by local judges, found this legislation distressing, but this time the Newport community adopted a wait-and-see attitude. For a time, at least, the *Mercury* was content to report the protests and debates from other colonies. Columnists repeated the oft-heard arguments over taxation and representation, but it seemed almost as if Newport had poured all its own energy into the Sugar Act protests.

In the summer of 1764 the Rhode Island General Assembly appointed a committee to meet with other colonial committees to procure the repeal of the Sugar Act. Almost as an afterthought it encouraged the group to try to prevent the levying of the Stamp Duty, repeating the well-known argument that it was inconsistent with the rights, liberties, and privileges of British subjects.[15] Outside Newport, debate over the Stamp Act may have reached epidemic proportions, but on Aquidneck Island the people were content to mull over the Resolves from Virginia and to repeat whig arguments penned in Massachusetts. Newport offered no constitutional statements of its own in opposition to the Stamp Act; nor did it contribute to the pamphlet war.

The people of Newport responded to the new British militancy with mob action. If customs officers were serious about seizing illegal cargo, Newport townsmen were just as serious about retrieving it. Following the example of a Providence mob which had recaptured a condemned ship some months previously, a riotous group of Newporters broke into Philip Tillinghast's store and reclaimed "7 casks of rum and molasses" confiscated earlier by customs officers. By such action Newporters implied that they would not pay the duties. This kind of lawlessness was a constant occurrence in Newport, and would continue as long as Britain tried to enforce revenue acts.[16]

With mobs achieving a high rate of success in their war with customs officials, it is not surprising that Newporters responded in the same way to other British provocations which threatened their livelihood. Impressment also rankled the townspeople, and the economic dislocation resulting from it increased already existing tensions. Fishermen refused to go out, coasters feared to come in, and wood purveyors declined to deliver fuel for fear of being taken by the British ships hovering nearby. Already inflamed by news of the recently enacted revenue measures, unruly crowds reacted violently to the added threat of impressment. They skirmished with His Majesty's ship *St. John* in Newport harbor in July 1764, and with the *Maidstone* a year later.[17]

According to an eyewitness to the first event, an incensed mob of about fifty made its way to Goat Island and fired at the *St. John*.[18] The British did not heed the warning, impressment was stepped up, and in June 1765 a more serious conflict took place. A bitter crowd, "consisting chiefly of sailors, Boys and Negroes to the number of above Five Hundred," seized and burned a boat from the *Maidstone*. In justification, the *Mercury* declared that the *Maidstone*'s impressment policy was "fatal to the inhabitants of the town." The irate publisher of the newspaper, Samuel Hall, maintained that since impressment had been accelerated "Seamen's wages advanced nearly one Dollar and one half per month; our wood wharves [are] almost clear of wood, the coasters from Neighboring Governments [are] shunning our port to escape press. . . . our Fish Market, a considerable Support of the Town, is greatly distressed, as few of the Fishermen dare venture out."[19]

Having played this dress rehearsal scarcely two months earlier, the Newport "rabble" was determined not to be outperformed when news of the Boston Stamp Act riots reached Newport in mid-August 1765.[20] From all accounts, the riots that took place in Newport were instigated by three of the town's most influential merchants, Samuel Vernon, William Ellery, and Robert Crook. These respectable citizens did not speak openly of their motives in fomenting unrest, but since two of the three at least were known smugglers (that is to say, lawbreakers) they would have been standing on very shaky ground in talking of their rights under English common law. As it was, when one of the intended victims, Dr. Thomas Moffatt, demanded to know why he and Martin Howard were singled out to be burned in effigy along with the Stamp Master, Vernon replied that "your Friend Howard . . . has publickly justified all the Parliamentary restraints upon the commerce of the American colonies. . . ."[21] In short, anything that threatened Newport's trade warranted retaliation.

From the very beginning, Vernon, Ellery, and Crook were bent on greater destruction than the mere burning of effigies. According to eyewitness accounts they not only directed but took part in the actual plunder. Moffatt testified that "the chief contrivers" (meaning Vernon, Crook, and Ellery) "with some chosen Ruffians at their heels having their faces painted and being prepared and furnished with broad axes" demolished Howard's house. In a second letter Moffatt also asserted that "the chief ringleader of yesterday's spectacle" (the effigy burning) wielded axes along with the mob.[22] What must have astonished the leaders—and worried them not a little—was to see how easily the mob got out of hand. Deference was forgotten those humid August days as the "rabble" surged and pillaged and grew increasingly incensed under the direction of one John Webber. Several days after the rioters had finally dispersed, the Newport town meeting somewhat belatedly instructed its delegates to the General Assembly to devote their "utmost attention to those important objects the Courts of Admiralty and the Act for levying Stamp Duties."[23] The deputies were to "assert . . . with a becoming firmness" the right of self-taxation and trial by jury. At the same time as the General Assembly engaged in intellectual protest, still another mob prevented the customhouse in Newport from opening.[24]

By late-October everyone knew that the stamped paper was aboard the *Cygnet* in Newport harbor. Exhorting the townspeople to resist "slavery" by shunning the stamped paper in general, the *Mercury* also pinpointed the single most oppressive feature of the Stamp Act as far as Newport was concerned: stamped clearance papers. No vessel could leave Newport without such a document, and few merchants were willing to accept this incursion without protest. Samuel Hall, the newspaper printer, warned the customs collector that if he did not clear vessels without stamped paper he would be driven out of town, and that any merchant having stamped clearance papers would meet with the "highest displeasure." With the Stamp Act due to take effect on November 1, 1765, the last week in October saw an extraordinary number of vessels clear Newport harbor.[25]

Agitation on both sides of the Atlantic brought repeal, and news of the Stamp Act revocation reached Newport in May 1766. "A True Friend of Great Britain and her Colonies" congratulated the town "on the Prospect of an Enlargement of Trade. . . ." The *Newport Mercury* reported public rejoicing as news of the repeal spread—noting, at the same time, that orderly "Gentlemen and Ladies . . . met with no kind of indecent Treatment from the Populace."[26] Did the commentator mean to imply that in the past ladies and gentlemen could very well have been abused by the "populace"?[27]

To add a touch of color to the festivities, an 8 × 14 foot painting was displayed, presumably designed by local talent. In order to show "the Advantages which LIBERTY gives to COMMERCE," the artist had drawn "a fine Prospect of the Harbour of Newport." In so doing Newport demonstrated its commitment to a whig principle—and connected it to the town's economic well-being. A month later, the newspaper supplied a fitting footnote to a turbulent chapter in Newport's history when it reported that "the Lords of the Treasury have transmitted orders for the Stamped Papers ... to be returned home."[28]

The repeal of the Stamp Act gave notice to one and all that Great Britain, if pressed hard enough, would retreat. But the "detested" legislation was only one thorn in Newport's side, and scarcely had the rejoicing over repeal quieted when rumors of the Townshend duties reached Newport.[29] With a sigh heard around the world, Rhode Island petitioned—and petitioned again—to have its economic burdens reduced.[30] Governor Wanton expressed his gratitude to "Lord Hillsbro" that His Majesty stood "ever ready to hear and redress any real grievances" Rhode Islanders might have. Then in a rush of frustration, Wanton added that in his opinion "the power exercised by Parliament ... of raising monies upon us without our consent (which ... may be extended to our last penny) is a real grievance."[31] Again, whig rhetoric was attached to financial considerations. Very soon, the British would look upon Newporters as "men who considered any restraint on their commerce as an intolerable grievance."[32]

The king supported Townshend, the duties stuck, and the revenue cutters harassed Newport shipping. The townspeople, threatened once again, reverted to mob violence. In August 1768 His Majesty's storehouses were broken into and large quantities of molasses stolen. Later that year men armed "with stones and other weapons" forced customs officers to give up a cargo of smuggled goods.[33]

The following summer a more serious conflict erupted. This time the fury was directed at His Majesty's ship *Liberty*, at anchor in Newport harbor. In July 1769 the *Liberty* had seized two vessels for "Breach of Acts of Trade," and had impressed three sailors from them. Thus, when Captain Packwood of New London, Connecticut, was not only "detained" by the *Liberty* on July 10, but shot at by an overly anxious crew member, the town needed little encouragement for a full-scale riot.[34] Captain William Reid of the *Liberty* made the mistake of appearing in full view of the mob that had collected on Long Wharf. That many of the sullen-looking group were disguised and armed with bludgeons indicates premeditation rather than spontaneity. Reid was immediately taken and, according to his deposition, told by the mob that he " 'had seized many of their vessels and by God [he] should now pay for all.' "[35] Threatening the captain's life, the mob (egged on by Packwood) demanded that Reid send for his entire crew. Still not suspecting what lay in store, Reid complied. Late that night a small band of men cut the *Liberty* loose, and scuttled her after hacking Captain Reid's cabin and possessions to pieces. That the group was composed of three eminent townsmen— Captain John Goddard, George Scott, and one Captain Hull—is another indication that the genteel sort had no intention of letting the "populace" have all the fun.[36]

As British harassment continued, Newporters retaliated in kind. In June 1770, a "mobb" drove the customs officers off the wharf after the latter had seized seven hogsheads of French rum. One of the agents, Nicolas Lechmere, "applied to the Governor for Protection and Assistance but was refused, and that same evening the goods were carried off." As Thomas Vernon noted with disgust, law and order no longer meant very much in Newport.[37] Giddy with success, mobs continued to operate throughout the 1770s. In 1772, Edward Thurston, Jr., reported in his journal that the night following a customs seizure "a number of persons (said to be in disguise) took away all the goods that there was on board said vessel, except a quantity equal to what was at first entered."[38] Frustrated customs officers offered rewards, but never announced they had been claimed.

When a mob burned the customs schooner *Gaspee* in 1772 after it had run aground, the British automatically assumed the incident occurred in Newport harbor. Offended by this unwarranted presumption, Governor Wanton penned a hasty letter to Lord Dartmouth in which he assured the angry minister that the event took place "at least 30 miles off and none of the Newport people could have had any hand in it."[39] What he did not say was that the Newport mob stood ready to support its Providence counterparts had it been necessary.

While Newport mobs tormented customs officials, other colonial communities tried alternative methods of protest. One such response was nonimportation, which, not surprisingly, met with little enthusiasm in Newport. Townspeople were not moved by entreaties to "SAVE YOUR MONEY AND YOU WILL SAVE YOUR COUNTRY," although this was the closest the community ever came to developing a Revolutionary ideology. Merchants in Newport may have been sympathetic to the goals of non-importation, but it was difficult for a community completely dependent on trade to deny itself even a small part of that trade. Thus Newport did not subscribe to the non-importation agreements of 1765–1766, thereby earning the suspicion of those towns which did present a united front. Those suspicions were justified two years later when Boston and New York invoked non-importation in response to the Townshend duties and Newport's cooperation was still only half-hearted.[40]

Between 1768 and 1771, Newport vacillated between disregarding the non-importation agreements of its urban rivals and imposing (and breaking) its own non-importation strictures. With the *Newport Mercury* urging a non-importation agreement, and pressure mounting from outside, townsmen signed a non-importation agreement early in November 1769. At best only 47 of the principal merchants subscribed to the agreement, which was designed to extract Newport from its "distressed circumstances." At worst, the majority of merchants blithely ignored the agreement on the supposition that if Britain's regulations could be defied, so could those designed by other colonies unsympathetic to Newport's desperate need to trade. Committees of merchants in Boston and Philadelphia alternately criticized and threatened Newport for violating the pact. Merchants in the "Great Town" on Massachusetts Bay not only refused to trade with Newport, but refused to trade with anyone who did.[41] Newspapers in New York and Boston circulated rumors that Rhode Island's intent was to "take an Advantage of the Sister Colonies."[42] There was probably some truth to the rumor, and if pressure from other towns brought about any compliance at all, it was for self-serving motives. According to Stephen Ayrault, a leading merchant and future loyalist, "the merchants here are beholden to the Western Collonies for Flower and some other Articles for to make up West India cargoes, otherwise there would be no Difficulty here abt. Importing."[43] In other words, if Newport had not been dependent on the good will (not to mention the cargoes) of other colonies, local merchants would have ignored non-importation completely.

Josiah Hewes wrote from Philadelphia that "The day before yesterday Thurstons brig Capt Brown arrived here from Newport and tho she had no Cargo in, was Immediately ordered Back to Newport and is gone; By this you see the people here are determined to keep the port shut against you until you order the goods lately imported contrary to your agreement back again to England. . . ."[44] Nicholas Roosevelt informed the Vernons that "the [New] Brunswick people have Resolved to have no trade with you . . . ," and John Sleight certainly understated the rising hostility between Newport and other urban communities when he wrote that he was "very Sorry that there is such a difference between Newport and the other Colonys. . . ."[45] Sleight probably forgot—or may not have realized—that Rhode Island's strained relationship with its neighbors went back 130 years and needed little fuel to erupt once again.

In May 1770 New York drew up a formal set of Resolves declaring to all the world that the community would not trade with Newport if the latter did not adhere to the non-importation agreements, and arguing that since the merchants of Newport acceded to non-importation both begrudgingly and belatedly, "they have greatly advanced their private interests, and injured the cause of Liberty. . . ." Even worse, they had been "influenced by a sordid Regard to private gain"[46]—something supposedly unknown in New York.

The Charlestonians were just as exasperated, but their accusation was implied rather than expressed outright. In an appeal to the Rhode Island Sons of Liberty for total non-importation, they suggested that although "it would be a capital crime . . . to suspect the public Virtue of our Countrymen," they nonetheless realized that "Individuals will be found in every Colony, who . . . will sacrifice [liberty] to the dirty Considerations of present Emolument."[47] No names were mentioned.

If Newport's merchants decided to continue English and East India trade, they stood to alienate themselves completely from the other colonies, which held fast for non-importation. As independent as the community was, it simply could not risk economic ostracism by its neighbors and most important trading partners. Succumbing to peer pressure, the leading merchants of Newport publicly renewed their non-importation agreement and appointed a committee of inspection which was empowered to confiscate all goods imported contrary to the pact.[48] In the end, Newport's foot-dragging and breaching of agreements earned it the temporary enmity and lasting suspicion of New York, Philadelphia, and Boston. This was a heavy price to pay for the "trifle" of British goods that its merchants were determined to bring in.[49] And those who condemned Newport for what appeared to be unpatriotic behavior were unwavering in the belief that "had the colonies all stood firm to the non-importation agreement we should have work'd out our political salvation and have Rode Triumvant over the british ministry. . . ."[50] Newport was in the unenviable position of having to resist coercion from Britain as well as pressure from its supposed allies. Surely this urban rivalry exacerbated already existing tensions within the community.

"The Poor People of Newport . . ."

From the flurry of activity at the Newport customhouse in 1772, 1773, and early 1774, one would have guessed that the colonies had indeed "Rode Triumvant." The number of ships clearing and entering the harbor soared during these years despite continuous harassment by British cutters and men of war.[51] Indeed, Newport merchants might have put up with British provocations if Parliament had not closed Boston Harbor in a fit of rage over a tea party.[52]

The people of Newport were clearly aware of the ramifications of the Boston Port Bill.[53] At a town meeting on May 20, 1774, the freemen of Newport agreed that unless Boston was defended, Britain "may at pleasure destroy the trade and shut up the Ports of every other Colony . . . so that there will be a total end of all prosperity."[54] Nevertheless, their patriotic enthusiasm lagged when it came time to offer relief to the poor of that city. Perhaps Newporters remembered the harsh words Bostonians hurled at Newport during the non-importation crisis of 1770; perhaps older indignities and rivalries came to mind. Whatever the reasons, while money and supplies poured into Boston from other New England towns, Newport was still considering "what method to take" to relieve the poor and suffering of Massachusetts Bay. Finally, in March 1775, the *Mercury* noted that Boston was worth the munificent sum of £78 3s. 9d.[55] Boston took note and in Newport's time of trial responded even less kindly.[56]

For Newport, the Parliamentary bill closing Boston harbor was the beginning of the end. Once the Continental Association decided to retaliate against Great Britain by means of non-intercourse, Newport had nowhere to turn for relief.[57] If the town abided by the British restrictions, it became a colonial pariah; if the town ignored the British restrictions, it earned the animosity of and persecution by Great Britain—both of which cut deeply into profits. If Newport adhered to the non-importation agreement, not only was its trade curtailed, but whatever legal trade the community carried on was subject to confiscation by the British, who were undiscriminating when it came to seizing cargoes. For a town owing its existence to trade, each path led to disaster. Since the coastal and West Indies shipping was bread and butter to Newport—the slave trade was the jam—the community never really seriously considered throwing in its lot with Great Britain. And since the Continental Congress had the good sense to suspend non-exportation until the following September (in the hope that the British would retreat before that time), some merchants probably considered a favorable cash flow worth the drawbacks of non-importation.

In any case, with British war ships hovering about Newport harbor, and the Continental Association threatening to boycott any merchants who breached the Association agreement, the Rhode Island delegates to Congress had no trouble deciding that the tiny colony's only hope for survival lay in a united defense. As Governor Nicholas Cooke wrote to the Continental Congress: "Every idea of partial and colonial [i.e., individual] defence ought to be given up. There must be a supreme, superintending power, to exert and direct the force of the whole, for the safety and defence of all." Cooke was undoubtedly thinking of Rhode Island when he added that "otherwise . . . colony after colony may be subdued without chance of making resistance."[58]

If Newport expected the support of the other colonies, the other colonies could rightly expect Newport to cooperate by obeying whatever Resolves the Continental Congress passed. Not all merchants resisted the idea of non-importation: some felt that in the end it would force Great Britain to repeal the odious legislation; others realized that a shortage of goods would force prices up, which was not all bad from their standpoint. Former Governor Samuel Ward admitted that he could not predict "how the stopping [of] all commerce with the West Indies will be considered in Newport," but he argued for the measure "until the Islands will join us in a non-Importation and Exportation Agreement" against Great Britain. By pressuring the islands, "we [can] force them to it. . . ."[59]

The Continental Congress, realizing that lax enforcement of the Resolves would ruin their effect, encouraged local committees of inspection to see that merchants played by the rules. Remembering Newport's behavior in 1769–1770, New Yorkers were quick to warn that the moment they heard of "any provisions being shipped from Newport to supply the enemy," they were "determined to stop all ... provisions from being shipped from New York to the town."[60] It probably says something about Newport's previous reluctance to abide by non-importation that a 37-man committee was appointed to watch over the community—and each other. As evidence that the final battle lines had not been drawn even by this late date (December 1774), the committee did include several men who later joined the loyalist camp.[61]

Six months later Newporters tried one last time to stave off disaster when 74 prominent merchants put animosity aside and signed a petition acknowledging allegiance to His Majesty and offering to support civil authority until Great Britain and the colonies were reconciled. The leading spokesmen for both the colonial and the loyalist causes signed the document.[62]

As despondent merchants tried to support the colonial cause and eke out a living at the same time, they ran a hazardous course. While molasses and brown sugar were on the prohibited list, rum and plain sugar were not; therefore William Vernon was engaged in legal trade—from all standpoints—when he loaded up with rum and sugar at Jamaica in June 1775. Though Vernon's trade for once was conducted according to British regulations, Captain James Wallace, commander of the *Rose*, seized Vernon's ship *Royal Charlotte* and sent it to Admiral Graves in Boston. Vernon, usually a temperate writer, was furiously agitated. "The depridations committed by this petty tyrant [Wallace] upon our Trade and the defenceless Town of Newport is shocking to human nature. He is savage beyond belief and description. . . ."[63] Protest as he might, the response from Admiral Graves's headquarters was that the Admiral "cannot permit the Property of men in open Rebellion to be disposed of for their benefit. . . ."[64]

In the third week of July 1775, Wallace opened fire on the town of Newport. According to the newspaper accounts, this "greatly terrified the women and children, especially those women who were with child. . . . Many women and children were running about, wringing their hands and crying." Presumably, the men were not bothered at all, although many women fainted and a number "absolutely miscarried by the fright." This scene took place late in the evening. The men on the *Rose* allegedly told the townspeople that they intended to burn down the city the following morning. Wallace did not burn down the city the next day, or the day after that.

But he continually threatened to do so, and sporadically fired on the town. Wallace indicated that he would follow orders: " 'The Destruction of a Great Town . . . is a serious matter; however something must be done for the King's Service. . . .' "[65]

The psychological warfare took its toll, and "a great many of the inhabitants moved part [of or] all their effects out and many families . . . left town. The carts, chaises, riding chairs and trucks, were so numerous that the streets and roads were almost blocked up with them. . . ."[66]

In the hope that Wallace would spare the town and permit boats "to pass and repass unmolested with . . . the common and usual necessities for life," the General Assembly permitted the town of Newport to negotiate with the captain for supplying his ships "with beef, beer, etc."[67] Having received this permission, the inhabitants of Newport sent off a memorial to Congress in order to placate those who harbored ill will against the town and deliberately misinterpreted Newport's intentions. Speaking in a language that all the colonies understood, the memorial pointed out that the town of Newport paid 1/6th of all Rhode Island taxes and would probably pay a great share of the cost of a war with Great Britain. No matter what resentments Bostonians, Philadelphians, New Yorkers, and Charlestonians might be incubating, "the destruction of the town of Newport" could not possibly "promote or serve the common cause."[68]

Despite these efforts at public relations, the other colonies continued to look at Newport's actions in the worst possible light. In a letter to the Continental Congress, the Rhode Island General Assembly tried to justify the supplying of Captain Wallace, citing the "unhappy state of the town," which was "daily threatened with . . . immediate destruction." The letter assured the delegates that these conditions prompted the people of Newport to supply Wallace rather than "want of spirit or love of their country."[69] In truth, Wallace did have orders to "lay the Town in Ashes" if his ships were not supplied, but so powerful were the radicals in Newport by the winter of 1775–1776 that they frequently confiscated supplies destined for the *Rose* even though the majority of townspeople were in favor of a truce.[70]

Hoping to salvage whatever was left of Newport's reputation, Governor Cooke requested the Continental Congress to inform the General Assembly of "any letter . . . respecting the . . . supplying of Captain Wallace with provisions; and of any reflections that have been cast by such letters upon any part of this Colony."[71] Cooke need not have worried; the truce between

Wallace and Newport was short-lived. According to the *Mercury* of December 11, 1775, Wallace intended to celebrate Christmas by ordering the destruction of Newport. He insisted that the inhabitants "should be burnt in their houses if they did not instantly turn out." The newspapers reported that British soldiers plundered half the townspeople's possessions while fire consumed the rest. According to the account, "Some women were stripped of their . . . clothes."[72] Because of Wallace's assaults, "the once flourishing town of Newport" was forced to admit to the "cessation of all business."[73]

By January 1776 the Rhode Island General Assembly could honestly report to the Continental Congress that Newport "had been reduced to so deplorable a state" that "many of the wealthy inhabitants have not only left the town but the Colony."[74] Even before Wallace's Christmas raid over 14% of the town's taxpayers had fled inland or abroad.[75] They were not necessarily the very wealthy; it appears from the separate list of those taxpayers who absented themselves between 1772 and 1775 that the "lesser sort" were more likely to leave Newport than those with a larger stake in the community.[76] On January 2, 1776, Ezra Stiles noted in his diary that "more than three quarters of the Inhabitants are removed" from Newport, despite the reassuring presence of General Charles Lee.[77]

Before the exodus, however, individual religious groups tried to cope with the mounting demands for charity. The Quakers, in particular, took up collections, recognizing "an increase of our poor" and noting that "the present commotions . . . affect us more than in many other places." In an attempt to stem the flow from their meager reserves the Friends decided that instead of paying out "a large Rent for houses for our poor," it would be more economical "to erect a Bldg suff[icient] to Contain Eight Families."[78]

Of those who remained in Newport, an increasing number fell back on the town for support, and when the town's treasury registered empty, the Rhode Island General Assembly reached into its own pocket to provide for the "support of their poor." The people who remained were in "such distress" for wood that in desperation the Town Council petitioned Captain Wallace of the *Rose* for assistance. When the wood supply finally ran out, and the usually mild Newport winter turned severe, bitter people tore down fences and empty houses for firewood.[79]

Providence charitably offered to take and support 400 of Newport's poor. Those who could not remove up river on their own were given financial assistance by the Newport Town Council.[80] Samuel Vernon, Jr., noted agreeably that "the [General] Assembly have taken every measure to have them removed and maintained," but he drew the line at supporting those left in town by an outright dole: "To keep such in the town by *charitable Acts* ... *which are not* is a great damage to them and the Publick." While there were some who probably felt as Vernon did that "as long as they can be supported in their Idolness by donations ... the greater part will prefer that method of living before any other," others might disagree: "To ... feed upon the cold hand of charity is mortifying to those who have always lived Independent."[81] Nevertheless, pride proved no match for an empty stomach, and some of the less fortunate were forced to turn to the more affluent for help: "I must Inform you that I am in want of Sumthing for my famely to Eat at present which I could not do without. If you could Spair a little meat and flower. . . ."[82] With an increase in the number of poor, the question of responsibility for them must have strained relations in an already tense city, as economic ruin inched toward the well-to-do.

Merchants tried to carry on trade, but the few ships returning from long voyages were seized by Captain Wallace as they entered Newport harbor— unless they belonged to merchants who were known friends of the crown. If the vessels carried supplies needed by the ministerial troops, Wallace sent them to Boston. More often the vessels were "stripped of their sails and rigging [and] turned adrift." Hostility increased, and the *Mercury* angrily noted that many of "these vessels ... belonged to poor laborious people, the whole support of whose families depended on what they made by freighting wood."[83] Merchants, who were once the support of the town, could no longer provide the base from which tangential industries developed in this maritime community. "Times are very dull and everybody [is] out of employ with us," reported William Vernon dispiritedly.[84] With the army paying bounties to enlistees, some men, at least, must have found themselves allied with the whig cause by virtue of their desperate economic circumstances.

There was little left in Newport by the spring of 1776 to remind the merchants of their former golden days. "Seeing this town wou'd give you more pain than pleasure . . . ," despaired one correspondent. Trade was at a standstill due to the self-imposed non-importation and non-exportation agreements. William Vernon's shipping empire was shattered: "all intercourse with every part of the world is stopped in N. America—a scene too melancholy to dwell on." By the time Congress reversed itself on non-importation and offered a bounty on rum, sugar, and molasses, it was too late. Except for the thunder of guns from the *Rose,* and the frightened squawks of the sea gulls, the once bustling harbor was still.[85]

It was almost an anticlimax when Rhode Island withdrew its allegiance from the king and became the first American independent state on May 4, 1776. Rhode Island had maintained a *de facto* independence for so long that for some, at least, the break was nothing more than a formality. For others it was more difficult, and the vote in the General Assembly was six less than unanimous.[86] The *Newport Mercury* waited until June 10 to print the Rhode Island declaration of independence, by which time the event was stale news. Solomon Southwick acted a little more quickly when the Continental Congress passed its own Declaration of Independence on July 4, and offered for sale a limited edition "on one side of a large sheet." Then remembering who his audience was, he added: "Those of our readers who don't chuse to buy it in this form may see it in the *Newport Mercury* next Monday, at furthest."[87]

10

A Town at War with Itself

N OT ONLY DID BRITISH IMPERIAL POLICY create economic havoc in Newport and provide the setting for inter-urban rivalry; it also fostered an atmosphere that caused social harmony to disintegrate and submerged hostilities to break forth. In Newport's golden days, deep-seated prejudices were suppressed for the sake of common goals. But as soon as the community was frustrated by economic dislocation, old animosities erupted, political and religious discord surfaced, and the interdependent network was strained beyond endurance.

The Ward–Hopkins "controversy" of the 1750s and early 1760s affected the political struggles of the following decades only indirectly.[88] As it turned out later, both parties could count whig and tory members, and in 1774 Samuel Ward and Stephen Hopkins walked arm in arm into Carpenter's Hall and the First Continental Congress.

Nevertheless, because of the unseemly nature of Rhode Island politics in the 1750s, the foundations on which both loyalists and whigs would build were well defined by 1764 when Revolutionary agitation began in earnest. The excesses of the Ward–Hopkins squabbles had produced a number of Newporters who argued that the hotly contested gubernatorial elections spawned factions that threatened the public good. By the early 1760s, a coterie of like-minded people was becoming vocal in opposition to the democratic character of Rhode Island politics and the popular election of the governor and assembly. A number of these people (mainly crown officers and others with close English connections) had petitioned the crown to revoke Rhode Island's self-governing charter and replace it with one which provided for an appointed royal governor and council. The philosophy of the clique was summed up by George Rome: " 'The colonies have originally been wrong founded—They ought all to have been regal governments, and every executive officer appointed by the King.' "[89]

This kind of talk made Rome and his followers highly unpopular in Newport, where most people had found local elections—and control—much to their liking for over one hundred years.[90] News of this challenge to Rhode Island's charter spread to Boston where James Otis uncharitably labeled the royalists as a "little, dirty, drinking, drabbing, contaminated knot of thieves, beggars, and transports . . . collected from the four winds of the earth, and made up of Turks, Jews, and other infidels, with a few renegado Christians and Catholics."[91] Despite the calumny and invective, the group (which by this time was referred to as the "tory junto") applauded the efforts of the British to tighten colonial administration and assert sovereignty over the independent-spirited colony. Beyond name-calling this controversy produced few overt tensions, however, and Newport's merchants did not let business suffer because of the opinions of a few misguided souls. Indeed, Rhode Island being the sort of place it was, these royalists probably would have remained no more than political gadflies had Britain not chosen this moment to pass the Sugar and Stamp acts. By so doing, Parliament turned royalists into loyalists as members of the original "junto" became vociferous proponents of the new Parliamentary legislation.

As a *cause célèbre* the Sugar Act was a poor choice for the royalists because most Newporters were united in their opposition to any interference with the molasses trade. Unfortunately, the crown and its supporters refused to see that neither Rhode Island nor Newport could prosper without a constant and inexpensive supply of molasses. If Great Britain tried to collect the taxes on these goods, Newporters could and would resist. Stephen Hopkins futilely tried to explain Rhode Island's position by dashing off *The Rights of Colonies Examined*. In this pamphlet, written to protest the Sugar Act, Hopkins argued that "this high duty will not affect all the colonies equally, nor any other near so much as . . . Rhode Island, whose trade depended much more on foreign molasses and on distilleries than that of any others. . . ."[92]

Although his economic argument was sound, the governor was not a first-rate political thinker, and his ideas on empire were ambiguous at best, untenable at worst. He never did resolve the question as to whether Parliament could or could not tax the colonies, an omission providing a perfect opening for a response by the so-called tory junto. In *A Letter from a Gentleman at Halifax*, Martin Howard, an articulate spokesman for the crown, tore Hopkins' political theories to shreds, and dismissed the economic argument in one paragraph.[93] The jurisdiction of Parliament, Howard insisted, could not be apportioned; it was "transcendent and entire, and may levy internal taxes as well as regulate trade."[94] This argument justified the Stamp Act as well as the Sugar Act, but in his haste to assert the power of Parliament, Howard only reinforced Hopkins' claim that England was unresponsive to Rhode Island's interests. In other words, Hopkins was talking on one level; Howard and Parliament answered on another. Hopkins explained the economic facts of life in Rhode Island; the tories responded with a treatise on the empire.

If Howard, Thomas Moffatt, George Rome, and the other royalists could not see the logic of the economic argument, it was because they were blinded by the lawless atmosphere of Newport which consistently worked to the detriment of Great Britain. To them, this situation was intolerable; the need for law enforcement was paramount:

> If . . . customs are due to the crown; if illicit commerce is to be put an end to as ruinous to the welfare of the nation; if by reason of the interested views of traders and the connivance of courts and customhouse officers, these ends could not be compassed or obtained in the common and ordinary way, tell me, what could the government do but to apply a remedy desperate as the disease? . . . When every mild expedient to stop the atrocious and infamous practice of smuggling has been tried in vain, the government is justifiable in making laws against it, even like those of Draco, which were written in blood.[95]

Those most eager to see "an enforcement" of both the Sugar Act and the Stamp Act were the same people who had sought a royal charter. The latter legislation drew enough people to the royal cause for Ezra Stiles to claim that "in Newport was the greatest body of advocates for the Stamps of any one town in America." Stiles was wrong. They did not advocate the stamps. They advocated the right of Parliament to make and enforce colonial law. Stiles listed 55 people who supported the Stamp Act. Fifty-three would remain loyal to the crown throughout the next decade. At the same time, 36 of the 40 men committed to "Liberty" in 1765 constituted the nucleus of the Revolutionary movement and would support the cause of independence in 1776.

According to Stiles's comprehensive notes, the advocates of the Stamp Act were "the Custom House Officers, officers of three men of war, and about one hundred gentlemen Episcopalians."[96] He might have added that among those gentlemen were some of the principal merchants in Newport. A few

Wantons had already taken a stand, as well as Stephen Ayrault, Benjamin Mason, John Bours, and Silas Cooke. Under the banner of liberty the Ellerys, Samuel and William Vernon, John Collins, and Robert Crook, among others, opposed the Stamp Act.

Since the most visible and consistent advocates of the British regulations were Anglicans, Newporters divided along church lines in the decade following the Stamp Act. The members of Trinity Church (the only Anglican church in Newport) supported the loyalist cause overwhelmingly, and a list of both early royalists and later loyalists reads much like Trinity's register. With each crisis the schism between Episcopalians and the rest of the community widened, and animosities were less easily suppressed.

What makes the division difficult to understand is that both whig and tory leaders were dependent on the sea for their livelihood. Moreover, their commercial interests were similar, and most of the leaders on both sides were long-time Newport residents. Some of the loyalist families could claim ancestors among the founders of Rhode Island. With this in mind, it becomes tempting to stress the disproportionate wealth of the Anglican churchmembers in Newport as a reason for their conservatism. If at least half the top 50 tax-payers in 1772 (and 43 of the top 100) remained loyal to the crown, perhaps it was because they realized that in any upheaval they had more at stake.[97] And yet, wealth cannot be the entire answer because several of the rebel leaders were extremely affluent as well.

If most of these loyalists were members of the Trinity congregation, and most of the whigs were not, the key to their political affiliation may have been the sermons heard at the different churches each Sunday. Anglican ministers were bound by oath to support the English sovereign, and the Anglican liturgy contained prayers for both the king and his family. With such a commitment to the status quo, it is hardly surprising that the Rev. George Bisset would argue that God would never send a teacher who "encourages lawless riots and disorders among men." Bisset insisted that "the doctrine which tends to introduce into the world an universal deluge of vice and violence cannot be consistent with the will of him, who is the author of peace and lover of concord,"[98] and he consistently preached submission to legitimate authority. As the local violence increased in tempo, a regular churchgoer was likely to be persuaded that anarchy and radical whiggery were one and the same, especially since Bisset's reasoning "seldom failed to force conviction on the minds of his hearers."[99]

The sermons marking crucial moments in the Revolutionary drama also aggravated the growing cleavage between Anglicans and others. For example, Rhode Island set aside June 30, 1774, to protest the Intolerable Acts[100] with public fasting and prayer. The members of Trinity Church willingly joined in prayer, but toward a different end: according to the notes made by the Rev. Stiles, "Mr. Bisset the Church Clergyman took his Text —fast not as the Hypocrites—and preached a high tory Sermon inveiging (by allusions) against Boston and N. England as a turbulant ungoverned people."[101] Less than a year later, members of Newport's Anglican Church refused to observe a day of fasting and prayer at all.

Four blocks from Trinity Church Ezra Stiles confirmed the worst fears of Newport's Churchmen. Stiles, minister of the Second Congregational Church, spent his Sunday mornings assuring his congregation that only independence from Britain stood between them and slavery. He was convinced of a ministerial plot to subvert the dissenting churches and singled out the Anglicans for particular abuse, as the Revolutionary movement gained in momentum and long-suppressed fears overcame common sense.

It was no secret that the Congregationalists and Presbyterians feared that the British would send bishops to oversee the Anglican churches in America. This was a particularly frightening thought to the anti-Episcopalians in Newport, who had maintained an uneasy but long-standing truce with members of the Church of England. To Ezra Stiles, at least, bishops would upset the delicate balance of religious and civil power in Newport. He agreed with most Congregational ministers that bishops were politicians who held court, demanded taxes, and encroached on the rights of dissenters, and he feared that if the Anglican Church became powerful enough in America, it could persuade Parliament to pass laws denying civil or military power to dissenters.

In a small community in which few things escaped a watchful eye, Stiles could not have failed to notice that a number of Quakers and Baptists were enhancing their prestige and status by converting to Anglicanism. He periodically counted the number of families belonging to each of those denominations, and must have become increasingly uneasy to find that the Congregational churches were not growing as rapidly as the others. Quakers and Baptists were neutral toward Presbyterians and Congregationalists but if the British were able to woo members of the former groups to the British cause via Anglicanism, that neutrality could easily be converted into hostility.

TABLE VI

Religious Denominations, by Number of Families,
1760 and 1770

Denomination	Year Founded	Number of Families 1760	Number of Families 1770
Congregationalists	1st—1695 2nd—1728	Both meetings 228 (41 widows—in 2nd, 40 bachelors)	1st Cong.: 135 2nd Cong.: 130
Episcopalians	1706	169—18 widows and 31 bachelors	200
Friends	1656	105	150
First Baptist	1648	25	40
Sabbath Baptists	1671	15	40
Second Baptist	1656	150	200
Jews	17—	15	30
Moravians or United Brethren	1758	15	35
Baptists	1770		20
		772	980 families

Source: Adapted from the figures of Ezra Stiles in the Second Congregational Church
Records, 1728, Binder 838B, p. 122, NHS; *Itineraries*, p. 13.

Each action by the British ministry convinced Stiles that its ultimate goal
was to subvert the colonies and enslave them through the Anglican church.
Thus his constant and outspoken support of the whig cause earned him a
reputation as a "seditious"[102] preacher. But Stiles's seditious preaching was
acceptable to his congregation because his arguments flowed from the Bible.
For example, when news of the Boston Port Bill reached Newport, he se-

lected his text from Esther 4:3 and declaimed against "the cruel edict" in Biblical terms. Psalms 79 and 80 were useful on two similar occasions: the passage of the non-importation agreement in October 1774, and in recognition of Lexington and Concord when Stiles "adapted" them "to the present melancholy occasion." The verses—and Stiles—spoke of the vine God planted, how it took root and spread from the sea to the Great River, and how its wall had been leveled "for every passer by to rob it of its fruit." He alluded to heathen who shed the blood of God's servants "like water"—a reference which could hardly have been misinterpreted by his incensed audience on April 23, 1775. Stiles assured his flock that the current calamities stemmed from an absence of virtue and an excess of sin. Mindful of the increasing number of Anglican converts, he insisted that God would neither tend nor revive His vine if Newporters courted "the gods of other nations."[103]

If Stiles sermonized to the "very crouded Assembly of all Denominations" with the same passion as he wrote to his friends, he must have contributed greatly to the rising tensions in that troubled city. And if the wealthy merchants in his congregation hesitated at the risk they were taking or needed any justification to oppose British policy, Stiles was quick to remind them that they were God's chosen people and, by extension, that they acted in God's name. It is hardly surprising that his church, after spawning so many rebels, was called the Church of the Patriots.

Yet neither Bisset nor Stiles convinced everyone, and although the overwhelming majority of Trinity's congregants were loyalists, there were two very prominent rebels, John Collins and Captain Robert Elliott, among the congregation. In all likelihood, they either attended services less frequently or, like Henry Marchant, renounced their affiliation altogether—perhaps in favor of Dr. Stiles's church. In turn, two of Newport's most stalwart royalists were Samuel Freebody and Simon Pease, who turned away from their inherited religions and joined Trinity Church. Long-time friends and business correspondents went their separate ways, as angry spokesmen aired their grievances and committed themselves to one side or the other.

But it was not merely the Anglicans and the Congregationalists who were swept up in the Revolutionary frenzy. Religious groups which had reluctantly tolerated each other for a century and more suddenly found they could not keep up the façade. As each event precipitated another crisis, people turned on one another. For example, the Jewish community of Newport had suffered indignities in apparent silence for a century. In the decades preceding the Revolution, Jews listened while the General Assembly referred to them as strangers, watched while two of their co-religionists were denied naturalization, and waited to see if persecution would follow discrimination. According to the statutes, they, along with Catholics, had been denied the privilege of voting and holding office since 1663, making them long-term guests of the community rather than citizens.[104] Furthermore, this may have been one of the few laws which Newporters scrupulously obeyed, since there were no Jewish town officials or even voters in the years for which records survive.

In prosperous times it was possible to suppress anti-Semitic incidents for the sake of good business, but in times of economic stress this fault line in the community appeared to widen and add to already heightened tensions. There is ample evidence that the Jewish people in Newport were considered less trustworthy patriots in the Revolutionary era than other members of the community. Early in 1774 John Collins, a successful merchant in the town, expressed fear that " 'the jews at Newport' " would not boycott dutied tea—a suspicion that Collins himself later admitted was unjustified.[105] Nevertheless, accusations flew back and forth as both loyalists and rebels realized that the Jewish community had little reason to be devoted to either side. Thomas Vernon complained to a friend that "the trifle of goods we have Imported here chiefly by the Jews this Spring and Summer, has caus'd the resentment of the colonies. . . ."[106] If there was any truth to the charges, it was only because *many* of the merchants chose to ignore the non-importation agreements. The violations were hardly limited to Jewish merchants, although they were blamed for them—even by the usually fair-minded Ezra Stiles.

In 1773 the *Newport Mercury* noted with satisfaction that a Jewish merchant, "Mr. Aaron Lopez, owner of the Ship Jacob, . . . has assured us, in Riting, that said ship has no India Tea on board and that he thinks himself happy in giving such assurance." Meanwhile, scarcely a month later, a captain and part-time merchant, Peleg Clarke, made elaborate plans to conceal his own trade in this commodity: "I have sold 20 lbs of it [tea] at 21/ lawful, provided it will suit, so I must beg you will send a small mustard bottle full by Post. . . . please let it be wraped in paper and not let him know what it is. . . ." Undoubtedly, Lopez was not "happy" to be pressed for such "assurances" in the absence of similar guarantees from other suspected smugglers. Besides, what good were assurances compared to an invoice dated March 4, 1774, for ten chests of Bohea tea shipped to "St. Eustatia on account of Aaron Lopez"?[107]

It was the Quakers, however, who found themselves in the most difficult position in the pre-Revolutionary era. They were bound by their beliefs to support legitimate political authority. At the same time, astute Quaker merchants realized that the British restrictions hampered their trade. There seemed to be no way to reconcile Britain's right to regulate commerce with their own need for a steady supply of molasses. Indeed, the whole question of political legitimacy was becoming tangled in the sticky stuff.

The theoretical question was whether Quaker neutrality undermined the colonial cause. By taking no affirmative action in support of the rebels, were they not, in fact, aiding and abetting Newport's loyalists? Stiles denounced both stand and principle as petty compared to the larger issue of "American Liberty." At the very least he expected the Quakers to "pray for us and wish us well, especially in our commercial war."[108]

What made the matter even worse was that although the official stand of the Quakers dictated neutrality, unofficially they were as divided as the rest of the community. Their neutrality set them at odds with the rest of the town; their conflicting opinions set them at odds with themselves. Thomas Robinson, a leading Quaker merchant, openly supported the crown and was one of two people Ezra Stiles credited with being a five-star tory.[109] Other Quakers received fewer stars, but were, nevertheless, far from impartial. Early in 1777, seventy-six Newport Quakers declared "their allegiance to the King" in an address to the British commander, General Henry Clinton, and reminded him that they had disowned "such as have appeared openly in taking up Arms."[110] Yet the fact that the Quakers were forced to expel members for supporting the rebel cause was evidence of their internal division. For the most part it was the younger Quakers who became too restless to remain unaligned, and it was probably with great regret that the Quaker elders disowned William Bennett (son of Jonathan) since he "hath enlisted as a soldier and gone into the army" which was "directly contrary to the peaceable principles we profess." A short time later John Coggeshall (son of Elisha Coggeshall) was roundly criticized for entering on board a vessel of war to go "out on a Cruise."[111] Job Townsend, Gideon Shearman, and Seth Thomas were among those Quakers whose own principles forced them to deviate from the principles of their Society.

For some, the neutral stance of the Society of Friends provided the means for avoiding conflict altogether, and as war became inevitable there was a rash of conversions and requests to be taken under the protection of the Society. Quaker parents who had put off seeking admission for their children suddenly brought them in front of the appropriate committee.[112] As time went on, many non-Quakers who had committed themselves to one side or the other spoke harshly of former friends and business associates who refused to take sides in the escalating conflict.

With members of individual families interspersed among the various churches in town, it is not surprising that these same families were divided politically as well. In a great many cases brothers took sides against brothers, fathers against sons, and husbands against wives.[113] Most prominent families (and this probably holds true for the not-so-prominent as well) could claim both loyalist and rebel soldiers.[114] The saddest stories of all must have been told by those families with members in opposing camps. Such was the case with the Coggeshalls whose paths crossed on the way to Trinity Church, the First and Second Congregational Churches, the Second Baptist Church and the Quaker Meeting House.[115] And yet, despite the strains, some people managed to balance family loyalty with support for either the British or the American cause. Thus, when the rebels were in command of Newport before the British occupation, exiled loyalist Thomas Vernon wrote to his whig brother William acknowledging assistance: "I thank you for the tea. . . . I also thank you for every instance of your kindness in soliciting in my behalf in this very disagreeable business. . . ." He implied that he really had no choice but to "be content with my present lott, I had almost said hard. . . ."[116]

As time went by and commerce suffered, some of the more vocal rebels began to have second thoughts, and the components of backlash and uncertainty were added to the forces already disturbing the distressed town. At least three people cited by Ezra Stiles as super-patriots in the 1760s became champions of the British in the years that followed. Thomas Freebody started out as a Son of Liberty and ended up as a four-star tory. By the end of 1774 there were many more who pleaded that resistance had gone far enough, and that the risk was too great. They cursed the "Demagogues" who in their "blind and mistaken zeal" were leading Newport "into downright Perdition." Speaking for this group was Godfrey Malbone, who argued that nonconsumption and non-importation was one thing, but "to persevere in our Folly, and suffer ourselves to be led by the nose by a set of miserable wretches, and compelled to stake, like losing Gamesters, our All, at one Cast, against such mighty odds, is the very Acme of Madness."[117] Malbone blamed the "shortsighted, very young, raw and inexperienced Politicians" for the calamities besetting the colonies and advised his brother in Newport to submit with "patience and Resignation" in the hope that all would turn out well. When the final sides were chosen, Godfrey Malbone opted for Great Britain.

Governor Joseph Wanton was another who, at first, zealously, violently, and unstintingly supported the colonists in their opposition to Parliamentary encroachments, but changed his mind in the final minutes before independence. When the British revenue cutter *Liberty* was attacked in Newport Harbor by a mob in 1769, Wanton was accused of being "well pleased with what was going forward." It was said that one of his sons not only instigated the riot but "stood there in order to encourage" it. Yet when it came time to sign an order for raising troops to fight Great Britain, the governor stayed his quill, since it would have been an "open violation" of his oath of allegiance to the king.

Ironically, Wanton based his reluctance on the well-being of Rhode Island. Fearing "fatal consequences to our charter," he refused to hurl the stroke that would "involve the colony in the horrors of a civil War."[118] Born into an old Rhode Island family that once was largely Quaker, Wanton was indeed "closely united" to the inhabitants of Rhode Island "by every endearing tie." There can be no doubt that he sincerely believed that he was "preserving the good people" from "ruin and destruction" by refusing to sign the order. The governor knew as well as anyone the financial condition of "this once Happy Colony." If he felt that supporting an army of 1,500 men "must unavoidably bring on universal bankruptcy," he probably had good reason to think so. Furthermore, Wanton could not be sure that the other colonies would support Rhode Island with men and arms. Nevertheless, the Rhode Island General Assembly took his hesitancy as opposition to the whig cause and removed him from office, as bitterness increased and positions polarized in the months following Lexington and Concord.

Wanton defended his stand and then added dispiritedly: "I have ever considered it as the distinguishing privilege of an Englishman to give his opinion upon any public transaction, wherein the welfare and happiness of the community to which he belonged was immediately concerned, without incurring public censure therefor."[119] Wanton should have known by this time that this was true only if one's opinions happened to coincide with those of the majority. Dissent and uncertainty—that is, less than unswerving support for the radical patriot cause—were simply not tolerated any more, even though uncertainty showed only that people did not know which side best served their interests. Governor Joseph Wanton retained his ties with Britain, but more than one Wanton disagreed with his decision and marched off with rebel regiments.[120]

Governor Wanton's reluctant decision was reached after much soul-searching. His shipping interests, after all, varied little from those of William Vernon or John Collins, who were rebel leaders. Few loyalists—or whigs—had a specialized trade. No one confined his commerce to dry goods in a town known for its liquid assets. Loyalist merchants were as dependent on a constant flow of ships as the rebels. What divided them were the best means to that end.

Most of the loyalists were even willing to put up with a little lawlessness. Some of them had engaged in smuggling or bribery; at best they were unenthusiastic about the commercial restrictions. What they feared, however, was a complete breakdown of law and order. They felt that Newport's commerce was as much threatened by anarchy as by any navigation act. If the rebels saw themselves as defenders of liberty, the loyalists saw them as outlaws devoted "to Sedition, privy Conspiracy and Rebellion."[121] The loyalists cast themselves as patriots and watched as the Revolutionary drama unfolded and their deepest fears were realized. Rebellious merchants had "a multitude at their call, to perpetrate any villany."[122] And villainy as the loyalists perceived it was " 'instigating the Populace, and endeavoring to point their Fury against the Person and Interest of a Man meerly because he happens to differ in opinion from his countrymen.' "[123] What the loyalists feared most was that the rebel leaders would unleash the mob against them.

In good times much of the younger male population (the most obvious candidates for a mob) were likely to be away at sea. In bad times—times of unemployment—they were on the spot and a potential danger. Restless, resentful, perhaps looking for someone to blame for their distress, this amorphous group of unemployed mariners could be manipulated by the rebel leaders, and their anger deflected toward the loyalists. After all, mobs had scuffled with British officials at the instigation of the merchants for decades. What could be more natural than to expand the struggle to include those who supported the British position? To make matters worse, there was no recourse. According to the loyalists, local government, somewhat unstable to begin with, had become an instrument of the rabble. Those in political power applauded mob rule, and denied assistance to legitimate authority. One crown supporter argued that " 'Law instead of being a permanent and uniform rule to society is ever vague and transitory. . . .' "[124]

There is no reason to suppose that the loyalists were less devoted to liberty than the rebels. Indeed, what the tories resented most was the refusal of the "Sons of Liberty so called" to extend to conservatives "the same Privilege, which they claim and enjoy."[125] The charge was hypocrisy, and it was well-founded. Instead of being allowed to express themselves and to offer alternatives, loyalists were reduced to silence. Those who tried to speak for the rule of law rather than any particular British law, found themselves threatened or intimidated or the objects of violence. With each crisis the breach between the loyalists and the rest of the community broadened. It did the loyalists no good to "speak aloud for Justice."[126] As resistance became the popular choice, as supporters of the whig cause grew in number, there were few who would bother to listen. Incident after incident gave the loyalists good reason to fear the mob more than the monarch. They had the most to lose should law and order disintegrate completely. It was not unreasonable for them to assume that their best interests were served by the benign dictatorship of the British.

George Rome certainly had reason to feel this way. He had negotiated with Captain James Wallace to supply the *Rose* with 84 barrels of flour. The "Dastardly Rebel Rabel" had other ideas, however, and according to Wallace's account " 'from three to Seven hundred men' " armed with " 'Musquets, Bayonets, Sticks and Stones' " ran through the street shouting " 'kill the Tories.' " The rioters seized and destroyed the flour, and dispersed only when Wallace promised to release a captured rebel. Although Rome had bought and paid for the flour, the times were such that former Governor Samuel Ward announced he was "heartily glad the People had the Spirit to Seize it."[127]

The Brenton family also suffered from the mob's wrath when "a number of persons" visited their farm and carried off 1,000 sheep and from 40 to 50 head of cattle in retaliation for alleged loyalist activity. Shortly thereafter, the Brentons put the farm up for sale. When an anonymous merchant offered General Gage 40 blankets, a group of townspeople "waited on him," and the blankets were returned to the store. "This may be a warning to other merchants not to attempt to support our enemies."[128]

Loyalists, whose strong attachment to the crown encouraged them to ignore that threat, used discretion and deception in order to support their cause while avoiding reprisals by their countrymen. As Vice Admiral Samuel Graves advised Captain Wallace:

> A vessel will be freighted by [John Mansfield] of Newport with Fuel and Victual, and will purposely throw herself in the way of some of your ships to be seized. And it will be necessary, to preserve the Master from the Resentment of his Countrymen on his Return, to put on the Appearance of compelling him to come to Boston, but it will be proper also to take out some of the People and send yours instead, as the Crew may not be depended on.[129]

While these events demonstrate the growing strength of the Revolutionary movement, each incident also lends support to the idea that radical whigs were determined to suppress opposition thought and activities by extra-legal means. This was nothing new for the rebellious Newporters, of course. They were old hands at circumventing people and laws with which they disagreed. And they had little patience with people who challenged their methods, making their opponents bitterly critical of the tactics used in the name of liberty: "liberty so much talked [of] that one would think it was the best known of anything, but by some late conduct one would think it was not known at all."[130] Furthermore, there can be little doubt that the increasing violence threw a number of people into the loyalist camp.

In the end, how many loyalists were there in Newport? How many people actively supported the crown when the final break came? There were perhaps 100 "principal and active tories," who remained in Newport when the British took what was left of the town in December 1776.[131] Stiles singled out 28 for special mention, and it is clear from the "List of those who are objected against, as persons not to be trusted with arms" that at least 110 persons were suspected.[132] Once the whigs deserted Newport on those cold December days, many loyalists who feared to speak out earlier finally declared their allegiance. Denouncing both "factions" and "designing men" for effecting an "unnatural Separation from the Parent State . . . ," 444 people signed a petition to General Clinton, declaring their "Loyal and

Dutiful Allegiance to his Majesty King George the Third."[133] Though some may have signed to accommodate themselves to the occupying forces, a great many were undoubtedly glad to see the stability the British represented.

Many of the suspected tories in Newport were probably, like Christopher Champlin or Aaron Lopez, trying to hedge their bets, ply their trade, straddle the fence, and when the world turned upside down, land on their feet. Some honestly did not know until the last minute which way they would turn. Others were sure of their allegiance until the very last minute—and then, like Metcalf Bowler, switched sides. Judge Bowler was a Son of Liberty who had thrown an open house to celebrate the repeal of the Stamp Act, but found spying for the British more to his liking.[134]

Everyone in Newport probably wanted the same thing—a peaceful environment in which to live, carry on trade, and pursue profit. The townspeople differed over means, not ends, because no one really knew which side would serve them better. In the last analysis, they may have traveled different routes but they had the same goal in mind. And even when the final lines were drawn, the most ardent royalist harbored second thoughts and the firmest rebel wavered a bit in his commitment.

REFLECTIONS

In the end, what can be said about this rebellious city in an age of rebellious cities? What can be said about a community at loggerheads with Great Britain, other colonies, and itself? Above all, there is good reason to believe that the Revolution was fought for economic reasons which Newporters were able to translate into specific whig principles. The entire structure of the town was built and became dependent on an ever-expanding trade. By threatening this trade, the British threatened the very life of the community, as well as its prosperity. The Revolution, therefore, was of necessity a struggle to sustain that life and prosperity.

So desperate was their situation, in fact, that Newporters were left very little time for a consistent Revolutionary rhetoric. Each side claimed to be the true guardian of the British constitution and charged that the other had abandoned its sacred trust. At the same time, impartial observers insisted that both "whig and Torey Nostrums [have] ruined the Constitution."[135] Thus although the words "slavery," "liberty," and "equality" were frequently aired, they had no commonly acceptable definition since they were used by both whigs and tories. Newporters were uncomfortable with the concept of slavery in the 1770s. Because Newport was a community receptive to black slavery and reaping profits from the trade itself, townspeople could argue only awkwardly that they were fighting to prevent their own enslavement. Thus "slavery" was connected vaguely to any number of grievances. When Ezra Stiles spoke about "slavery," he was referring to domination by an Episcopal bishop who might not limit taxes to his own flock. William Vernon defined "slavery" as obedience to laws which threatened his commercial empire. A number of married women saw their confining lives as a kind of "slavery," and at the height of the controversy "eloped" from their husbands in record numbers.[136] "Liberty" was important to whigs because it was advantageous to commerce. It was no less important to tories, and they counterclaimed that they were being denied "that very liberty they [the rebels] are so loudly Bawling out to Preserve."[137] If rebellious Rhode Islanders sought to separate themselves from England's "poisonous Luxury and Venality," loyalists shrank from Newport's excessive "luxury and dissipation."[138] For the rebels "equality" was bound up with the rights of Englishmen. To most Newporters it suggested the "right to carry on trade upon an equal Footing with the people in England. . . ."[139] It also meant the right to manufacture products to compete with English goods.

In fact, by 1774 the idea of manufacturing had become so important to the Newport community that the thwarting of it was listed as a major grievance—which rather suddenly dated retroactively to the end of the "last war." An article in the *Mercury*—perhaps written by printer Southwick himself—summed up what Newporters were thinking on the eve of the Revolution. The author asserted that Britain treated the colonists as slaves and that the mother country thought it had a right to "all the fruits of our labor and all the produce of our lands." The article went on to argue that

Our country abounds with iron, but we are cruelly forbid the use of mills for manufacturing; and thus denied the use of what God hath so liberally bestowed upon us, and what is so highly necessary for us.

By one act, the wool raised upon our islands cannot be brought to market; by another act, a few felt hats, or a piece of flannel, made in one town and sent by water to another, endangers the seizure of the vessel that carries them: By others our foreign trade is embarrassed, that we can hardly make an advantageous voyage to any part of the world. And to enforce these arbitrary acts, our streets are crowded with collectors, tide waiters, and other tribute gatherers; and our harbours (formerly peaceful avenues of commerce) filled with armed ships and cutters.

If the lawyers of Pennsylvania, Virginia, and Massachusetts are revered as the spokesmen of an American constitutional doctrine, no less credit should be awarded to the Rhode Islanders who translated those arguments into economic language. It was not the principle of the revenue measures that disturbed the Newport community but the probable consequences: "By taxing . . . the article of tea [the British] will assume the same right to lay a tax on all you eat, drink, wear and possess until you have nothing to be taxed for." Practical to the end, the Rhode Islanders immediately went to the heart of the matter and reduced the rhetoric to an expression of self-interest.

They rejected a heavy tax burden—even when it came to taxes that were self-imposed. Townspeople were constantly chided for their delinquency in paying local and colony-wide assessments. The General Treasurer of Rhode Island was forced to file a warrant against the treasurer of the town of Newport for this reason. In an ironic twist of the legal system, the town treasurer was jailed for failing to collect the required taxes.[140] George Rome was close to the truth when he insisted that merchants hoped to " 'obtain a total exemption from all taxation.' "[141]

Furthermore, Newport itself (although neither England nor Newport may have been more than vaguely aware of it) was becoming the hub of a mini mercantile empire. By converting molasses into rum, and by pursuing a never-ending search for markets for raw materials and finished products, Newport actually confronted England as a competitor rather than as a smooth-fitting component of her mercantile network. By 1773 the farsighted were insisting that "we could, in a few years, beat Great Britain in manufactures."[142] This was totally unacceptable to Great Britain, as it should have been under the rules and expectations of the eighteenth-century mercantilist system.

Newport had matured quite independently while its indifferent parent busied herself elsewhere. Britain had encouraged this particular colony to elect its own governor, frame its own laws, and eschew an established church. Without encouragement, Rhode Island had become economically independent of England as well. Given Rhode Island's upbringing, it was perfectly reasonable for Governor Stephen Hopkins to ask as early as 1756 " 'what have the king and Parliament to do with making a law or laws to govern us by, any more than the Mohawks have?' "[143] As irritated as England may have been by such outbursts, it was too late for the mother country to reassert authority. Newport could not have remained in the British empire, given the circumstances of the 1760s and 1770s. Despite an active number of loyalists, rebels remained unconvinced that war was potentially more disruptive to trade than the British duties. The deeper Newport's economic distress, the closer the town came to *de jure* independence.

The law underwent many curious twists in those heady days prior to the Revolution. Clearly, there was a connection between the mild-mannered smugglers of the mid-eighteenth century and the violent resisters of the 1770s. Evading the law by means of smuggling and bribery helped build a prosperous community; it was merely a step further to protecting this investment by use of force. The new leaders of the Republic would argue in retrospect that "Smuggling was formerly not disreputable because it was the evading of Laws which were not made by proper Authority and therefore not obligatory."[144] By general agreement and long habit, the laws could be bent to further one's ends. And if the ends justified the means, the law could be stretched enough to suppress free speech, deny civil liberties, and confiscate private property. In the end, Newporters paid dearly for their independence. Mid-war a saddened Ezra Stiles noted that "the town is in Ruins." He counted 300 houses destroyed; the actual number was closer to 500.[145] Even the British, who were responsible for the wreckage, admitted that Newport had become "a damd place to live in."[146] With more bravado than omniscience the good minister predicted that Newport would "be rebuilt and excede its former splendour."[147] And when it was all over, even those who chose crown over country would lament with Stiles the fate of their former home:

> I hope prospects brighten at Newport and that you begin to realize some of the many benefits which Independence and a new Constitution were to give you— A whole continent ruined to get rid of ideal Taxes— My attachment to our native country is so fervent and sincere that I could freely give up my life and Ten thousand more if I possessed them could I return dear Rhode Island to its former happy happy situation. . . .[148]

1. John Adams to William Tudor, Quincy, Massachusetts, Aug. 11, 1818, in *The Works of John Adams*, ed. Charles Francis Adams, 10 vols. (Boston, 1850–1856), x 345.

2. On October 18, 1774, Congress established the Continental Association, which agreed on behalf of the colonies to cease importing from Great Britain on December 1, 1774, and to stop exporting to Britain, Ireland, and the West Indies on September 1, 1775.

3. Governor Samuel Ward to Henry Ward, Oct. 5, 1775, *Correspondence of Governor Samuel Ward, May 1775 – March 1776*, ed. Bernard Knollenberg (Providence, 1952), p. 95.

4. Caleb Heathcote to the Board of Trade, Sept. 7, 1719, RICR, IV 259.

5. Thomas Vernon to I. R., Esq., June 27, 1770, Vernon Papers, Box 79, folder 3, NHS.

6. *A Letter to the House of Commons: The Importance of the Sugar Colonies to Great Britain and Some Objections to the Sugar Colony Bill* (London, 1731); Bigelow, "Commerce of Rhode Island with the West Indies," Part I, chap. 4, note 33.

7. *NM*, Nov. 28, 1763.

8. Throughout the last decade of Rhode Island's membership in the British empire, reports constantly flowed to England of the colony's "unbounded licentiousness." Moreover, Parliament's distress must have increased with the news that it was "obvious" to everyone "that illegal trading has been growing to an egregious excess in Rhode Island...." Chief Justice Smyth of New Jersey to Lord Dartmouth, Feb. 8, 1773, Chalmers Papers, p. 73, NYPL.

9. *The Rights of Colonies Examined* (Providence, 1765), as reprinted in *Pamphlets of the American Revolution. I. 1750–1776*, ed. Bernard Bailyn (Cambridge, Mass., 1965), pp. 513–14.

10. *NM*, Feb. 13, 1764.

11. "Remonstrance," RICR, VI 382.

12. *NM*, Feb. 13, 1764.

13. G. and J. Malbone to Messrs. Trecothick and Thomlinson, July 28, 1764, Malbone Papers, Box 174, folder 12, NHS. The Malbones also explained that they could not smuggle foreign molasses because the British were keeping a "very strict watch."

14. *NM*, May 27, 1765.

15. *NM*, Apr. 30, Aug. 6, 1764.

16. *NM*, May 7, Oct. 8, 1764; see also the issues of Apr. 22, 1765, and Aug. 8, 1768, for reports of Newporters reclaiming what they felt was rightfully theirs.

17. Rudolph, "Merchants of Newport," pp. 118ff.; *NM*, May 7, July 16, 1764.

18. Deposition of Daniel Vaughn, Newport, July 8, 1764, Chalmers Papers, p. 41, NYPL.

19. *NM*, June 10, 1765.

20. *NM*, Aug. 19, 26, 1765.

21. See Thom. Moffatt's "Minutes" of the riots (1765), Chalmers Papers, p. 99, NYPL. They are included in *Prologue to Revolution: Sources and Documents on the Stamp Act Crisis, 1764–1766*, ed. Edmund S. Morgan (Chapel Hill, N.C., 1959), pp. 109–13. Martin Howard was the author of *A Letter from a Gentleman at Halifax to His Friend in Rhode-Island* (Newport, 1765), which supported the right of Great Britain to tax the colonies. It has been reprinted in *Pamphlets of the American Revolution*, ed. Bailyn, pp. 532–44.

For a full account of the Stamp Act riots in Newport, see Lovejoy, *Rhode Island Politics*, pp. 100–10; Edmund S. and Helen Morgan, *The Stamp Act Crisis* (New York, 1962), pp. 144–48; Pauline Maier, *From Resistance to Revolution* (New York, 1972), pp. 57, 59, 60; *NM*, Sept. 2, 1765.

22. Thom. Moffatt's "Minutes" of the riots, p. 99. This would appear to contradict Pauline Maier's conclusion that the elite were likely to eschew force in favor of legal remedies and that they directed rather than participated in mob violence. *From Resistance to Revolution*, pp. 59–60. When the *Gaspee* was burned in June 1772 Midshipman Dickinson testified that "the greatest part" of those he saw on board the *Gaspee* as it was burning were shopkeepers, merchants, and masters of vessels, "wearing ruffled shirts and other good apparel." Chief Justice Oliver to Lord Dartmouth (1773), Chalmers Papers, p. 77, NYPL. Another eyewitness noted that among the perpetrators were "a number of armed people, many of whom by their dress appeared much above the rank of common people. . . ." Report of the Commissioners of Inquiry about the Burning of the *Gaspee*, ibid., p. 79.

23. Town Meeting Records, 1679–1779, Book 2007, p. 804, NHS.

24. *NM*, Sept. 9, 1765.

25. *NM*, Oct. 2, 28, 1765. See the letter from William and Samuel Vernon to Richard Adams, dated Oct. 1, 1765, showing the deliberate attempt by Newport merchants to clear vessels before November 1, "the time limited for the detested Stamp Act to take place." Vernon Letter Book #77, NHS.

According to Pauline Maier, Hall was one of the Sons of Liberty. Other members were Christopher Ellery (merchant), Henry Marchant (lawyer), Henry Ward (Secretary of the Province), Metcalf Bowler (deputy and judge), Josias Lyndon (clerk of the General Assembly and inferior court of common pleas, Newport County), William Ellery (merchant), John Channing (merchant), Thomas Freebody (merchant), Robert Crook (merchant), John Collins (merchant), Jonathan Otis (gold- and silversmith), and Charles Spooner ("'from among middling and lower life'"). Professor Maier compiled her list from Ezra Stiles's Stamp Act notebook, Yale University. *From Resistance to Revolution*, pp. 309–10. See also a letter from Newport to the Providence Sons of Liberty, Apr. 4, 1766, RIHS MSS XII, f. 67, Providence.

26. *NM*, May 26, June 2, 1766.

27. Carl Bridenbaugh noted that Newport townspeople did not necessarily show the proper deference to wealthy summer visitors: "To be a gentleman was sufficient to expose the bearer of that name to mockery and rudeness. . . ." "Colonial Newport," 12.

28. *NM*, June 2, July 14, 1766.

29. In an effort to meet the objections levied against the Stamp Act, the Townshend duties were applied only to imports of glass, paper, paint, lead, and tea.

30. S. and W. Vernon to Richard Adams, Oct. 1, 1765, Vernon Letter Book #77, NHS; see *NM*, Mar. 14, 1768, for evidence that some Newporters were convinced of the efficacy of petitions.

31. J. Wanton to Lord Hillsbro, May 5, 1769, Chalmers Papers, p. 43, NYPL. Lord Hillsborough was Secretary of State for the Colonies.

32. Thoughts on the Outrage committed on HM Schooner *Gaspee* in Rhode Island, ibid., p. 65.

33. *NM*, Aug 8, Dec. 12, 1768.

34. Capt. William Reid to Gov. Joseph Wanton, "Weds. Eve., 11 o'clock July 19, 1769," Chalmers Papers, p. 55, NYPL.

35. Deposition of William Reid, July 21, 1769, ibid., p. 57.

36. The Captain Hull referred to was probably John Hull, a well-known Newport resident, and friend of Goddard's.

37. Thomas Vernon to I. R., Esq., June 27, 1770, Vernon Papers, Box 79, folder 3, NHS.

38. The well-publicized Boston tea dumping was not the first colonial masquerade party. "Extracts from Edward Thurston, Jr.'s Almanac, 1772," *Newport Historical Magazine*, 1 (July 1880 – April 1881), 125.

39. Gov. Wanton to Lord Dartmouth, Jan. 30, 1773, Chalmers Papers, p. 71, NYPL; Rudolph, "Merchants of Newport," p. 199.

40. *NM*, Nov. 30, 1767, Nov. 4, 1765, Sept. 19, 1768, Aug. 21, 1769.

41. *NM*, Nov. 6, 13, 1769; June 4, 1770.

42. *New York Journal*, June 29, Nov. 30, 1769; *Massachusetts Gazette*, July 10, 1769. See also Arthur M. Schlesinger, *Colonial Merchants and the American Revolution, 1763–1776* (New York, 1918; repr. 1968), pp. 152–53, 195–96.

43. Stephen Ayrault to Messrs. Welchs, Wilk[i]nson, and Startin, Aug. 30, 1770, Box marked "Stephen Ayrault's Letters to Friends and Business Associates, 1767–1778," NHS.

44. Josiah Hewes to Messrs. Vernon and Tanner, Philadelphia, June 2, 1770, Box 656, folder marked "Champlin Letters, Vernon Letters, 1743–77, transferred from Book 652," NHS.

45. Nicholas Roosevelt to Samuel and William Vernon and James Tanner, New York, June 25, 1770, Vernon Papers, Box 79, folder 17, NHS; John Sleight to Samuel and William Vernon, New Brunswick, June 19, 1770, Box 656, folder marked "Champlin Letters, Vernon Letters, 1743–77, transferred from Book 652," NHS.

46. Document signed by Thomas Cox and Robert Lawton, New York, May 30, 1770, Box 2, #143, NHS.

47. John Neufville to the Sons of Liberty in Rhode Island, Apr. 25, 1770, Haight Collection, NHS.

48. *NM*, June 4, 1770.

49. Thomas Vernon to I. R., Esq., June 27, 1770, Vernon Papers, Box 79, folder 3,

NHS. According to *NM*, in 1774 Connecticut, Rhode Island, and New Hampshire together imported only £12,000 sterling worth of goods from Great Britain, while Massachusetts imported £395,000 worth of goods, New York £531,000, and Philadelphia £611,000. The crisis of 1770 may have looked like an excellent opportunity to divert some of the British trade to Newport—even at the expense of other seaports. In 1776 the small amount of merchandise coming directly from England may have made it easier for Rhode Island to cut the colonial apron strings. Compare with the figures in Table Z21–34 in Census Bureau, *Historical Statistics of the United States* (1960), p. 757.

50. Josiah Hewes to Messrs. S. and W. Vernon, Philadelphia, Aug. 14, 1770, Box 656, folder marked "Champlin Letters, Vernon Letters, 1743–77, transferred from Book 652," NHS.

51. Bigelow, "Commerce of Rhode Island with the West Indies," Part I, chap. 7, p. 12. See customs entries in *NM* for 1772, 1773, 1774.

52. The Boston Tea Party was incidentally reported in the *NM* on December 20, 1773. The importation of tea had long been an object of contention in Newport, and it was with unconcealed delight that the newspaper printed the following story on February 14, 1774: "Last Friday morning a countryman, stepping out of a sloop at Brown's wharf with a small bag of the accursed East India tea in his hand, fell into the dock [water].... Be cautious how you travel with this baneful article about you; for the salt-water seems of late to attract it as a loadstone attracts iron."

53. To force the Bostonians to compensate the East India Company for losses incurred as a result of the Tea Party, Parliament passed the Boston Port Bill in the spring of 1774. The Act prohibited the loading or unloading of vessels in Boston harbor, with the exception of those carrying military supplies, food, and fuel.

54. Town Meeting Records, 1679–1779, Book 2007, p. 1044, NHS.

55. See the *NM*, May 30, July 18, Aug. 22, Sept. 5, Oct. 17 and 31, 1774; Mar. 27, 1775. Individuals in Newport who had family and friends in Boston were quick to send whatever they could in response to the mounting number of pleas. Francis Brinley (a Newport merchant, ropewalk owner, and loyalist) sent cider, ducks, turkeys, and cheeses to Boston in the summer of 1775 to at least three different families who reported that they were near starvation: "Our situation is truly distressing that obliges us to trouble our friends that are so happy as not to [chance] the same fate...." Mary Gerrish to Francis Brinley, Sept. 6, 1775, Box 174, folder 1, NHS; George Brinley to Francis Brinley, July 27, 1775, ibid.; Jonathan Murray to Francis Brinley, July 18, 1775, ibid., folder 3.

56. Perhaps the beseiged city of Boston was not in a position to help, but the town was conspicuously absent from the list of those Newport formally thanked for donations in March 1776. Town Meeting Records, 1679–1779, Book 2007, p. 1113, NHS.

57. On October 20, 1774, the Continental Congress resolved that as of December 1, 1774, the colonies could not import anything from Great Britain or Ireland; nor could they reimport any English or Irish products from anywhere else. In addition, no East India tea could be imported or molasses, syrup, paneles, coffee, or pimento

from British plantations. At the same time, the Continental Association prohibited both slavery and the slave trade after December 1, 1774. Non-exportation was suspended until September 1, 1775. *Journals of the Continental Congress*, edd. Ford et al., I 76–77.

58. Jan. 21, 1776; see *Rhode Island in the Continental Congress*, ed. William Staples (Providence, 1870), p. 56.

59. Samuel Ward to ——, May 23, 1774, Box 43, folder 6, NHS.

60. *NM*, May 15, 1775. At the same time as the other colonies were warning Newport to abide by the non-importation agreements, the British continued to squeeze Newport from the other side, leaving William Vernon to puzzle "Why we are . . . stigmatized beyond our neighbors[. I] cannot assign any reason as our whole Trade and Commerce is strictly conformable to the late acts of Parliament." William Vernon to Geo. Erving, Aug. 16, 1775, Vernon Papers, Box 45, folder 1, NHS.

61. The names of the Committee of Inspection were printed in *NM*, Dec. 19, 1774. J. G. Wanton, Francis Malbone, George Gibbs, and Samuel Dyre remained loyal. The Committee of Correspondence also lost a member, John Mawdsley, to the tories.

62. William G. Roelker and Clarkson A. Collins, "The Patrol of Narragansett Bay (1774–1776) by H.M.S. *Rose*, Captain James Wallace, [Part II]," *Rhode Island History*, 8 (July 1949), 82.

63. Vernon also felt that Wallace was discriminating in his seizures, releasing those vessels whose owners supported the British. S. and W. Vernon to George Hayley, Esq., London, Aug. 23, 1775, Vernon Letter Book #77, NHS.

64. John Knowles to William Vernon, Boston, July 4, 1775, Box 656, folder marked "Champlin Letters, Vernon Letters, 1743–77, transferred from Book 652," NHS.

65. *NM*, July 24, 1775. Wallace to Admiral Graves, Dec. 28, 1775, as quoted in Roelker & Collins, "Patrol of Narragansett Bay . . . by H.M.S. *Rose* . . . [Part IV]," *Rhode Island History*, 9 (April 1950), 54.

66. *NM*, Oct. 9, 1775.

67. Proceedings of the General Assembly, October 1775, RICR, VII 382.

68. "Memorial of the Inhabitants of the Town of Newport, Rhode Island, to the Delegates of the United Colonies of America, in Congress at Philadelphia in 1775," *Rhode Island Historical Magazine*, 6, No. 1 (July 1885), 8–9. Apparently some Newporters felt even Providence might benefit from Newport's distress: "Some of the inhabitants of Newport are very jealous of the views of the town of Providence; fearing that the latter has in view the destruction of Newport, for their own private advantage. . . ." Nathanael Greene to Jacob Greene, Dec. 20, 1774, in *The Papers of Nathanael Greene*, ed. Richard K. Showman, 3 vols. to date (Chapel Hill, N.C., 1976–1984), I 166–67. Even Captain Wallace noticed that many Newporters were " 'jealous of the Providence people.' " Wallace to Admiral Graves, June 30, 1775, as quoted in Roelker & Collins, "Patrol of Narragansett Bay . . . by H.M.S. *Rose* . . . [Part II]," 81.

69. "Memorial of the Colony of Rhode Island to the Continental Congress," May 20, 1776, RICR, VII 550–51.

70. Nathanael Greene to Samuel Ward, Oct. 23, 1775, in *Correspondence of Governor Samuel Ward*, ed. Knollenberg, p. 108.

71. Nicholas Cooke to the Continental Congress, Jan. 21, 1776, in *Rhode Island in the Continental Congress*, ed. Staples, p. 57.

72. *NM*, Dec. 11, 1775. Solomon Southwick, patriot printer of the *NM*, needed no lessons in propaganda if his goal was to incite the townspeople to riot. According to Southwick, the ministerial troops "pillage," "plunder," "butcher," "murder," "rape," etc., while the Americans "collect together," "wait on people," and are consistently pictured as the placid victims of British assaults.

Southwick never described the activities of roving mobs of Newporters in the early 1770s as dramatically and emotionally as he described the actions of British soldiers a few years later. It may not be fair to say that Southwick was distorting events to suit his purpose, but his aim clearly was to enlist as many people as possible in the patriot cause.

See *NM*, Mar. 29, Apr. 3, May 29, July 24, Dec. 11, 1775, for examples, and note the different approaches to the accounts of the flour riots in June 1775. See also James Wallace to Admiral Graves, June 5, 1775, as quoted in Roelker & Collins, "Patrol of Narragansett Bay . . . by H.M.S. *Rose* . . . [Part II]," 81; and *NM*, June 5, 1775.

73. General Assembly of Rhode Island to Continental Congress, Jan. 1776, in *Rhode Island in the Continental Congress*, ed. Staples, p. 54.

74. Ibid.

75. The 1772 tax list for Newport claims 1,210 persons. The tax list for August 1775 shows approximately 985 people, a decline of 225 persons. The entire tax collected in 1772 was £1,200; the amount collected in 1775 was £800.

76. A list of those "who left the island on the breaking out of the war, with the amount of tax paid by them in 1772" was published in *NM* along with the 1775 tax assessment on Feb. 12, 19, 26, and Mar. 5, 1853. Furthermore, that all but 20 of the 86 people assessed £10 or more in 1760 are listed in the tax assessment of 1775 suggests that even in times of economic stress the people with the most to lose found it neither necessary nor advantageous to leave Newport. The next semi-official count, in September 1776, reported 5,299 persons left in town. See RICR, VII 616.

77. *Diary*, I 649.

78. Friends Records, Monthly Meetings, 6th and 9th, 1775, 1773–1790, Book 810, pp. 56, 65, NHS.

79. General Assembly of Rhode Island to Continental Congress, Jan. 1776, in *Rhode Island in the Continental Congress*, ed. Staples, p. 54; Town Meeting Records, 1679–1779, Book 2007, p. 1110, NHS; *NM*, Jan. 22, 1776.

80. Town Meeting Records, 1679–1779, Book 2007, p. 1104, NHS.

81. S. Vernon, Jr. to Isabel Marchant, Newport, Mar. 20, 1776, Vernon Papers, Box 49, folder 5, NHS; Nathanael Greene to Governor Nicholas Cooke, Feb. 6, 1776, in *Papers of Nathanael Greene*, ed. Showman, I 192.

82. Benjamin Chappel to Aaron Lopez, Feb. 22, 1775, Lopez Papers, Haight Collection, NHS.

83. *NM*, Aug. 7, Sept. 18, 1775.

84. William Vernon to Mr. John Glazier, Newport, Dec. 15, 1775, Vernon Letter Book #77, NHS.

85. Walter Chaloner to Col. Godfrey Malbone, May 18, 1776, Malbone Papers, Box 174, folder 10, NHS: William Vernon to Geo. Hayley, Oct. 19, 1775, Vernon Letter Book #77, NHS; *Journals of the Continental Congress*, edd. Ford et al., IV 257–59; Josiah Hewes to Wm. Vernon, June 4, 1776, Box 656, folder marked "Champlin Letters, Vernon Letters, 1743–77, transferred from Book 652," NHS. From November 1775 onward, the *NM* reprinted no customhouse entries or departures.

86. David Lovejoy says that these six votes might well have been cast by the deputies from Newport. It is unlikely that this was the case, however, since this would have meant a unanimous vote by the Newport delegation, and there is no reason to believe that the whigs in the group voted for less than independence. *Rhode Island Politics*, p. 192. See RICR, VII 510, for the names of the deputies.

87. *NM*, July 15, 1776.

88. Since the political bickering of that decade is a subject through which political historians have thoroughly sifted, there is little point in presenting the whole story here. Suffice it to say that the controversy revolved around a power struggle between Newport and Providence—or the northern *vs.* the southern parts of the colony—and disputes over currency. For an excellent presentation of the entire story, see Lovejoy, *Rhode Island Politics*; for shorter studies, consult James, *Colonial Rhode Island*, pp. 294–313, and Mack E. Thompson, "The Ward–Hopkins Controversy and the American Revolution in Rhode Island: An Interpretation," *William and Mary Quarterly*, 16 (1959), 365–75.

89. George Rome to Thomas Moffatt, Dec. 22, 1767, as quoted in Weeden, *Early Rhode Island*, p. 293.

90. Whig partisans probably never forgot Rome's early and vociferous condemnation of Rhode Island politics. Town meeting records suggest that a number of representatives gave Rome a difficult time when he petitioned to embark on a road construction project in 1771. The "greatly agrieved" Mr. Rome eventually won the day, but only after a great deal of haggling. Town Meeting Records, 1679–1779, Book 2007, p. 954, NHS.

91. *Brief Remarks on the Defence of the Halifax Libel on the British-American-Colonies* (Boston, 1765), p. 5.

92. In *Pamphlets of the American Revolution*, ed. Bailyn, p. 514.

93. In ibid., pp. 523–44.

94. In ibid., p. 538.

95. In ibid., p. 541.

96. Ezra Stiles Papers, Bancroft Transcripts, pp. 95, 37, 87, 51, NYPL.

97. Newport Tax List, 1772. In 1775, 15 of the top 25 people on the tax assess-

ment were Anglicans. Newport Tax List, 1775, NHS. Loyalists have been identified by using the "List of Names of Some of the Inhabitants left in the Town of Newport, Dec. 8, 1776," in Stiles's *Diary*, II 131; the List of Persons "Gone with the Enemy" in Gov. William Greene to General Nath. Greene, Nov. 14, 1779, Redwood Library, Newport; the "List of those . . . not to be trusted with arms," Box 44, folder 5, NHS; the "List of Congregation [Trinity] before Revolution and dead 1807," NHS; and the List of Loyalist Property Confiscated, George Richardson Scrapbook, p. 65, NHS.

98. *The Trial of the False Apostle, A Sermon Preached in Trinity Church, Newport, Rhode Island, Sunday, Oct. 24, 1773* (Newport, 1773), pp. 12, 10. A copy of this sermon may be found at the Redwood Library in Newport.

99. *Newport Herald*, Apr. 24, 1788.

100. More formally known as the Coercive Acts, this legislation was passed by an angry Parliament in 1774 in response to the Boston Tea Party. It included the Boston Port Bill (Mar. 25), the Administration of Justice Act (May 20), and the Massachusetts Government Act (also on May 20).

101. *Diary*, I 447–48, 550–51.

102. Chief Justice Smyth of New Jersey to Lord Dartmouth, Feb. 8, 1773, Chalmers Papers, p. 73, NYPL.

103. *Diary*, I 447–48, 461, 538, 550–51.

104. A fear that the welcome mat would be pulled from under their feet may have prompted the congregation to add an escape tunnel to the original plans of Touro Synagogue, which was dedicated in 1763. Although there is no hard evidence that the passageway, which still exists, was designed with a hasty exit in mind—and no historian even mentioned the area (which leads to the pulpit in the center of the synagogue) until the 1930s when the synagogue was being restored after a period of disuse—the religious climate in Newport at the time could hardly have encouraged peace of mind. Two of Newport's leading Jewish citizens, Aaron Lopez and Isaac Elizer, were denied naturalization in 1761–1762 at the same time as the Jewish community reluctantly formed a social club of its own after being excluded from the prestigious Artillery Company. See Elaine F. Crane, "Uneasy Coexistence: Religious Tensions in Eighteenth-Century Newport," *Newport History*, 53, No. 3 (Summer 1980), pp. 101–11. One might also add that the 1663 law has been the subject of historical controversy for at least a century. Both Sidney Rider and Samuel Arnold maintain that the 1663 law was a figment of the imagination of the 1719 committee instructed by the General Assembly to compile Rhode Island's statutes. The first known reference to the law appeared in that compilation, and it is Rider's contention that subsequent digests merely perpetuated the error or hoax. Whether this law was passed at the 1663 session, a few years earlier or later—or not at all—is not really relevant. During the eighteenth century, Rhode Island jurists and legislators recognized the statute as law and enforced it. For example, when Aaron Lopez was denied naturalization, it was on the grounds that "by a law made and passed in the year 1663, no person who does not profess the Christian religion can be admitted free of this colony. This court, therefore, unanimously dismiss this petition as wholly inconsistent with the

first principles upon which the colony was founded and a law of the same now in force." Superior Court Records, March Term, 1762, Providence College Archives.

The General Assembly went so far as to repeal this legislation in 1783 as it related to Catholics. For a copy of the 1663 law, see *Acts and Laws of His Majesty's Colony of Rhode-Island* . . . (1730), p. 4. For a discussion of the controversy (and a weak—if vigorous—repudiation of the law), see Sidney S. Rider, *An Inquiry Concerning the Origin of the Clause in the Laws of Rhode Island (1719–1783) Disfranchising Roman Catholics*, Rhode Island Historical Tracts, Second Series, No. 1 (Providence, 1889), pp. 7–53; and Samuel Arnold, *History of the State of Rhode Island and Providence Plantations*, 2 vols. (New York, 1878), II 490–96.

105. John Collins to Governor Samuel Ward, January 4, 1774, as cited in *Correspondence of Governor Samuel Ward*, ed. Knollenberg, p. 24.

106. Thomas Vernon to I. R., Esq., Newport, June 27, 1770, Vernon Papers, Box 79, folder 3, NHS.

107. *NM*, Dec. 27, 1773; Peleg Clarke to Herman Brimmer (in Boston), Newport, Jan. 22, 1774, Peleg Clarke Letter Book, NHS; Lopez Papers, Haight Collection, NHS.

108. *Diary*, I 494.

109. Stiles ranked tories according to the number of stars he assigned them. *Diary*, II 131–34.

110. The Address of the people called Quakers on Rhode Island in Monthly Meeting Assembled the 2nd day of the [1st] mo. 1777. Friends Records, Monthly Meetings, 1773–1790, Book 810, p. 101, NHS.

111. Ibid., pp. 77, 93.

112. Friends Records, Testimonies, 1718–1827, Book 821, pp. 96, 98, 99, NHS.

113. Since there was so much intermarriage in Newport, many people ended up with the same surname. In addition, they received similar given names even within the same generation. This makes it impossible to identify a great number of tories and whigs within the same family.

114. The Coggeshalls, Wantons, Vernons, Malbones, and Almys were among the families with divided allegiances. An amusing anecdote, related by a rebel spy from Newport, gives illustration of the divisiveness within the community. The story is narrated by John Trevett, a Newporter who was serving in the Continental Navy. In 1777 during the British occupation of Newport, his vessel was moored near the town and was short of water: "A short time before daylight the officer turned to me and says, 'Jack, do you know where you can get water handy?' I informed him that I had sailed from this place sometime before, and that there was some good water near Long Wharf. 'Jack,' says the officer, 'step into the boat with 2 hands. . . .' And the officer gave us strict charge not to be gone more than 20 minutes. This was just what I wanted. I went into Mr. Philip Wanton's desk, took out a great cask, and my 2 midshipmen carried it up. I went with them into Mr. Wanton's washroom, where they had a pump, with good water, who should I see there but Mr. George Lawton,

washing his hands; I asked him to lend me a funnel to fill the cask; he told me he had none, but that Mrs. Battey had one, on the Long Wharf. I saw Mr. Lawton looked hard at me, but I made myself scarce. I went to Mrs. Battey's and found her alone, making a fire. I knew her well. I asked her to lend me a funnel; she answered me very short 'no.' As no soul was near I goes up to her and told her she *should* lend me one: she knew my mode of speaking and said, 'for God's sake! where did you come from?' I informed her that I came from Providence. 'How did you leave my son,' says she, meaning Capt. Henry Dayton. I informed her, well. 'Now,' said she, 'speak low, for I have got, overhead, several of the British officers boarding with me, and I expect Mr. Battey ashore this morning, as he is a pilot on board one of the ships of war, and if he sees you he may know you. Here is the funnell; will you eat or drink anything?' I told her no. I must remark 4 or 5 months before, I took up this same Battey for a Tory." John Trevett's Diary, during the Revolution, Box 44, folder 1, NHS.

115. Daniel Coggeshall	Tory	Trinity
Deacon Nath. Coggeshall	Whig	First Congregational
Billings Coggeshall	Whig (?)	Second Congregational
Caleb Coggeshall	?	Second Baptist (12/74)
James Coggeshall	Tory	Quaker
Thomas Coggeshall	Tory	Quaker
John Coggeshall	Whig	Quaker

116. Thomas Vernon to William Vernon, Warwick, Rhode Island, Sept. 30, 1776, Vernon Papers, Box 79, folder 3, NHS. Eventually Thomas Vernon was permitted to return to Newport, and when the British occupied the town in December 1776, he was in a position to repay the favors his brother had generously extended. When the tide of war finally turned in favor of the Americans, Thomas was reduced to different circumstances once again, and was forced to admit that "I have tasted the bitter cup . . . and do daily." His name does not appear on the list of those whose properties were confiscated by the rebels (there were 45 names), and it may be that his influential brother William (by this time president of the Continental Navy Board) had prevented the confiscation. Thomas Vernon to George Rome, Newport, Sept. 23, 1781, quoted in *Thomas Vernon's Letters* (New York, 1880), p. 50. See the List of Loyalist Property Confiscated, George Richardson Scrapbook, p. 65, NHS, and a very similar, though less extensive, list in Box 45, folder 5, NHS.

117. Godfrey Malbone to John Malbone, Dec. 23, 1774, Malbone Papers, Box 174, folder 16, NHS.

118. Deposition of Ebenezer Bradford, Chalmers Papers, p. 61, NYPL; Gov. Wanton to Lord Dartmouth, Apr. 22, 1775, ibid., p. 93.

119. *Rhode Island in the Continental Congress*, ed. Staples, pp. 26–27, 31, 32. See James, *Colonial Rhode Island*, pp. 345–46, for an explanation of Wanton's removal from office.

120. Benjamin Cowell, *The Spirit of '76 in Rhode Island* (Boston, 1850), passim.

121. Godfrey Malbone to John Malbone, Dec. 23, 1774, Malbone Papers, Box 174, folder 16, NHS.

122. Thomas Vernon to I. R., Esq., June 27, 1770, Vernon Papers, Box 79, folder 3, NHS.

123. Quoted in Lovejoy, *Rhode Island Politics*, pp. 103–104.

124. Quoted in *Pamphlets of the American Revolution*, ed. Bailyn, p. 525. See also *NM*, Jan. 24, Apr. 18, 1763; Apr. 13, 1764.

125. Stephen Ayrault to Messrs Vardon and Franklin, Nov. 10, 1769, Ayrault Papers, NHS.

126. Thomas Vernon to I. R., Esq., June 27, 1770, Vernon Papers, Box 79, folder 3, NHS.

127. Jonathan Murray to Francis Brinley, July 18, 1775, Haight Collection, NHS; James Wallace to Admiral Graves, June 5, 1775, quoted in Roelker & Collins, "Patrol of Narragansett Bay . . . by H.M.S. *Rose* . . . [Part II]," 89; Samuel Ward to Henry Ward, June 15, 1775, *Correspondence of Governor Samuel Ward*, ed. Knollenberg, p. 47. Samuel Southwick of the *NM* described the event less dramatically: "A number of people collected together and insisted on having the flour given up, which was accomplished before sunset." *NM*, June 5, 1775.

128. *NM*, Oct. 9, 1775, Jan. 1, 1776, Oct. 31, 1774.

129. Vice Admiral Samuel Graves to Capt. James Wallace, Boston, Sept. 30, 1775, in *Naval Documents of the American Revolution*, ed. William Bell Clark, 4 vols. (Washington, D.C., 1964——), II 253.

130. Stephen Ayrault to Mr. Thomas Swanson, Aug. 7, 1770, Ayrault Papers, NHS.

131. Stiles, *Diary*, II 134.

132. This list may be found in Box 44, folder 5, NHS.

133. Stiles, *Diary*, II 125–27; *Newport Gazette*, Jan. 16, 1777.

134. Jane Clarke, "Metcalf Bowler as a British Spy," *Rhode Island Historical Society Collections*, 23 (1930), 101–17.

135. Felix O'Hara to Aaron Lopez, Gaspee, Nov. 24, 1775, Lopez Papers, Haight Collection, NHS.

136. *NM*, Sept. 9, 1765; Oct. 25, 1773, Mar. 14, Aug. 22, Sept. 5, Oct. 3, Dec. 5, 1774.

137. Stephen Ayrault to Thomas Griffity, Dec. 27, 1770, Box marked "Stephen Ayrault's Letters to Friends and Business Associates, 1767–1778," NHS.

138. Henry Marchant to Catharine Macauly, Newport, Nov. 21, 1772, Marchant Journal, September 1772 – March 1773, Box 45, NHS: Bisset, *Trial of a False Apostle*, p. 11.

139. John Anderson, *The Rhode Island Almanack for 1775*, *in National Index of American Imprints Through 1800: The Short-Title Evans*, edd. Clifford K. Shipton and James E. Mooney, no. 13115.

140. *NM*, Apr. 24, 1775; Apr. 28, 1776; Feb. 7, 1774; Nov. 22, 1773; Aug. 29, 1763; Sept. 13, 1773; Apr. 10, Aug. 7, 1775.

141. Quoted in Weeden, *Early Rhode Island*, p. 293.

142. *NM*, May 31, 1773.

143. As quoted in Arnold, *History of the State of Rhode Island*, II 514–15.

144. Robert Morris to the Governor of Rhode Island [William Greene], Aug. 2, 1782, Morris Letter Book, Library of Congress.

145. *Diary*, II 427; Downing & Scully, *Architectural Heritage*, p. 92.

146. Edmund Dixon to William Wakefield, Newport, Feb. 20, 1777, in Charles M. Andrews, *Guide to the Materials for American History, to 1783, in the Public Record Office of Great Britain*, 2 vols. (Washington, D.C., 1912; repr. 1965), II 325.

147. *Diary*, II 427.

148. James Clarke to Miss A. Coggeshall, Halifax, Feb. 5, 1786, Box 45, folder 5, NHS.

Epilogue

FROM THE DREARY APPEARANCE OF THE TOWN in the 1780s few strangers would have guessed that before the war Newport was " 'one of the pleasantest places in the world.' "[1] No longer was the community a cultural haven whose very name was synonymous with elegance and urbanity. Instead of prosperity and conviviality a post-war visitor encountered a "reign of solitude . . . only interrupted by groups of idle men standing with folded arms at the corners of the streets, houses falling to ruin, miserable shops which present nothing but a few coarse stuffs or baskets of apples, and other articles of little value; grass growing in the public squares in front of the court of justice, rags stuffed in the windows."[2] The destruction of Newport seemed to extend to the very spirit of the people.

So many houses had been destroyed during the war that although the population had been reduced to half, a number of people were forced to live together in single dwellings. The 1782 census showed 5,530 people living in Newport.[3] Most of the names on the list were carryovers from pre-war days; some were new. Both English and French forces had occupied the town in the intervening years. With their departure, the curious mixture of whigs and tories was left to get on with each other as best they could. Not surprisingly, by 1782 the whigs had the upper hand. Their ascendancy began in the fall of 1779 when the British troops withdrew from Newport and the Rhode Island General Assembly passed legislation enabling the state to confiscate the property of any British sympathizer. At the same session the legislature deprived loyalists of the right to vote. Whig retaliation for real and imagined injuries reached its height in the summer of 1780 when the Assembly banished the leading tories from Rhode Island, presumably forever.[4]

Forever turned out to be a somewhat shorter period of time than one would have expected from the passionate language of the legislative act. By November 1780 Stephen Ayrault's confiscated lands were reassigned so that he could collect rent on them. By 1783 this "principal and active tory," as Ezra Stiles had labeled him, had resumed his place among the town's leading taxpayers.[5] Due to whig opposition, it took Robert Stoddard and John Mawdsley a little longer to receive permission to return home. Their return to the fold started in the fall of 1782 when Francis Malbone, no ardent whig himself, circulated a petition, hoping to gain support for their return. The whigs circulated a counter petition, which "prevented a great number from subscribing" to Malbone's.[6] Despite the hostility, this was one of the last outbursts against the loyalists. By 1784 John Mawdsley's lands had been returned to him, and Mawdsley and Stoddard were restored to full citizenship, along with John Freebody, a two-star tory.[7] By the mid-1780s, former enemies were commercial partners.

What the records only barely suggest is the suffering caused by the banishment and confiscation legislation. Although the wives of many loyalists fled with their husbands into the wilderness of Nova Scotia, New York, or London, some chose to remain in Newport. Whether political consciousness or economic self-interest dictated the choice is not so much at issue as the fact that the separation of husband and wife created great hardship, especially for the women left behind.

The Rhode Island statute governing confiscation of property was particularly harsh toward women, and assumed that a wife's loyalty to her husband superseded her loyalty to the state. Thus, in October 1780 the General Assembly declared that "widows of loyalists are, and shall be, taken and deemed to be forever barred and excluded from any claim of dower. . . ." Having vented its anger in this manner, the General Assembly then sat down to deal with the problem of loyalist wives and widows who had no other visible means of support. Faced with a petition from the widow Elizabeth Wightman whose loyalist husband left her "utterly unable to support herself and family," the General Assembly softened its position and allowed her to collect one-third of the rents and profits from his confiscated estate. Sarah Wanton, widow of Colonel Joseph Wanton, also pleaded with the General Assembly for assistance, since she was without "the necessaries of life," and they permitted her to collect the rents from her former home—a less than magnanimous gesture, since a considerable amount of that property had been hers prior to marriage. Eunice Hazard, whose husband was a loyalist refugee in New York, begged the legislature to consider her "unhappy case" and return some of her husband's property to her. In much the same way as former holdings were restored to avowed loyalists, the General Assembly meted out property to women like Eunice

Hazard whose husbands, for whatever reason, did not return to Newport.[8]

Another such woman was Kitty Dudley, who followed her exiled husband, Charles, to England in 1778, but returned to Newport without him six years later. As one of the king's men, Charles Dudley hoped to receive a post in Nova Scotia, but the mournful correspondence between him and his wife indicates that his great expectations went unfulfilled, and he died in England about 1790.[9]

As time went on, the former loyalists who trickled into town created little animosity and less furor. The people, like the town itself, were spent. Both sides had lost so much that further protest seemed a waste of time and resources. Moreover, once the census taker reported his findings in 1782, both whig and tory probably welcomed any man who wanted to return to Newport, no matter what his former or future political persuasion.

Most striking about the census returns of 1782 was the tremendous imbalance in the number of women over men in the community. This trend, evident in 1774, was glaring in 1782. In the latter year white males made up only 37% of the community; white females, 51%. But as imbalanced as those figures are, they become even more skewed when children under 16 are eliminated from the calculations. Adult white males constituted only 17.6% of the town, while adult white females accounted for 30.6% of the population.[10] The sex ratio was even more disproportionate when the white population is extracted from the total community.

The situation had improved slightly by 1790 when the census takers made their next rounds, but the sex ratio was still nowhere near balanced. White females represented 50% of the community; white males, 40%. The percentage of white males above 16 climbed from 17.6% in 1782 to 21.6% in 1790, but women still heavily outnumbered men.[11] As the proportion of women in Newport's population escalated during the Revolutionary years, there may have been a growing concern about the economic viability of the community, and a great deal of worry over the way to support the growing number of widows and poor families who were dependent on the town for survival. The remaining men may also have been concerned about the erosion of the town's political base and the way in which this might affect its relationship with other communities throughout Rhode Island. When Newport dominated Rhode Island both economically and numerically, no one seriously challenged the town's disproportionate representation in the colonial legislature. With Newport's decline, however, rumblings of discontent were heard from people in the country towns who urged more equal representation in the state legislature.[12]

Furthermore, though the number of people in Newport in 1782 remained virtually unchanged from its low of 5,299 in September 1776, the composition of the population changed dramatically during that time.[13] When the British withdrew in 1779, many sympathizers who were fearful of reprisals left with them. A number of whigs who had fled on the eve of occupation in December 1776 returned in time to cheer the French on their arrival in the summer of 1780. Thus, by 1782, partisans from both camps had already lived side by side for some time.

With these considerations as background, it becomes understandable why there was so little resistance to the former British sympathizers who returned to Newport. They would have no political power in the sense of party politics, yet their very numbers would lend weight to Newport's position in the General Assembly in relation to the other towns—no small matter. Inherently pragmatic, Newporters may have reasoned that any person who could help reverse the tide would be tolerated despite previous political affiliation. Yet it must have been difficult to face a former enemy. What rules of etiquette governed the patriot confronting a tory neighbor bereft by loss? How did a loyalist father greet a rebel son on his return from the war? The rebels became patriots only by virtue of victory. Had victory eluded them, had the tables been turned, they would have been traitors, and the loyalists patriots.

Some of the most dedicated—and affluent—loyalists could not or would not return to Newport. Many remained in Canada; some, in England. The Society for the Propagation of the Gospel reassigned the Rev. George Bisset to a mission in New Brunswick, a gesture which greatly pleased the tory minister. In a letter from England to the former customs collector, Charles Dudley, Bisset showed an unabashed eagerness to return home. "I think if I once more get a hold of American ground the Devil will not be able to make me lose it. . . ."

Former Governor Joseph Wanton died toward war's end, and his brother William was apparently content eking out an existence in New York and reminiscing with another Newport loyalist, Samuel Goldthwaite. John Bell died bearing arms in His Majesty's service. From England George Rome continued to petition for compensation. He might have done better to wait out the war in Newport. In the end, Rome lost everything by casting his future among the British. Not so for other loyalists who were, perhaps, not as vociferously tory as Rome, but clearly as sympathetic to the crown. According to a 1783 tax assessment, those loyalists and patriots who emerged from the war physically unscathed were in the same relative financial position as they had been in in the pre-war years. The town's leading taxpayer in 1783 was an unabashed tory: Stephen Ayrault.[14]

At first glance, then, the tax assessment gives no clues to the civil disorders that had rocked the community for at least seven years. But further inspection suggests that certain disturbances had taken place. First, the total number of taxpayers was reduced from a pre-war high of 1,210 in 1772 to 628 in 1783. Table VII, which compares the concentration of wealth in 1783 to the pre-war years, indicates that wealth was becoming less concentrated. Furthermore, 63% of adult white males were assessed, an increase of 6% over 1772. Women, on the other hand, accounted for less than 3% of the total number of taxpayers, which was a slight retreat from their pre-war position.

The 1782 census figures also suggest upheaval in Newport, and not only in terms of a disproportionate sex ratio. Since the 1774 tally, the proportion of blacks in the town had dropped to 11% of the total population. A third of the blacks were free. Runaways were partly responsible for the decline in number, and the general economic downturn during the war may have precipitated many of the manumissions. Perhaps as many as twenty-five earned their freedom by serving in the Continental Army under Colonel Christopher Greene. Masters who sacrificed their slaves in the cause of liberty were well compensated for their loss, and it is interesting that both loyalists and rebel owners took advantage of this offer by the Rhode Island General Assembly.[15]

At the same time, there can be little doubt that Revolutionary oratory stimulated emancipation to some extent. When the Rhode Island General Assembly finally provided for the gradual abolition of slavery in 1784, it was because "all men are entitled to life, liberty, and the pursuit of happiness." And in a complete turnabout, the legislature placed responsibility for the support and education of blacks with the town rather than with former owners.[16] The loophole in the act, of course, was that it only freed children born of slaves after March 1784. Nevertheless, by 1790 when legislation encompassing Jefferson's catchy phrase was six years old, there were more free blacks than slaves in Newport for the first time.[17]

161

TABLE VII

Concentration of Wealth in Highest Taxpayers,
1760, 1772, 1775, 1783

33 highest taxpayers

year	% of tax paid	% of total taxpayers
1760	27	3.4
1772	30	2.7
1775	34	3.3
1783	28.5	5.2

86 highest taxpayers

year	% of tax paid	% of total taxpayers
1760	50	8.9
1772	51	7.1
1775	57.5	8.7
1783	49.8	13.6

Source: "Assessment List of . . . June 1760," Rhode Island State Archives, Providence;
Tax assessments for 1772, 1775, NHS; 1783, RIHS.
Total number of taxpayers:
   1760: 962
   1772: 1210
   1775: 985
   1783: 628

Legislation providing for abolition of the slave trade was a stickier problem, given Newport's history. The Rev. Samuel Hopkins, who continued to agitate against slavery and the slave trade, was less than satisfied with the scope of the emancipation legislation and in 1784 was somewhat "gloomy" about the prospects of ever abolishing the trade itself. "This town . . . will be the last in the State to do what they ought to do, and be foremost in it, respecting that most abominable traffic. . . ."[18] Despite his forebodings and much to his surprise, the Assembly did pass "An Act to prevent the slave trade, and to encourage the abolition of slavery" in October 1787, with only four dissenting votes.[19] Dr. Hopkins knew his congregation all too well to be encouraged by the bill. Realizing that the act as worded permitted the re-exportation of slaves from the West Indies, Hopkins worried that "this law will soon be like some other Rhode Island laws"—i.e., circumvented.[20] His assessment was correct. Sullen merchants continued to outfit ships for the African coast as if the legislation had never existed, justifying their actions by arguing that "it is the African trade that prolongs the existence of this declining town; and the poor of this place well evince who benefits them most, the African Trader or the Abolition Man."[21]

But even though Newport retained its role as the major American carrier in the immediate post-war years, the general economic slump, a lack of markets, legislation against the traffic, and French privateering combined to thwart Rhode Island slave traders. The town fitted out approximately 149 African ventures between 1783 and 1807, handling considerably less volume than in the pre-war years.[22] Writing at the end of the eighteenth century, historian Jeremy Belknap noted that because of this decline, " 'the town of Newport has gone to decay.' "[23]

Decay and deterioration were not easy to erase. At least three whig churches had been converted to hospitals during the war years, and it was not until 1785 that the Rev. Stiles's "dear exiled Flock"[24] regathered in its newly refurbished meeting house to hear their former minister—now president of Yale University. Trinity Church suffered no abuse during the occupation since it suited the needs of both occupying forces; nor did harm come to the Friends' Meeting House—presumably because it housed ambivalent neutrals. In 1781 the French army took possession of the Quaker meeting house, but released it after intercession by the governor.[25] The physical structure of Touro Synagogue was also spared, perhaps because its congregation was considered "foreign" or, more likely, because some of its members supported the British cause. So few Jews remained in Newport after the war, however, that the synagogue saw no communal worship for nearly forty years, and only sporadic services during the following decades.

If joining the rebels was less an option than a forced gamble for Newporters in 1776, the outcome of the Revolution hardly justified the risks. Their independence was confirmed, to be sure, but in terms of what they had hoped to gain by it, they had little to show. Some, but surely not all, might point to the gradual abolition of slavery as a Revolutionary achievement; a few might add that the few Jews left in Newport were enfranchised in 1777, and therefore were no longer "deprived . . . of the invaluable rights of free citizens," as they had "hitherto been." Others might note that Catholics were given the same "rights and privileges" as Protestants in 1783.[26] All this was small comfort to those who remembered the heady days when "the four winds of the earth" filled the harbor with ships and brought prosperity to the island town.

For Newport, independence brought dislocation rather than benefit, and the tories could have said I-told-you-so. The seaport was in shambles, and although the merchants tried to resuscitate their failing commercial empire, they were unable to restore it to its pre-war eminence. Former merchant magnates, such as Christopher Champlin, attempted to open a correspondence with shipping houses in Portugal, France, Germany, and Russia. Along with the usual cargoes, they began to market tobacco and rice, but the crops from Maryland and South Carolina were scarce, and of poor quality.

A British Order in Council closed the West Indies to American shipping, a turn of events the colonists had never seriously contemplated.[27] Although Newport merchants were hardly unfamiliar with illegal trading, the British action could only be termed catastrophic to a community so heavily dependent on the Caribbean trade. At the same time, the British placed a heavy duty on the importation of whale oil and eliminated one more means by which merchants could pay for manufactured goods. With American ports open to all, Newport's merchants faced additional competition from foreigners. This turned out to be a considerable burden when it came time to assemble cargoes for shipment abroad.

Newport merchants even turned to their old tricks in a vain attempt to recapture their former commercial prominence. Before the war was formally over the Quakers showed "an unwarrantable desire after the perishing things of this world," and were found "guilty of falshood and deceit in clearing out vessels and other Clandestine dealing" by their brethren in New York.[28]

It was all to no avail. By the 1780s merchants had "intirely relinquished all trade both foreign and domestick and [were] compelled to live penuriously on their diminished capital." This diminished capital allowed them only minimal participation in the infant China trade, and merchants who had once offered support to those who were poor, out of work, and "destitute of the means of subsistence" could no longer afford to do so.[29] Since this dependence on the more affluent was part of the natural order of eighteenth-century society, a lack of it was almost revolutionary in itself.

Independence for the rest of the American colonies meant that people could direct their attention to the West. Colonists moved west; eastern urban centers quickly saw the possibility of new markets. Thwarted from trading with the English islands, Newport merchants were in no position to capitalize on this new prospect. The city—what was left of it—was on an island, severed from the mainland by water on all sides. Newport's predicament was Providence's opportunity. As the relatively undamaged cities of Providence, Boston, New York, and Philadelphia expanded their spheres of influence, Newport stagnated, unable to compete for markets best served by highways, canals, and eventually railroads. Newport had always looked east; the time had come to look west.

Internal controversies also rocked Newport's stability in the post-war era. Intensive squabbling over paper money resulted in a repeal of Newport's city charter a scarce three years after it had been granted in 1784.[30] Rhode Island's snub of the federal Constitution irked its sister states, and once again Newport was the subject of calumny and economic sanctions. Although the merchants of that town were no more eager to turn over revenue to the federal government than to England, it became increasingly evident that Rhode Island was too small and weak to remain an independent country. Newport threatened to secede from Rhode Island and rejoin the United States if the General Assembly did not authorize a ratifying convention.[31] Finally, in 1790 Rhode Island invited the United States to join its company.

In the first decade of the nineteenth century, efforts at small manufacturing failed, and it was not until nearly mid-century that Newport began to regain some reputation as a resort community. Sails filled the harbor once more, but they belonged to pleasure craft rather than to merchant vessels as in the old days. Today Newport is again recognized as the "queen of the summer places," by no less an authority than *The New York Times*, but it has never regained its pre-Revolutionary commercial stature.[32]

After the Revolution the loyalists could claim rightly that they had the more accurate perception of what a war would do to the city's mercantile interests. It did little good to dwell on the past, however; what was done, was done. "Liberty" had been sacrificed to "ambition and rebellion," and the "Garden of Eden" had been transformed into "a field of blood." For the loyalists, consolation lay in the thought that they had resisted this "public ruin" to the best of their ability. Indeed, tory consciences could be clear because they had not been "accessary to the ruin of [their] country."[33]

If those Newporters demanding independence could have foreseen the future in 1776, would they have been so eager to sever the bonds of empire? Perhaps not. But as it was, their actions and commitment to the cause surely encouraged the faint-hearted and brought other Americans more swiftly to a decision for independence than might otherwise have been the case.

NOTES

1. Unpublished journal of the Baron du Bourg, aide-de-camp to General Rochambeau, as quoted in Thomas Willing Balch, *The French in America During the War of Independence of the United States, 1777–1783* (Philadelphia, 1891), p. 143.

2. Brissot de Warville, *New Travels in the United States*, pp. 144–45.

3. "The Rhode Island Census of 1782," *New England Historical and Genealogical Register*, 127 (1973), 5–17, 138–42; "A Summary of the Inhabitants in the several Towns in the State of Rhode Island, taken A.D. 1782, by order of the General Assembly of Said State," RICR, IX 653. The original MS census is at RIHS.

4. "An Act for the confiscating the estates of certain persons Therein described," RICR, VIII 609–14; see also ibid., 605–606, as well as "An Act to prevent certain persons Therein named, and others, who have left this State, or either of the United States of America, and joined the enemy; or who have joined the enemy in this State, from being admitted within this State," ibid., IX 139–42.

5. RICR, IX 289; Stiles, *Diary*, II 134; Town Rate, July 31, 1783, Newport, Rhode Island, RIHS.

6. Samuel Vernon III to William Vernon, Oct. 30, 1782, Vernon Letter Book #77, NHS.

7. RICR, IX 728, X 10, 46–48; Stiles, *Diary*, II 132.

8. RICR, IX 252, 15, 350–51, 530; X 43, 116.

9. Correspondence between Charles and Kitty Dudley, 1775–1785, Haight Collection, NHS.

10. In 1774 white males made up 39.7% of the town; white females, 46.2%. Though the proportion of women in the population grew steadily during the war years, the number of female heads of households did not keep pace with this demographic change. Women headed 20% of the households in Newport in 1774, and 22% in 1782. Of these 22%, 17% were widows.

11. United States Bureau of the Census, *Heads of Families at the First Census of the United States Taken in the Year 1790: Rhode Island* (Washington, D.C., 1908).

12. Polishook, *Rhode Island and the Union*, pp. 23, 44–45.

13. RICR, VII 616. Ezra Stiles, who continued to compile statistics both during the war and after, estimated that only ⅓ of the town's pre-war population remained by the fall of 1776, despite official estimates. *Diary*, II 111, 112.

14. George Bisset to Charles Dudley, Dec. 20, 1785, Simon Gratz Collection, Historical Society of Pennsylvania. Aaron Lopez, the leading taxpayer in 1772 and 1775, never returned to Newport. He drowned accidentally in March 1782; Town Rate, July 31, 1783, Newport, Rhode Island, RIHS.

15. Charles Battle, *Negroes on the Island of Rhode Island* (Newport, 1932), pp. 9–10; *At the General Assembly . . . of the State of Rhode Island . . . February 1778 (Attleborough)* (Newport, 1778), pp. 14–18.

16. "An Act authorizing the manumission of Negroes, mulattoes, and others, and for the gradual abolition of slavery," RICR, X 7–8.

17. In 1790, 3% of the community were slaves; 6%, free blacks. Census Bureau, *Heads of Families at the First Census*, pp. 9, 19–23.

18. Dr. Samuel Hopkins to Moses Brown, Newport, Apr. 29, 1784, *Documents*, III 336. Hopkins must have known that Rhode Island was "the last New England colony to forego the trade before the war [and] the first state to resume it when peaceful commerce was again possible." Donnan, "New England Slave Trade," 225.

19. RICR, X 262.

20. Samuel Hopkins to Levi Hart, Nov. 27, 1787, as cited in *Documents*, III 344n2.

21. *Newport Herald*, Sept. 2, 1790.

22. Hamm, "American Slave Trade with Africa" chap. 3.

23. As quoted in *Commerce*, I 398–99n1.

24. *Diary*, II 216.

25. Arthur Mekeel, *The Relation of the Quakers to the American Revolution* (Washington, D.C., 1979), p. 222.

26. Richard B. Morris, "Civil Liberties and the Jewish Tradition in Early America," in *The Jewish Experience in America*, ed. Abraham Karp, 5 vols. (Waltham, Mass., & New York, 1969), I 417; Moses Seixas to George Washington, Aug. 17, 1790, in *A Documentary History of the Jews in the United States*, ed. Morris U. Schappes (New York, 1971), p. 79; RICR, IX 674–75.

27. "The King's proclamation, respecting the trade between the British West India Islands and the United States, has very much surprised and alarmed the people of the latter, who, having formerly traded freely with those islands, confidently expected always to do it." Edward Bancroft to William Frazer, Nov. 8, 1783, Bancroft Papers, America and England, 1783–1786, I 91, NYPL. See also the second volume of *Commerce*, passim.

28. Friends Records, Monthly Meetings, 29th of 1st mo. 1782, 1773–1790, Book 810, p. 222, NHS.

29. Memorial of the Town of Newport to the General Assembly, October 1781, NHS.

30. "An Act to incorporate the town of Newport into a city," RICR, X 30, 217, 234.

31. Polishook, *Rhode Island and the Union*, pp. 209–10.

32. *The New York Times*, July 8, 1979, Section 10, p. 7.

33. Rev. George Bisset, *Honesty the Best Policy in the Worst of Times, Illustrated and Proved from the Exemplary Conduct of Joseph of Arimathea, and Its Consequent Rewards with an Application to the Case of the Suffering Loyalists: A Sermon Intended to have been Preached at Newport, Rhode Island, on the Sunday preceding the Evacuation of that Garrison by His Majesty's troops, and Afterwards Preached at St. Paul's and St. George's Chapels, New York, on Sunday, October 7, 1780* (London, 1784), pp. 16–17.

BIBLIOGRAPHY

Bibliographic Aids

Andrews, Charles M. *Guide to the Materials for American History, to 1783, in the Public Record Office of Great Britain.* 2 vols. Washington, D.C., 1912, 1914.

Bartlett, John Russell. *Bibliography of Rhode Island.* Providence, 1864.

Brigham, Clarence. *Bibliography of Rhode Island History.* Boston & Syracuse, 1902.

——. *History and Bibliography of American Newspapers, 1690–1820.* 2 vols. Worcester, Mass., 1947.

——. "Report on the Archives of Rhode Island." *American Historical Association Annual Report,* 1 (1903), 543–70, 606–609.

Evans, Charles. *American Bibliography: A Chronological Dictionary of All Books, Pamphlets, and Periodical Publications Printed in the United States of America from 1639–1820.* 14 vols. New York, 1941–1959.

Greene, Evarts B., and Morris, Richard B. *Guide to Sources for Early American History in New York City, 1600–1800.* New York, 1953.

Griffin, G. G. *A Guide to Manuscripts Relating to American History in British Depositories.* Washington, D.C., 1914.

Hammett, Charles E. *A Contribution to the Bibliography and Literature of Newport, Rhode Island.* Newport, 1887.

Index to the Printed Acts and Resolves of Petitions and Reports to the General Assembly of the State of Rhode Island and Providence Plantations from the year 1758–1850. Ed. John Russell Bartlett. Providence, 1856.

Manuscript Sources in the Library of Congress for Research on the American Revolution. Edd. John Sellers et al. Washington, D.C., 1975.

The New-York Historical Society: Guide to the Manuscript Collections. Ed. Arthur J. Breton. 2 vols. Westport, Conn., 1972.

Rhode Island Imprints: A List of Books, Pamphlets, Newspapers, Broadsides, Printed at Newport, Providence, Warren, Rhode Island Between 1727 and 1800. Providence, 1915.

Rhode Island Imprints, 1727–1800. Ed. John E. Alden. New York, 1949.

Repositories, Special Collections, Manuscripts

The Library of Congress

Newport County Court House

Newport Historical Society (NHS)

Great Britain, Public Record Office,
Treasury I, Vol. 471

Ayrault, Stephen
Banister, John
Bennett, John
Bowler, Metcalf
Brenton, Jahleel
Brett, John
Brinley, Francis
Brown, John
Carpenter family
Champlin, Christopher
Channing family
Clarke, James
Coggeshall, James and family
Collins family
Collins, Josiah
Dudley, Charles (collector of customs)
   account books
Durfee family
Ellery family
Franklin family
Freebody family
Greene family
Hall, Samuel
Hazard family
Hookey family
Hopkins family
Hopkins, Stephen
Hunter family
Isaacks, Jacob
Lawton family
Lopez, Aaron
Malbone family
Marchant, Henry
Mumford family
Osborne, Samuel and Jeremiah
Peckham family

Redwood, Abraham
Richardson family
Rome, George
Scott family
Taggart, Henry
Thurston family
Trevett, John
Vernon family
Wanton family
Whitehorne, John
Wickham, Benjamin
Wightman family

Baptist Church records
Bonds and Indentures
Charters
Congregational Church records
Court Cases Pending
Court Papers
Freemen lists
Friends' Records
Killington, Vermont, plot of lots, 1764
Loyalists
Peleg Clarke letter book
Revolution
Sheriff Papers
Slave Trade
Slavery
Vice Admiralty Court
Town Meeting Records
Town Council Records
John Trevett's Diary during the
  Revolution
Woodstock, First Division of the
  Township

New-York Historical Society (NYHS) Papers Pertaining to the Slave Trade
New York Public Library Chalmers Papers
Redwood Library, Newport
Rhode Island Historical Society (RIHS)
Rhode Island State Archives

Newspapers

Newport Mercury, 1758–1776.
Newport Gazette, selected issues
Massachusetts Gazette and News Letter, selected issues
Newport Herald, 1790

Census and Tax Lists, Account Books, Court Records

Colony of Rhode Island: Amount of People, 1730, 1748, 1755. NHS.

Customs 16/1. Customhouse reports. A record of American imports, exports, tonnage and duties, by port. 1768–1773. Public Record Office, Great Britain; transcript, Library of Congress.

"Account of the People in the Colony of Rhode Island, Whites and Blacks, Together with the Quantity of Arms and Ammunition in the hands of private persons" (1755). NHS.

"Assessment List of £3110 Lawful Money made By Us the Assessors by Order of the General Assembly of the English Colony of Rhode Island and Providence Plantations in New England—In America began and holden by adjournment at Newport in Said Colony, The Second Monday of June, 1760." Rhode Island State Archives, Providence.

"A List of the Polls and Estates Real and Personal of the Proprietors and Inhabitants of the town of Newport in the Colony of Rhode Island taken persuant to an Act of the Rhode Island General Assembly passed in June 1767." NHS.

"A List of the Names of the Persons who Proxed for General Officers of the Government for the Ensuing Year [April 15, 1767]." Rhode Island State Archives, Providence.

Tax Assessment for the town of Newport, 1772. NHS.

"An Account of the Number of Families and Inhabitants of the Town of Newport, 1774." Rhode Island Archives.

Tax Assessment for the town of Newport, 1775. NHS.

Town rate, Newport, Rhode Island, July 31, 1783. RIHS.

Occupants of Houses in Newport During the Revolution. NHS.

Manuscript Census, Newport, 1782. RIHS.

Account Book B, Treasurer 1761–1796. NHS.

Miscellaneous Records, Newport, Rhode Island (1 vol.). NHS.

Records of the Inferior Court of Common Pleas, Newport County (Newport County Court House).

Records of the Superior Court of Judicature, Newport County (Newport County Court House).

Customs Office Letters 1767–1775. Book 90, NHS.

Printed Sources: Primary

Acts and Laws of His Majesty's Colony of Rhode-Island, and Providence Plantations. In America. Boston, 1719.

Acts and Laws of His Majesty's Colony of Rhode-Island, and Providence Plantations. In America. Newport, 1730.

Acts and Laws of the English Colony of Rhode-Island and Providence Plantations, in New England, in America. Revised Codification. Newport, 1767.

Acts and Laws of His Majesty's Colony of Rhode-Island and Providence Plantations, Made and Passed Since the Revision in June, 1767. Newport, 1772.

Adams, John. *The Works of John Adams.* Ed. Charles Francis Adams. 10 vols. Boston, 1850–1856.

"Address of the Colony of Rhode Island to the Continental Congress Relative to Its Condition." *The Newport Historical Magazine,* 7 (July 1886 – April 1887), 304.

The American Revolution: An Atlas of Eighteenth-Century Maps and Charts. Ed. W. B. Greenwood. Washington, D.C., 1972.

Anderson, John. *The Rhode Island Almanack for 1775.* Newport, 1774. In *National Index of American Imprints Through 1800: The Short Title-Evans.* Edd. Clifford K. Shipton and James E. Mooney. No. 13115.

Berkeley, George. *The Works of George Berkeley.* Ed. Alexander C. Fraser. 4 vols. Oxford, 1901.

Bisset, George. *Honesty the Best Policy in the Worst of Times, Illustrated and Proved from the Exemplary Conduct of Joseph of Arimathea, and Its Consequent Rewards with an Application to the Case of the Suffering Loyalists: A Sermon Intended to have been Preached at Newport, Rhode Island, on the Sunday Preceding the Evacuation of that Garrison by His Majesty's troops, and Afterwards Preached at St. Paul's and St. George's Chapels, New York, on Sunday, October 7, 1780.* London, 1784.

———. *The Trial of the False Apostle, A Sermon Preached in Trinity Church, Newport, Rhode Island, Sunday, Oct. 24, 1773.* Newport, 1773.

Bridenbaugh, Carl. "Patrick M'Roberts' Tour through Part of the North Provinces of America." *The Pennsylvania Magazine of History and Biography,* 59 (1935), 134–80.

Brissot de Warville, Jacques Pierre. *New Travels in the United States of America Performed in 1788.* London, 1792.

Browne, James. *The Letter Book of James Browne of Providence, Merchant, 1735–38.* Freeport, N.Y., 1971.

Census of the Inhabitants of the Colony of Rhode Island and Providence Plantations, 1774. Ed. John Russell Bartlett. Providence, 1858.

Chastellux, François Jean Marquis de. *Travels in North America in the Years 1780, 1781, and 1782 by the Marquis de Chastellux.* Trans. Howard C. Rice. 2 vols. Chapel Hill, N.C., 1963.

Commerce of Rhode Island, 1726–1800. Collections of the Massachusetts Historical Society. 7th Series. Nos. 9 and 10. Boston, 1914, 1915.

Cooke, Nicholas. "Revolutionary Correspondence of Governor Nicholas Cooke." *Proceedings of the American Antiquarian Society,* 46 (1926).

The Correspondence of the Colonial Governors of Rhode Island, 1723–1775. Ed. Gertrude Kimball. 2 vols. Freeport, N.Y., 1969.

A Documentary History of the Jews in the United States. Ed. Morris U. Schappes. New York, 1971.

Documents Illustrative of the Slave Trade. Ed. Elizabeth Donnan. 4 vols. Washington, D.C., 1930–1935.

Documents of the American Revolution. Ed. K. C. Davies. 21 vols. Colonial Office Series. Dublin, 1972——.

Drowne, Solomon. "Solomon Drowne's Journal." *The Newport Historical Magazine,* 1 (July 1880 – April 1881), 67–68.

Greene, Nathanael. *The Papers of Nathanael Greene.* Ed. Richard K. Showman. 3 vols. to date. Chapel Hill, N.C., 1976–1984.

Hamilton, Alexander. *Gentleman's Progress: The Itinerarium of Dr. Alexander Hamilton, 1744.* Ed. Carl Bridenbaugh. Chapel Hill, N.C., 1948.

Hopkins, Samuel. *Timely Articles on Slavery.* Miami, 1969.

——. *The Works of Samuel Hopkins.* 3 vols. Boston, 1854.

Hopkins, Stephen. *The Rights of Colonies Examined.* Providence, 1765.

Howard, Martin. *A Letter from a Gentleman at Halifax to His Friend in Rhode-Island.* Newport, 1765.

Journals of the Continental Congress, 1774–1789. Edd. Washington C. Ford et al. 34 vols. Washington, D.C., 1904–1937.

Lees, John. "Rhode Island in 1768." *Rhode Island Historical Society Collections,* 14 (1921), 123.

"Memorial of the Inhabitants of the Town of Newport, Rhode Island, to the Delegates of the United Colonies of America, in Congress at Philadelphia in 1775." *Rhode Island Historical Magazine,* 6, No. 1 (July 1885), 8–9.

Morris, Robert. *The Papers of Robert Morris, 1781–1784.* Edd. E. James Ferguson and John Catanzariti. 5 vols. Pittsburgh, 1973——.

Naval Documents of the American Revolution. Ed. William Bell Clark. 4 vols. Washington, D.C., 1964——.

"Newport Anti-Stamp Act Resolutions, 1769–1770." *The Newport Historical Magazine,* 3 (July 1882 – April 1883), 253.

Otis, James Jr. *Brief Remarks on the Defence of the Halifax Libel on the British-American-Colonies.* Boston, 1765.

Pamphlets of the American Revolution. I. *1750–1776.* Ed. Bernard Bailyn. Cambridge, Mass., 1965.

Prologue to Revolution: Sources and Documents on the Stamp Act Crisis, 1764–1766. Ed. Edmund S. Morgan. Chapel Hill, N.C., 1959.

Records of the Colony of Rhode Island and Providence Plantations. Ed. John Russell Bartlett. 10 vols. Providence, 1862.

Records of the Vice Admiralty Court of Rhode Island, 1716–52. Ed. Dorothy S. Towle. Washington, D.C., 1936.

"The Rhode Island Census of 1782." *New England Historical and Genealogical Register,* 127 (1973), 5–17, 138–42.

Rhode Island in the Continental Congress. Ed. William Staples. Providence, 1870.

A Rhode Island Slaver: Trade Book of the Sloop Adventure. Ed. Robert Champlin. Providence, 1922.

Simitière, Pierre Eugène du. "Du Simitière's Notes on Newport in 1768." *Rhode Island Historical Society Collections,* 12 (1919), 47–52.

Stiles, Ezra. *Extracts from the Itineraries and Other Miscellanies of Ezra Stiles, D.D., LL.D., 1755–1794.* Ed. Franklin B. Dexter. New Haven, Conn., 1916.

———. *The Literary Diary of Ezra Stiles.* Ed. Franklin B. Dexter. 3 vols. New York, 1901.

Thurston, Edward Jr. "Extracts from Edward Thurston, Jr.'s Almanac, 1772," *The Newport Historical Magazine,* 1 (July 1880 – April 1881), 125.

———. "Letter from Edward Thurston, Jr. to James Coggeshall, March 5, 1767." *The Newport Historical Magazine,* 2 (July 1881 – April 1882), 58.

"Travel Diary of Dr. Benjamin Bullivant [1697]." *New-York Historical Society Quarterly,* 40, No. 1 (January 1956), 58–60.

Tucker, St. George. *A Dissertation on Slavery, With a Proposal for the Gradual Abolition of It, in the State of Virginia.* Philadelphia, 1796. Repr. Westport, Conn., 1970.

United States Bureau of the Census. *A Century of Population Growth.* Washington, D.C., 1909.

———. *Heads of Families at the First Census of the United States Taken in the Year 1790: Rhode Island.* Washington, D.C., 1908.

———. *Historical Statistics of the United States: Colonial Times to 1957.* Washington, D.C., 1960.

———. *Historical Statistics of the United States: Colonial Times to 1970.* Bicentennial Edition. 2 vols. Washington, D.C., 1975.

Valuation of the Cities and Towns in the State of Rhode Island from 1860–1869 for Purposes of Taxation. Together with the Census of the Colony in 1730 and 1775 and Other Statistics. Ed. Elisha Dyer. Providence, 1871.

Vernon, Thomas. "The Diary of Thomas Vernon, a Royalist." *Rhode Island Historical Tracts,* 13 (1881), 1–116.

———. *Thomas Vernon's Letters.* New York, 1880.

Vital Records of Rhode Island, 1636–1850. Ed. James M. Arnold. 4 vols. Providence, 1892–1901.

Ward, Samuel. *Correspondence of Governor Samuel Ward, May 1775 – March 1776.* Ed. Bernard Knollenberg. Providence, 1952.

Woolman, John. *The Journals and Essays of John Woolman.* Ed. Amelia M. Gummere. New York, 1922.

Printed Sources: Secondary

Anstey, Roger. "The Volume of the North American Slave-Carrying Trade from Africa, 1761–1810." *Revue Française d'Histoire d'Outre-Mer,* 62 (1975), 47–66.

Appleton, M. "Richard Partridge: Colonial Agent." *New England Quarterly,* 5 (1932), 293–309.

Arensberg, Conrad. "The Community as Object and as Sample." *American Anthropologist,* 63 (1961), 241–64.

Arnold, Samuel. *History of Rhode Island.* 2 vols. New York, 1859.

Atlas of Early American History: The Revolutionary Era, 1760–1790. Edd. Lester Cappon et al. Princeton, N.J., 1976.

Aykroyd, W. R. *Sweet Malefactor: Sugar, Slavery, and Human Society.* London, 1967.

Balch, Thomas Willing. *The French in America During the War of Independence of the United States, 1777–1783.* Philadelphia, 1891.

Baldwin, Alice. *The New England Clergy and the American Revolution.* Durham, N.C., 1928.

Barrow, Thomas. *Trade and Empire: The British Customs Service in Colonial America, 1660–1775.* Cambridge, Mass., 1967.

Bartlett, Irving. *From Slave to Citizen: The Story of the Negro in Rhode Island.* Providence, 1954.

Battle, Charles. *Negroes on the Island of Rhode Island.* Newport, 1932.

Baxter, W. T. *The House of Hancock: Business in Boston, 1724–1775.* Cambridge, Mass., 1945.

Bigelow, Bruce. "The Commerce of Rhode Island with the West Indies, Before the American Revolution." Unpublished Ph.D. dissertation, Brown University, 1930.

Bolhouse, Gladys E. "Abraham Redwood, Reluctant Quaker, Philanthropist, Botanist." *Newport History*, 45, Part 2, No. 146 (Spring 1972), 17–35.

Bridenbaugh, Carl. "Charlestonians at Newport, 1767–75." *South Carolina Historical Magazine*, 41 (1940), 43–47.

———. *Cities in Revolt: Urban Life in America, 1743–1776*. London & New York, 1971.

———. "Colonial Newport as a Summer Resort." *Rhode Island Historical Society Collections*, 26 (1933), 1–23.

———. *Fat Mutton and Liberty of Conscience*. Providence, 1974.

———. *Mitre and Sceptre: Transatlantic Faiths, Ideas, Personalities, and Politics, 1689–1775*. New York, 1962.

———. *Peter Harrison*. Chapel Hill, N.C., 1949.

Brown, Robert E. *Middle Class Democracy and the Revolution in Massachusetts, 1691–1780*. Ithaca, N.Y., 1955.

"Bull's Memoirs of Rhode Island, 1636–1783." *Rhode Island Republican*, 1832–1839.

Calhoon, Robert McCluer. *The Loyalists in Revolutionary America, 1760–1781*. New York, 1965.

Channing, George R. *Early Recollections of Newport, Rhode Island*. Newport, 1868.

Chapelle, Howard I. *The History of American Sailing Ships*. New York, 1935.

Chapin, Howard. *Rhode Island Privateers in King George's War, 1739–1748*. Providence, 1926.

Chyet, Stanley F. *Lopez of Newport*. Detroit, 1970.

Clarke, Jane. "Metcalf Bowler as a British Spy." *Rhode Island Historical Society Collections*, 23 (1930), 101–17.

"A Club Formed by the Jews, 1761." *The Newport Historical Magazine*, 4 (July 1883 – April 1884), 58.

Cohen, Joel A. "Rhode Island Loyalism and the American Revolution." *Rhode Island History*, 27 (1968), 97–112.

Coleman, Peter J. "The Insolvent Debtor in Rhode Island, 1745–1828." *William and Mary Quarterly*, 22 (1965), 413–34.

———. *The Transformation of Rhode Island, 1790–1860*. Providence, 1963.

Cott, Nancy F. "Divorce and the Changing Status of Women in Eighteenth-Century Massachusetts." *William and Mary Quarterly*, 33 (1976), 586–614.

Coughtry, Jay A. *The Notorious Triangle: Rhode Island and the African Slave Trade, 1700–1807*. Philadelphia, 1981.

Cowell, Benjamin. *The Spirit of '76 in Rhode Island*. Boston, 1850.

Crane, Elaine F. "Uneasy Coexistence: Religious Tensions in Eighteenth-Century Newport." *Newport History*, 53, No. 3 (Summer 1980), 101–11.

Crawford, Walter. "The Commerce of Rhode Island with the Southern Continental Colonies in the Eighteenth Century." *Rhode Island Society Collections*, 14 (1921), 99–110, 124–30.

Curtin, Philip. *The Atlantic Slave Trade: A Census*. Madison, Wisc., 1969.

Davies, K. G. *The Royal African Company*. London, 1957.

Demos, John. "Families in Colonial Bristol, Rhode Island: An Exercise in Historical Demography." *William and Mary Quarterly*, 25 (1968), 40–57.

Dinkin, Robert J. *Voting in Provincial America: A Study of Elections in the Thirteen Colonies, 1689–1776*. Westport, Conn., 1977.

A Documentary History of Rhode Island. Ed. Howard Chapin. 2 vols. Providence, 1916, 1919.

Donnan, Elizabeth. "The New England Slave Trade After the Revolution." *The New England Quarterly*, 3 (1930), 251–78.

Dow, George, *Slave Ships and Slaving*. Port Washington, N.Y., 1969.

Downing, Antoinette F., and Scully, Vincent J. Jr. *The Architectural Heritage of Newport, Rhode Island*. Cambridge, Mass., 1952. Repr. New York, 1967.

Drescher, Seymour. *Econocide: British Slavery in the Era of Abolition*. Pittsburgh, 1977.

DuBois, W. E. B. *The Suppression of the African Slave Trade to the United States of America, 1638–1870*. New York, 1954. Repr. 1965.

Duignan, Peter, and Clendenen, Clarence. *The United States and the African Slave Trade, 1619–1862*. Stanford, Calif., 1963.

Dunn, Richard. *Sugar and Slaves: The Rise of the Planter Class in the English West Indies, 1624–1713*. Chapel Hill, N.C., 1972.

Durfee, Thomas. *Gleanings from the Judicial History of Rhode Island*. Rhode Island Historical Tracts, First Series, No. 18. Providence, 1883.

Dyer, Ceil. *The Newport Cookbook*. New York, 1972.

Easton, Arthur Wentworth Hamilton. "Rhode Island Settlers on the French Lands in Nova Scotia in 1760 and 1761." *Americana* (January 1915), 1–43; (February 1915), 83–103; (March 1915), 179–97.

Edward, James G. *The Newport Story*. Newport, 1952.

Ernst, Joseph A. *Money and Politics in America, 1755–1775*. Chapel Hill, N.C., 1973.

———, and Egnal, Marc. "An Economic Interpretation of the American Revolution." *William and Mary Quarterly*, 29 (1972) 3–32.

Ferguson, E. James. "Currency Finance: An Interpretation of Colonial Monetary Practices." *William and Mary Quarterly*, 10 (1953), 153–80.

Field, Edward. *State of Rhode Island and Providence Plantations*. 3 vols. Boston & Syracuse, 1902.

Flaherty, David H. *Privacy in Colonial New England*. Charlottesville, Va., 1967.

Foner, Philip. *Labor and the American Revolution*. Westport, Conn., 1976.

Foote, Henry W. *Robert Feke, Colonial Portrait Painter*. Cambridge, Mass., 1930.

Foster, William. *Stephen Hopkins, Rhode Island Statesman: A Study in the Political History of the Eighteenth Century*. Rhode Island Historical Tracts, First Series, No. 19. 2 vols. Providence, 1884.

Franklin, Ruth B. "Some Early Schools and Schoolmasters of Newport." Newport Historical Society *Bulletin*, No. 96 (January 1936), 13–31.

Genovese, Eugene. *Roll, Jordan, Roll*. New York, 1972.

Godfrey, W. S. Jr. "The Newport Puzzle." *Archaeology*, 2 (1949), 146–49.

———. "Newport Tower, II." *Archaeology*, 3 (1950), 82–86.

Goldenberg, Joseph A. *Shipbuilding in Colonial America*. Charlottesville, Va., 1976.

Greene, Lorenzo. *The Negro in Colonial New England*. New York, 1969.

Grigg, Susan. "Toward a Theory of Remarriage: A Case Study of Newburyport at the Beginning of the Nineteenth Century." *Journal of Interdisciplinary History*, 8 (1977), 183–220.

Gross, Robert. *The Minutemen and Their World*. New York, 1976.

Gutman, Herbert G. *The Black Family in Slavery and Freedom, 1750–1925*. New York, 1976.

Gutstein, Morris A. *The Story of the Jews of Newport*. New York, 1936.

Hamm, Tommy Todd. "The American Slave Trade with Africa, 1620–1807." Unpublished Ph.D. dissertation. Indiana University, 1975.

Hazeltine, Harold D. "Appeals from Colonial Courts to King in Council, With Especial Reference to Rhode Island." *American Historical Association Annual Report* (1895), 299–350.

Hedges, James B. *The Browns of Providence Plantations*. 2 vols. Cambridge, Mass., 1952.

Henretta, James. "Economic Development and Social Structure in Colonial Boston." *William and Mary Quarterly*, 22 (1965), 75–92.

———. *The Evolution of American Society*. Lexington, Mass., 1973.

Higgins, W. Robert. "The Geographical Origins of Negro Slaves in Colonial South Carolina." *South Atlantic Quarterly*, 70 (1971), 34–47.

History of Newport County. Ed. Richard Bayles. New York, 1888.

Holand, Hjalmar P. *America, 1355–1364: A New Chapter in Pre-Columbian History*. New York, 1946.

Hood, Graham. *American Silver*. New York, 1971.

Inikori, J. E. "Measuring the Atlantic Slave Trade: An Assessment of Curtin and Anstey." *Journal of African History*, 17 (1976), 197–223.

James, Sidney V. *Colonial Rhode Island: A History*. New York, 1975.

———. *People Among Peoples: Quaker Benevolence in Eighteenth-Century America*. Cambridge, Mass., 1963.

Jervey, Theodore. *The Slave Trade: Slavery and Color*. New York, 1969.

Johnston, William D. "Slavery in Rhode Island, 1755–1776." In *Slavery in the United States*. New York, 1969. Pp. 113–64.

Jones, Alice Hanson. "Wealth Estimates for the American Middle Colonies, 1774." *Economic Development and Cultural Change*, 18 (1970), Supplement, 1–172.

———. "Wealth Estimates for the New England Colonies about 1770." *Journal of Economic History*, 32 (1972), 98–127.

Jordan, Winthrop. *White Over Black: American Attitudes Toward the Negro, 1550–1812*. Baltimore, 1968.

Klein, Herbert S. *The Middle Passage*. Princeton, N.J., 1978.

———. "Slaves and Shipping in Eighteenth-Century Virginia." *Journal of Interdisciplinary History*, 5 (1975), 383–412.

Labaree, Benjamin. *Patriots and Partisans: The Merchants of Newburyport, 1764–1815*. Cambridge, Mass., 1962.

Lemisch, Jesse. "Jack Tar in the Streets." *William and Mary Quarterly*, 25 (1968), 371–407.

Lockridge, Kenneth. "Land, Population, and the Evolution of New England Society, 1630–1790; and an Afterthought." In *Colonial America*. Ed. Stanley Katz. Boston, 1971. Pp. 466–91.

Lough, George J. "The Champlins of Newport: A Commercial History." Unpublished Ph.D. dissertation. The University of Connecticut, 1977.

Loughrey, Mary Ellen. *France and Rhode Island, 1686–1800*. New York, 1944.

Lovejoy, David. *Rhode Island Politics and the American Revolution, 1760–1776*. Providence, 1958.

Lyman, E. B. *A Reminiscence of Newport Before and During the Revolutionary War*. Newport, 1906.

Mackesy, Piers. *The War for America, 1775–1783*. Cambridge, Mass., 1965.

Maier, Pauline. *From Resistance to Revolution*. New York, 1972.

Mannix, Daniel P., and Cowley, Malcolm. *Black Cargoes: A History of the Atlantic Slave Trade, 1518–1865*. New York, 1962.

Mason, George C. "The African Slave Trade in Colonial Times." *American Historical Record*, 1 (July–August 1872), 311–19, 338–45.

———. *Annals of Trinity Church, Newport, Rhode Island, 1698–1821*. 2 vols. Newport, 1890.

———. *Reminiscences of Newport*. Newport, 1884.

Mayer, Kurt B. *Economic Development and Population Growth in Rhode Island*. Providence, 1953.

McCusker, John James Jr. "The Rum Trade and the Balance of Payments of the Thirteen Continental Colonies, 1650–1775." Unpublished Ph.D. dissertation. University of Pittsburgh, 1970.

McKee, Samuel. *Labor in Colonial New York, 1664–1776*. New York, 1935.

Means, Philip A. *The Newport Tower*. New York, 1942.

Mekeel, Arthur. *The Relation of the Quakers to the American Revolution*. Washington, D.C., 1979.

Morgan, Edmund S. *The Gentle Puritan: A Life of Ezra Stiles, 1727–1795*. New Haven, Conn., 1962.

———. *Virginians at Home*. Williamsburg, Va., 1952.

———, and Morgan, Helen. *The Stamp Act Crisis*. New York, 1962.

Morison, Samuel Eliot. *The European Discovery of America: The Northern Voyages, A.D. 500–1600*. New York, 1971.

Morris, Richard B. "Civil Liberties and the Jewish Tradition in Early America." In *The Jewish Experience in America*. Ed. Abraham Karp. 5 vols. Waltham, Mass., & New York, 1969. 1 404–23.

———. *Government and Labor in Early America*. New York, 1946.

———. *Studies in the History of American Law: With Special Reference to the Seventeenth and Eighteenth Centuries*. New York, 1963.

Morse, Jarvis. "The Wanton Family and Rhode Island Loyalism." *Rhode Island Historical Society Collections*, 31 (1938), 33–34.

Mullin, Gerald W. *Flight and Rebellion: Slave Resistance in Eighteenth–Century Virginia*. New York, 1972.

Myres, William V. "The Private and Public Political Thought of Ezra Stiles, 1760–1795." Unpublished Ph.D. dissertation. The University of Dallas, 1973.

Nash, Gary. "Slaves and Slaveowners in Colonial Philadelphia." *William and Mary Quarterly*, 30 (1973), 223–56.

———. "Social Change and the Growth of Pre-Revolutionary Urban Radicalism." In *The American Revolution*. Ed. Alfred F. Young. DeKalb, Ill., 1976. Pp. 3–36.

———. "The Transformation of Urban Politics, 1700–1765." *Journal of American History*, 60 (1973), 605–32.

———. *The Urban Crucible: Social Change, Political Consciousness, and the Origins of the American Revolution*. Cambridge, Mass., 1979.

———. "Urban Wealth and Poverty in Pre-Revolutionary America." *Journal of Interdisciplinary History*, 6 (1976), 545–84.

Nelson, William H. *The American Tory*. Boston, 1961.

Norton, Mary Beth. *The British Americans: The Loyalist Exiles in England, 1774–1789.* Boston, 1972.

———. " 'My Resting Reaping Times': Sarah Osborn's Defense of Her 'Unfeminine' Activities, 1767." *Signs: Journal of Women in Culture and Society,* 2 (1976), 515–29.

"Notes of Silversmiths." *The Newport Historical Magazine,* 2 (July 1881 – April 1882), 187.

Ostrander, Gilman M. "The Colonial Molasses Trade." *Agricultural History,* 30 (1956), 77–84.

———. "The Making of the Triangular Trade Myth." *William and Mary Quarterly,* 30 (1973), 635–44.

Papenfuse, Edward. *In Pursuit of Profit: The Annapolis Merchants in the Era of the American Revolution, 1763–1805.* Baltimore, 1975.

Pares, Richard. *Colonial Blockade and Neutral Rights, 1739–1763.* Oxford, 1938.

———. *Yankees and Creoles: The Trade Between North America and the West Indies Before the American Revolution.* Cambridge, Mass., 1956.

Patten, William, D.D. *Reminiscences of the Late Rev. Samuel Hopkins, D.D.* Boston & New York, 1843.

Peterson, Edward. *History of Rhode Island.* New York, 1853.

Pitkin, Timothy. *A Statistical View of the Commerce of the United States of America.* Hartford, Conn., 1816.

Platt, Orville H. "Negro Governors." *New Haven Historical Society Papers,* 6 (1900), 315–35.

Platt, Virginia Bever. " 'And Don't Forget the Guinea Voyage': The Slave Trade of Aaron Lopez of Newport." *William and Mary Quarterly,* 32 (1975), 601–18.

———. "Triangles and Tramping: Captain Zebediah Story of Newport, 1769–76." *American Neptune,* 33 (1973), 294–303.

Polishook, Irwin. *Rhode Island and the Union.* Evanston, Ill., 1969.

Potter, Elisha R. "A Brief Account of the Emissions of Paper Money, Made by the Colony of Rhode Island." In *Historical Sketches of the Paper Currency of the American Colonies.* Ed. Henry Phillips. New York, 1865. Repr. 1969.

Preston, Howard W. *Rhode Island and the Sea.* Providence, 1932.

Price, Jacob. "Economic Function and the Growth of American Port Towns in the Eighteenth Century." *Perspectives in American History,* 8 (1974), 123–86.

———. "Quantifying Colonial America: A Comment on Nash and Warden." *Journal of Interdisciplinary History,* 6 (1976), 701–709.

Ransford, Oliver. *The Slave Trade: The Story of Transatlantic Slavery.* London, 1971.

Ray, John Michael. "Newport's Golden Age: A Study of the Newport Slave Trade." *Negro History Bulletin*, 25 (1961), 51–57.

Religion and the Coming of the American Revolution. Ed. Peter N. Carroll. Waltham, Mass., 1970.

"The Rhode Island Emigration to Nova Scotia." *Narragansett Historical Register*, 7 (1889), 89–136.

Richardson, David. "West African Consumption Patterns and Their Influence on the Eighteenth-Century English Slave Trade." In *The Uncommon Market: Essays in the Economic History of the Atlantic Slave Trade*. Edd. Henry A. Gemery and Jan S. Hogendorn. New York, 1979. Pp. 303–30.

Richman, Irving B. *Rhode Island: A Study in Separatism*. Boston & New York, 1905.

Rider, Sidney S. *The History of Denization and Naturalization in the Colony of Rhode Island, 1636–1790*. Providence, 1905.

——. *An Inquiry Concerning the Origin of the Clause in the Laws of Rhode Island (1719–1783) Disfranchising Roman Catholics*. Rhode Island Historical Tracts, Second Series, No. 1. Providence, 1889. Pp. 7–53.

Roelker, William G., and Collins, Clarkson A. "The Patrol of Narragansett Bay (1744–1776) by H.M.S. *Rose*, Captain James Wallace [Parts I–IV]." *Rhode Island History*, 7 (July 1948), 90–95; 8 (July 1949), 77–83; 9 (January 1950), 11–23; 10 (April 1950), 52–58.

Rothman, David. *The Discovery of the Asylum*. Boston, 1971.

Rudolph, Richard. "The Merchants of Newport, Rhode Island, 1763–1786." Unpublished Ph.D. dissertation. The University of Connecticut, 1975.

Sainsbury, John A. "Indian Labor in Early Rhode Island." *The New England Quarterly*, 48 (1975), 378–93.

Schlesinger, Arthur M. *Colonial Merchants and the American Revolution, 1763–1776*. New York, 1918. Repr. 1968.

Schumacher, Alan T. "Newport Literature and Printing, 1700–1850." *Newport History*, 50 (1977), 45–64.

Scott, Kenneth. "George Scott (1706–1740): Slave Trader of Newport." *American Neptune*, 12 (1952), 222–28.

Shea, Margaret. *The Story of Colonial Newport*. Newport, 1962.

Shepherd, James F., and Walton, Gary M. *Shipping, Maritime Trade, and the Economic Development of Colonial North America*. London, 1972.

Sheridan, Richard. *An Economic History of the British West Indies, 1623–1775*. Baltimore, 1974.

Smith, Billy G. "The Material Lives of Laboring Philadelphians, 1750 to 1800." *William and Mary Quarterly*, 38 (1981), 163–202.

Smith-Rosenberg, Caroll. "The Female World of Love and Ritual: Relations Between Women in Nineteenth-Century America." *Signs: Journal of Women in Culture and Society*, 1 (1975), 1–30.

Spears, John R. *The American Slave Trade: An Account of Its Origins, Growth, and Suppression.* New York, 1900.

Stampp, Kenneth. *The Peculiar Institution.* New York, 1956.

Stein, Robert. "The Profitability of the Nantes Slave Trade, 1783–1792." *Journal of Economic History*, 35 (1975), 779–93.

Stowe, Harriet Beecher. *The Minister's Wooing.* New York, 1859. Repr. Ridgewood, N.J., 1968.

Sumner, William G. *A History of American Currency.* New York, 1874. Repr. 1968.

Thomas, R. P., and Bean, R. N. "Fishers of Men: The Profits of the Slave Trade." *Journal of Economic History*, 34 (1974), 885–914.

Thompson, Mack E. "The Ward–Hopkins Controversy and the American Revolution in Rhode Island: An Interpretation." *William and Mary Quarterly*, 16 (1959), 365–75.

Thornton, John W. *The Pulpit of the American Revolution, Or the Political Sermons of the Period of 1776.* Boston, 1860.

Tuckerman, Arthur. *When Rochambeau Stepped Ashore.* Newport, 1955.

Updike, Wilkins. *History of the Narragansett Church.* 3 vols. Boston, 1907.

Walton, Gary. "New Evidence on Colonial Commerce." *Journal of Economic History*, 28 (1968), 363–89.

Warden, G. B. *Boston, 1689–1776.* Boston, 1970.

———. "Inequality and Instability in Eighteenth-Century Boston: A Reappraisal." *Journal of Interdisciplinary History*, 6 (1976), 585–620.

Warner, Samuel B. *The Private City: Philadelphia in Three Periods of Its Growth.* Philadelphia, 1968.

Weeden, William. "The Early African Slave Trade in New England." *Proceedings of the American Antiquarian Society*, 7–8 N.S. (1887–1888).

———. *Early Rhode Island: A Social History of the People.* New York, 1910.

———. *Economic and Social History of New England.* 2 vols. Boston, 1890.

———. "Ideal Newport in the Eighteenth Century." *Proceedings of the American Antiquarian Society*, 18 N.S. (October 1906), 106–17.

Weiner, Frederick. "Rhode Island Merchants and the Sugar Act." *The New England Quarterly*, 3 (1930), 464–500.

Wells, Robert V. "Demographic Change and the Life Style of American Families." *Journal of Interdisciplinary History*, 2 (1971), 273–82.

———. "Household Size and Composition in the British Colonies in America, 1675–1775." *Journal of Interdisciplinary History*, 4 (1974), 543–70.

———. *The Population of the British Colonies in America Before 1776: A Survey of Census Data*. Princeton, N.J., 1975.

Williams, Eric. *From Columbus to Castro: The History of the Caribbean, 1492–1969*. London, 1970.

Wilson, Joan Hoff. "The Illusion of Change: Women and the American Revolution." In *The American Revolution*. Ed. Alfred F. Young. DeKalb, Ill., 1976. Pp. 383–445.

Withey, Lynne E. "Household Structure in Urban and Rural Areas: The Case of Rhode Island, 1774–1800." *Journal of Family History*, 3 (1978), 37–50.

———. *Urban Growth in Colonial Rhode Island: Newport and Providence in the Eighteenth Century*. Albany, N.Y., 1984.

Works Progress Administration. *Rhode Island: A Guide to the Smallest State*. New York, 1937.

Zuckerman, Michael. *Peaceable Kingdoms*. New York, 1970.

INDEX

Adams, John, 107
Africa trade, 10, 11, 15–23 passim,
  29, 30, 31, 33, 36, 37, 51, 69,
  163
  see also Rum distilling and trade;
  Slave trade
Agriculture, *see* Farming and land-
  holding
Allen, Timothy, 50
Almay (family), 153*n*114
Anabaptists, 60
Anglicans (Episcopalians), 3, 52, 59–
  60, 130, 131, 163
  acrimony and discord, 3, 5, 129–
  30, 131–32
  conversions to Anglicanism, 59,
  130, 132
  see also Bisset, George
Anstey, Roger, 23
Arnold, Benedict, 1
Artillery Company (Newport), 152
  *n*104
Artisans, *see* Craftsmen and tradesmen
Ayrault, Stephen, 18, 29, 32, 117,
  129, 157–58, 161

Banister (family), 31
Banister, John, 13
Baptists, 3, 130, 131
Barbados: trade, 12, 17
Belcher, Edward, 100*n*72
Belknap, Jeremy, 163
Bell, John, 26, 160
Bennett, John, 100*n*72
Bennett, Jonathan, 134
Bennett, William, 134
Berkeley, George, 3, 59

Bigelow, Bruce, 13, 20
Bissell, Lydia, 72
Bisset, George, 129, 130, 132, 160
Black community, 47, 52, 76–83, 161
  education, 79, 161
  females, 51, 79
  free blacks, 78, 82, 161
    by manumission, 52, 82–83, 161
  housing, 51, 52
  indentured servants, 78, 82, 83
  mortality rate, 79–80
  self-"government" and "court,"
  78–79
  service in the Continental Army,
  161
  voting denied, 61
  see also Slavery; Slave trade
Boston, 2, 9, 165
  slaves, 20, 57, 103*n*111
  taxpayers before the Revolution,
  98*n*50
  trade, 2, 9, 14, 20, 165
  and relations with Newport, 1, 2,
    13, 14, 25, 117, 118, 119
  restrictions and protests, 113,
    117, 118, 119, 131–32,
    147*n*38, 152*n*100
Boston Port Bill, 119, 131–32,
  152*n*100
  see also Intolerable Acts
Bours, John, 26, 129
Bowers, Captain, 13
Bowler, Metcalf, 140, 146*n*25
Brenton (family), 138–39
Brett, Mary, 79
Brewer Street (Newport), 50
Brick Market Place (Newport), 3